General Will in Political Philosophy

Janusz Grygień

Translated by Dominika Gajewska

imprint-academic.com

Copyright © Janusz Grygieńć, 2013

The moral rights of the authors have been asserted.
No part of this publication may be reproduced in any form
without permission, except for the quotation of brief passages
in criticism and discussion.

Published in the UK by
Imprint Academic, PO Box 200, Exeter EX5 5YX, UK

Distributed in the USA by
Ingram Book Company,
One Ingram Blvd., La Vergne, TN 37086, USA

ISBN 9781845405588

A CIP catalogue record for this book is available from the
British Library and US Library of Congress

**This translation has been funded by the
Foundation for Polish Science**

Contents

Introduction	1
Chapter 1. From theology to politics. The evolution of the concept of general will	7
1.1. From St. Paul to Denis Diderot	8
1.1.1. Blaise Pascal	10
1.1.2. Nicolas Malebranche	12
1.1.3. Jacques-Bénigne Bossuet, François Fénelon, Pierre Bayle	17
1.1.4. Montesquieu	21
1.1.5. Denis Diderot	24
1.2. The general will in the thought of Jean-Jacques Rousseau	27
1.2.1. The general will. Definition and interpretations	30
1.2.2. The general will and natural law	38
1.2.3. The general will and the will of all	45
1.2.3.1. The will of all	46
1.2.3.2. The general will vs. the will of all	47
1.2.4. Two visions of community	48
Chapter 2. The community in the idealist perspective	52
2.1. Beyond the abstractions of reason	58
2.1.1. The rejection of apriorism	59
2.1.2. Against individualism. Theories of the first look	61
2.1.3. Against contractualism and modern natural law theory	67
2.2 The social sources of identity. Towards contextualism	73
2.2.1. My station and its duties (Francis Herbert Bradley)	74
2.2.2. The community of ideas (Bernard Bosanquet)	77
2.2.3. Moral duties and legal obligations (Thomas Hill Green)	80
2.3 Teleologism, historicism, moral ideal. Towards objective values	82
2.3.1. The moral ideal	84
2.3.2. Teleologism, historicism. The moral goals of the community and mankind	87
2.4. "The duties of citizenship" (Bernard Bosanquet and Francis Herbert Bradley)	91

Chapter 3. Idealist interpretations of the general will　　　　94

   3.1. Novelty and limitations of the thought of Jean-Jacques Rousseau　96
      3.1.1. From the utopia of atomism to the utopia of community　　97
      3.1.2. Ancient intentions, modern failures　　　　　　　　　　102

   3.2. The general will as…　　　　　　　　　　　　　　　　　　　105
      3.2.1. …universal will (Francis Herbert Bradley)　　　　　　106
      3.2.2. …congeries of the hopes and fears (Thomas Hill Green)　108
         3.2.2.1. Rejection of John Austin's positivism　　　　　110
         3.2.2.2. Between Jean-Jacques Rousseau and John Austin　113
         3.2.2.3. Between positivism and jusnaturalism　　　　114
      3.2.3. …a system of ideas (Bernard Bosanquet)　　　　　　　116
         3.2.3.1. Interpretations　　　　　　　　　　　　　　　118

   3.3. Further history of the concept of the general will　　　　123
      3.3.1. Criticism.
         Controversy over the metaphysical theory of the state　123
      3.3.2. Continuation. J.H. Muirhead, H.J.W. Hetherington, L.T.
         Hobhouse, J.A. Hobson　　　　　　　　　　　　　　133

Chapter 4. Idealism, the general will
       and the liberal-communitarian debate　　　　　　　　140

   4.1. Liberal communitarianism　　　　　　　　　　　　　　　　140

   4.2. Is idealism liberal-communitarian?　　　　　　　　　　　　150

   4.3. The idealist theory of rights　　　　　　　　　　　　　　　154
      4.3.1. The recognition-based character of rights　　　　　155
      4.3.2. The common good　　　　　　　　　　　　　　　　159
      4.3.3. Negative liberty–positive liberty.
         Negative rights–positive rights　　　　　　　　　　161

   4.4. What became of the idealist theory of rights　　　　　　　165

   4.5. Determinants of the liberal communitarianism of the idealists　169
      4.5.1 Teleologism　　　　　　　　　　　　　　　　　　　169
      4.5.2 The metaphysical foundation of politics　　　　　　170
      4.5.3 Ethico-political contextualism　　　　　　　　　　　171
      4.5.4 Between relativism and universalism　　　　　　　173
      4.5.5 Criticism of the concept of negative freedom　　　175
      4.5.6 Individualism　　　　　　　　　　　　　　　　　177

Conclusion　　　　　　　　　　　　　　　　　　　　　　　　　180

Bibliography　　　　　　　　　　　　　　　　　　　　　　　　184

Index　　　　　　　　　　　　　　　　　　　　　　　　　　　192

Introduction

The present book is about the role and place ascribed to the general will in modern and contemporary political philosophy. Despite the extensive nature of this subject matter, its aim is to explore three, strictly defined, research areas. The first is the history of how the category of the general will developed, from the eruption of the first controversies surrounding this issue, to the twentieth century and the writings of the last representatives of the British idealist tradition. The second is the nature of the category of *volonté générale* in the writings of Jean-Jacques Rousseau, in particular the misconceptions which have accrued around this question, as well as the potential ways of elucidating them, in addition to the implications each may have for the thought of Rousseau as a whole. The third area of research concerns the issues related to the idealist modification of this Rousseauian category and its potential significance for contemporary philosophical and political debates.

The fact that such a prominent place is given here to British thought is justified. The development and modification of the Rousseauian notion of *volonté générale* has nowhere been as significant as in Great Britain at the turn of the nineteenth and twentieth centuries. Until the publication of the first works of Rousseau, the term "general will" itself was mostly confined to the writings of French authors. After the French Revolution, the disdain in which writers representing nearly all existing world views held the author of the *Social Contract* led to the abandonment of the general will as a topic. And although there was no lack of authors in the British Isles explicitly, or implicitly, expressing their dissatisfaction with the theoretical constructs of the Citizen of Geneva, it was there that the subject was revived in the 1880s. Within this context, British political philosophy was largely represented by thinkers belonging to the idealist tradition. The potential they had noticed in the Rousseauian thesis on will as the underlying foundation of political communities blended perfectly with their own views on the nature of social and political reality.

The choice of subject matter always requires an appropriate justification. In our case, it is the scholarly importance of the subject as well as the degree to which it has been studied in the relevant literature.

As far as political philosophy and political science are concerned, the importance of reflecting on the category of the general will cannot be stressed enough. Many contemporary concepts refer to it, while an even greater number cannot avoid doing so. The theories of rational choice (K. Arrow, J. Buchanan, D. Gauthier) and public reason (J. Rawls, J. Habermas) developed by English-speaking thinkers and theorists need to be mentioned here. Not forgetting interpretations employing the concept of the general will for analyses in game theory (W.G. Runciman, A.K. Sen). References to the notion are also seemingly unavoidable when discussing topics such as natural law, public opinion, political decision-making, the legitimation of political power or sovereignty. It is difficult to overestimate the influence this Rousseauian concept has had on the theory of democratic government, or the debate on the limits of state interventionism, by supplying the theoretical foundations of social-liberal and socialist conceptions.

In spite of its significance, both for the history of thought and for political science, the concept of general will has not yet received satisfactory treatment from scholars. For can we regard the three works available on this subject, the most recent published nearly thirty years ago, as sufficient? Patrick Riley and Andrew Levine[1] – the authors of two of the works in question – respectively examined: the pre-Rousseauian meanings of the term *volonté générale* and its doctrinal affinity with communism in its Marxist guise. The oldest work on the subject, *Rousseau and the Concept of the General Will* by Frank Thakurdas,[2] published in 1976, examined the general will through Bernard Bosanquet's corrective revision of the concept, also surveying later reactions to this revision.

The political philosophy of British idealism is the next subject area we shall be exploring. The main exponents of this tradition are Francis Herbert Bradley, Thomas Hill Green and Bernard Bosanquet. Their writings – a distinctive mix of liberalism, republicanism, conservatism and socialism – have for years provided inspiration for thinkers representing nearly every political doctrine, and social liberalism in particular. As with Rousseau's general will, it is equally hard to overestimate the importance of British idealism for political theory and philosophy.

---

1 P. Riley, *General Will Before Rousseau: The Transformation of the Divine into the Civic*, Princeton, NJ 1986; A. Levine, *The General Will: Rousseau, Marx, Communism*, Cambridge 1993.

2 F. Thakurdas, *Rousseau and the Concept of the General Will*, Calcutta 1976.

There are historical reasons for this fact, namely the impact British thought has had on political theorists and philosophers, but also its role in shaping political practice in the United Kingdom at the turn of the century. Here we are of course talking about the New Liberals (J.A. Hobson, L.T. Hobhouse, W.H. Beveridge, Ch. Masterman, W. Clarke, Ch.P. Scott) — philosophers, economists, journalists and theorists responsible for the social reorientation of liberalism at the beginning of the twentieth century, explicitly appealing to the authority of Green and seeing him as the main firebrand of the "moralisation" of liberal thought. But they were not the only ones to refer to this thinker. There were other theorists and philosophers, sometimes also actively engaged in political affairs. First among them was Arnold Toynbee, the liberal and social activist, promoter of cooperative ideas and founder of the *Settlement Movement*, who was concerned with the moral and material condition of the British proletariat. Other engagé theorists included Richard Burdon Haldane, Sidney and Beatrice Webb and "Christian socialists" such as Richard Henry Tawney.

A somewhat lesser influence on Britain's political life was exerted by Bosanquet who never took an active part in politics, and who, on account of his somewhat early retirement from academia, was less influential in shaping the mentality of the British intellectual and political elites. Nevertheless, for several years he was one of the main activists and theorists of the Charity Organisation Society and of the London Ethical Society, charitable institutions aiding the poorest.

Apart from its historical significance, British idealist thought also has significant heuristic value. Combining elements native to many political doctrines, it spawned political concepts running counter to the traditional distinctions ingrained in political theory and philosophy. This is why the writings of the idealists can provide a special inspiration. Especially today, in the context of the ongoing (for nearly 40 years) attack on contemporary liberalism — still largely equated with the thought of Rawls as expounded in *A Theory of Justice* (and later modified in *Political Liberalism*). Certain scholars are right to point out that in the domain of political thought, the idealists managed to escape the perception of justice proper to neo-Kantian liberalism, where it was placed higher than the good, and to link the idea of justice with the ethea of particular communities, thereby avoiding the charge of ethical and political relativism. It is for this reason that idealist thought can today serve as an example of a non-standard approach to liberal theory, having on many occasions been compared in the relevant literature to the conceptions of Michael Oakeshott, Philip Pettit, Joseph Raz, Charles Taylor or Michael Walzer.

The above references and annotations indicate clearly that we will be occupied with a very diverse subject matter. A book devoted to such a broad topic must necessarily aim to fulfil multiple goals. These, I believe, can be divided into two groups. The first is to supply arguments in support of the book's main theses. These are, first, that in its programme the political philosophy of British idealism combined elements of the individualist and the communitarian position, being a precursor of today's liberal-communitarian position, and second, that a reading of the Rousseauian conception of the general will must inevitably have a dual nature. The general will can and should be viewed as a strictly ethical concept on the one hand, and as a political and legal one on the other.

Next to proving these theses, the goal of this book is also to serve a more descriptive, rather than argumentative, purpose. Its chief aim is to present the idealist vision of the general will. Furthermore, it narrates the development of the category of the general will prior to Rousseau, and outlines the social and political philosophy of British idealism. All of this is accomplished in four chapters, divided into sections, ordered chronologically, according to the issues raised in them and substantively allowing for a consistent presentation of the argumentation used to justify the two main theses of this work.

Chapter one discusses the history of the category of the general will prior to its transformation into the widely known Rousseauian concept of *volonté générale*. We will examine the various forms the idea took, also as a non-political category of strictly theological import, as well as the precisions given by the author of the *Social Contract* concerning its attributes. We will then enumerate potential interpretations of the general will and define its relation to natural law theories. Further on, we will attempt to define *volonté particulière/volonté de tous*, since only the prior definition of the relationship between the categories of *volonté particulière* and *volonté générale* can enable us to set down possible interpretations of the ideal of the community and of citizenship, as postulated by Rousseau.

Chapter two will focus on the political (and where necessary, the social, ethical or even metaphysical) philosophy of British idealism, concentrating on the three most important figures in this respect: Green, Bradley and Bosanquet. Their respective positions will be described in both their negative and positive aspects. Criticism of apriorism, individualism, contractualism and modern jusnaturalism will be presented first. This will be followed by a description of the fundamental political theses of the idealists. The first, proclaiming the social origins of human identity, found its expression in Bradley's concept of "my station and its duties", Bosanquet's notion of the community of ideas, as well as Green's view of the relationship between moral duties and legal obligations. All of these suggest the contextualism of idealist thought, which sought the sources of moral principles in custom and in the law of specific communities. It is only superficially that they appear to be in conflict with the idealists' second thesis, which underlines the teleological dimension of reality at the basis of Bradley's concept of the "moral ideal" and of the historicist outlook of the other idealists.

In chapter three, we will analyse the role and place ascribed to the general will in the writings of the British philosophers of interest to us here. The argumentation will once again follow a two-stage pattern. Firstly, we will present the idealist critique of the Rousseauian *volonté générale* as undertaken by Green, followed by Bosanquet (omitting Bradley, since he did not present one). The second stage will consist in showing how the idealists modified the concept. In Bradley's *Ethical Studies*, the general will becomes the will of the community, in Green — the "congeries of the hopes and fears of a people bound together by common interests and sympathy" — while it takes the form of a community of ideas in Bosanquet. The reflections of chapter three are supplemented by an outline of the subsequent fate of the idealist concept of the general will. In this context, we will relate the nature of Hobhouse's attack on Bosanquet's version of the concept, as well as the subsequent readings of it in the writings of the last prominent representatives of the British idealist tradition — John Henry Muirhead and Hector James Wright Hetherington, and finally the New Liberals — Hobhouse and Hobson.

Chapter four will aim to verify the validity of the statements appearing in the relevant literature regarding the importance of idealist thought in the context of contemporary philosophical and political debates. Since one of the two main arguments of this book is that idealist thought reconciles the individualist and communitarian positions, we shall need to analyse the contemporary position of liberal communitarianism. We will present its main representatives and their arguments, which state that the opposition between liberalism and communitarianism, as it is usually encountered in the literature, springs from a distorted image of liberal thought. We will also argue in favour of including representatives of the British idealist tradition among exponents of nineteenth-century communal liberalism. A key role will be played here by the theory of right found in their writings, especially by its three elements or theses: rights being based on recognition, their inevitable link to the common good and the fundamental importance of the notion of positive liberty. The book will end with a conclusion, summing up its most important findings as well as indicating potential areas for further research on topics thematically linked to the concept of the general will.

Chapter One

From Theology to Politics: The Evolution of the Concept of General Will

Whenever the term "general will" appears in scholarly literature we can be almost certain that the name of Jean-Jacques Rousseau will immediately follow. This category has become so inextricably entangled with the *Social Contract* and its author in the public awareness that it is practically impossible to examine them separately today. Most contemporary works devoted to political philosophy rightly speak of the concept of *volonté générale* as Rousseau's most important contribution to political theory and philosophy. Of course, Rousseau was neither the first nor the last to have developed this concept. The emerging question about the uniqueness of his approach can be answered in a number of ways. Compared to his predecessors (there were quite a few, after all), Rousseau effected a total secularisation of the general will (a distinctly theological concept before him), attaching it permanently to the theory of democratic government. Although the first step brought him the recognition of contemporary thinkers, his radical democratism—which the eighteenth century treated as a utopian anachronism undeserving of political or philosophical attention— gained him the affection of future generations. None of his successors were able to build a more intriguing political construct based on this concept. It is true that the German idealists employed it, in particular Georg Wilhelm Friedrich Hegel. But they did not relate it directly to political issues or make it their main concern. It is therefore hardly surprising that the British idealists, although doctrinally closer to classical German thought, built their own vision of the general will upon a critique of the work of Rousseau.

This chapter will present the history of the development of the idea of the general will. The subtitle of Patrick Riley's work on the subject— *The General Will before Rousseau: The Transformation of the Divine into the*

Civic—reflects the nature of these changes perfectly. The scholar with an interest in the history of the general will must become closely familiar with the theological controversies of the early Christian era, in particular the debate about predestination, and trace the gradual application of the concept, still strictly theological, to individual and social life in order to, finally, analysing the thought of the French Enlightenment, reach the end of this transformation and so the writings of Rousseau.

1.1. From St. Paul to Denis Diderot

Controversies surrounding the idea of general will, which at the time was not yet called by this name, appeared as early as the writings of St. Paul. Seldom has a single suggestion fostered a debate stretching for over a millennium.[1] It is equally rare for it to be treated as the cause of subsequent political revolutions. But this is exactly what happened in the case of the concept discussed here. The connection between certain fragments of the letters of St. Paul and the writings and actions of Maximilien Robespierre (by which I mean the French Revolution) is of course not direct. It leads through the ideas of St. Augustine, the debate between the Jansenists and the Jesuits, the works of Blaise Pascal, Nicolas Malebranche, Jacques Bénigne Bossuet, François Fénelon, Pierre Bayle and finally Montesquieu and Denis Diderot, all the way to Rousseau, whose writings are sometimes viewed as the direct inspiration for Jacobin terror. From the mere tone of the suggestion, contained notably in St. Paul's *Letter to Timothy*, it is difficult to infer any of its momentous political consequences: "[f]or this is good and acceptable in the eyes of God our Saviour; who will have all men to be saved, and to come unto the knowledge of the truth."[2] The object of the debate is this: the universality or particularity of God's will to save. Will all of us be saved, or only a few? "Is He the God of the Jews only? Is He not also of the Gentiles?",[3] or perhaps "many are called, but few are chosen"?[4]

Controversies surrounding this issue later became an addendum to the debate about Divine grace and predestination. This debate was initiated by the teachings of Pelagius, a British monk who lived in the fifth century, credited with the view that good deeds done of free will are sufficient for salvation, which does not require Divine grace. The

---

[1] This is why Patrick Riley describes the whole tradition of employing and interpreting the idea of the general will as "mere gloss on a passing phrase in a letter of St. Paul" (P. Riley, *General Will Before Rousseau*, p. 9).
[2] 1 Tim. 2:3–4.
[3] Rom. 3:29.
[4] Matt. 22:14.

conformity of this view with Catholic doctrine was questioned at the sixteenth synod in Carthage (418), whose final canons (especially 3-7) emphasised the importance of grace. Despite the condemnation of Pelagianism, its central tenets were to be revived on several occasions. They remained present in the writings of the Semipelagians, including Faustus of Riez, St. John Cassian, the Marseillans and the Molinists.

On the opposite side of this dispute were the predestinarians, who held to the view that salvation depends entirely on grace. No personal effort can alter the Divine will, which destines some for salvation and sentences others to damnation. Proponents of this view are usually thought to include St. Augustine (whose opinions in this respect were, however, subject to change), the monk Gottschalk, Johannes Scotus Eriugena (on account of the unorthodox nature of his *De divina praedestinatione*), Hincmar, archbishop of Reims (who with a number of other bishops signed a four-point memorial at Quierzy-sur-Oise (853) proclaiming that God wills the salvation of all men and that His grace is essential to salvation), John Wycliffe and Jan Hus, Martin Luther, Jean Calvin, Michel du Bay and — drawing inspiration from the works of the latter — Cornelius Jansen and other Jansenists such as Antoine Arnauld, Pasqiuer Quesnel and Pascal.

Both of these positions were firmly rejected by subsequent synods and councils of the Catholic Church. Following the Synod of Carthage, councils were held at Arles and Lyon (473), and at Orange (529), meant primarily to answer the Semipelagianism of Faustus of Riez and provide support to a moderate reading of St. Augustine. Numerous fragments of Scripture[5] were cited in the canons at the Council of Orange in order to prove the necessity of grace for salvation. Pelagian teachings were then condemned at Valence (855), where the theses ascribed to Eriugena and Hincmar were rejected, and at Sens (1140/1141); at the general council in Constance (1414-1418), where the views of Wycliffe and Hus were condemned ("All things happen from absolute necessity", and "The prayer of someone foreknown as damned profits nobody"[6]); while the sixth session of the Council of Trent (1547), which produced the *Decree on Justification*, also rejected the views of Luther. According to the *Decree*, all will not be saved, but only those who respond to the grace bestowed upon them by working towards their salvation. "But, though He died for all [2 Cor. 5:15], yet do not all receive the benefit of His death, but those only unto whom the merit of His

---

[5] Including: Isa. 65:1; Rom. 10:20; Prov. 8:35; Phil. 2:13; Phil. 1:6; Phil. 1:29; Eph. 2:8; 1 Cor. 4:7; 1 Cor. 7:25; 1 Cor. 15:10; Gal. 2:21.
[6] http://www.papalencyclicals.net/Councils/ecum16.htm
http://www.thecounciloftrent.com/ch6.html

passion is communicated."⁷ The main theses of the Jansenists were also condemned by Innocent X (*Cum occasione*), who found them to contain five statements incompatible with Church teaching (including: "[s]ome of God's precepts are impossible to the just, who wish and strive to keep them, according to the present powers which they have; the grace, by which they are made possible, is also wanting", "[i]n the state of fallen nature one never resists interior grace", "[i]t is Semipelagian to say that Christ died or shed His blood for all men without exception"⁸), Alexander VII (*Ad sacram beati Petri sedem*), Clemens XI (*Unigenitus*) and Pius VI (*Auctorem fidei*).

We must content ourselves here with this abbreviated account of the debate. We lack the room to discuss efficacious, sufficient, prevenient, actuating and helping grace, the connections between them and their consequences for the freedom of the human will. We need only note that it is in a work by one of the most loyal disciples and fervent defenders of Jansenius — the *Première Apologie pour M. Jansénius* (1644) by Arnauld (considered by some the most influential theologian of the seventeenth century) — and precisely in the context of the debate on predestination, that the term *volonté générale* first appeared. The author defined it as the Divine desire to save all people. Like Augustine and Michel du Bay, Arnauld himself took a specific position in the debate, arguing that God, initially intending to save everyone, changed his general will into a particular one after the fall of Adam and Eve, abandoning the salvation of all in favour of saving a small group of chosen individuals. Arnauld used the term *volonté générale* on many occasions in his later works, for instance in *Des vraies et des fausses idées*⁹ or in his commentary on Malebranche's *Traité de la nature et de la grâce*,¹⁰ sometimes employing it in a sense characteristic of this thinker, namely that of the unchanging laws governing the world. But before we move on to Malebranche, we must first discuss another thinker whose Jansenist leanings can be read within the context of the debate on the general will.

1.1.1. Blaise Pascal

Since the general will was turned into a weapon in the dispute between the Jansenists and Jesuits, it is hardly surprising that its next note-

---

7 http://www.thecounciloftrent.com/ch6.html
8 http://www.romancatholicism.org/jansenism/jansenism-condemnations.htm
9 A. Arnauld, *Des vraies et des fausses idées*, in: idem, *Šuvres philosophiques de Antoine Arnauld*, ed. J. Simon, Paris 1813, p. 163.
10 A. Arnauld, *Réponse du Pčre Malebranche au livre Des vraies et des fausses idées*, in: idem, *Šuvres philosophiques de Antoine*, pp. 293–294.

worthy mention should be found in the writings of Pascal, who after all remained a supporter of Port-Royal for most of his life. The concept of general will appears in two of his works: the popular, collected and posthumously published *Pensées*, as well as the *Écrits sur la grâce* (1656). In the latter, an opposition is made between two categories — *volonté absolue* and *volonté générale*. Pascal defines the first as the Divine will to save a few arbitrarily chosen people, attributing this view to the Calvinists. By general will, on the other hand, he means God's will to save all, regarding St. Augustine as the most prominent exponent of this view. The author of the *Pensées* agrees with St. Augustine's claim that God initially wanted to save everyone, but changed his plan after the fall of man.

A pre-eminently political context, though not bereft of theological reference,[11] was lent to the general will by Pascal in the *Pensées*: "If the feet and the hands had a will of their own [*volonté particulière* – J.G.], they could only be in their order in submitting this particular will to the primary will [*volonté première* – J.G.] which governs the whole body. Apart from that, they are in disorder and mischief; but in willing only the good of the body, they accomplish their own good";[12] "To make the members happy, they must have one will and submit it to the body."[13] It is easy to see parallels to the words of St. Paul here: "but God hath tempered the body together, having given more abundant honour to that part which lacked, that there should be no schism in the body, but that the members should have the same care one for another."[14] Generality and particularism are both valorised and strongly opposed to each other. Riley is therefore correct to discern here a distinct similarity to the later conceptions of Rousseau.[15] Such associations spring particularly to mind when we read:

> We must consider the general good; and the propensity to self is the beginning of all disorder, in war, in politics, in economy, and in the particular body of man. The will is therefore depraved.
>
> If the members of natural and civil communities tend towards the weal of the body, the communities themselves ought to look to another

---

[11] "God having made the heavens and the earth, which do not feel the happiness of their being, He has willed to make beings who should know it, and who should compose a body of thinking members. [...] But for this they would need to have intelligence to know it, and good-will to consent to that of the universal soul" (B. Pascal, *Thoughts*, transl. W.F. Trotter, ed. Ch.W. Eliot, New York, 1910, p. 162 [482]).

[12] *Ibid.*, p. 160 [475].

[13] *Ibid.*, p. 161 [480].

[14] 1 Cor. 12:24–25.

[15] P. Riley, *The General Will Before Rousseau*, p. 17.

more general body of which they are members. We ought therefore to look to the whole.¹⁶

Is it hard to see in this a foreshadowing of Rousseau's later apology of the general will, seeing in its rule the foundation of political order? Similar associations arise on a strictly ethical level: "Self-will will never be satisfied, though it should have command of all it would."¹⁷ Pascal — like Rousseau after him — pointed to the vicious circle of particular desires, impossible ever to satisfy since always turning to new objects. Even if they should all be realised, the individual — alienated from the harmony of the community — will remain empty and unhappy.

The importance of the above statements for the later fate of the idea of the general will is clear to see. With Pascal (a thinker as apolitical as Arnauld and Malebranche), this concept was implanted in the social and political spheres. Pascal equates particular will with self-will, which has no regard for the needs of the community and therefore acts to its detriment. Its antithesis, the general will, tends towards the welfare of the social whole. In order to achieve its aim, it must subjugate the wills of individuals and state institutions.

1.1.2. Nicolas Malebranche

Although the notion of *volonté générale* appeared as early as Arnauld, while Pascal was the first to use it in a socio-political context, it was only Malebranche who appreciated it enough to make it one of the chief categories of his *Traité de la nature et de la grâce*. The concept of general will expounded therein sparked commentaries and criticisms from the greatest minds of the time. It was commented upon by Gottfried Wilhelm Leibniz, John Locke and Rousseau, praised by Bayle, and criticised by Fénelon, Arnauld, Bossuet, Pierre Jurieu and Bernard Fontenelle — even though Malebranche had presented his views on the matter much earlier, in *De la recherche de la vérité* (1674–1675), and in particular in the *Éclaircissements*¹⁸ added to it in 1678. Let us recall that Malebranche, next to Arnold Geulincx (1624–1669), Johannes Clauberg (1622–1665) and Louis de La Forge (1605–1679), was one of the most prominent representatives of occasionalism — the philosophical doctrine denying both *raison d'être* ("Now, it is the will of God which gives existence to bodies and to all created things, the existence of which, certainly, is not necessary. As this will which has created them abides

---

¹⁶ B. Pascal, *Thoughts*, pp. 160–161 [477].
¹⁷ *Ibid.*, p. 159 [472].
¹⁸ P. Riley, *Introduction*, in: N. Malebranche, *Treatise on Nature and Grace*, transl. P. Riley, Oxford 1992, p. 15.

for ever, they too abide"[19]) and causative power to anything or anyone other than God. All that happens in the world happens on account of Divine will. *Dieu fait tout*. The existence and all the actions and workings of objects and people are dependent on His wish: "The Creator alone can be the mover, only He who gives being to bodies can put them in the places which they occupy."[20] It is a mistake to take credit for what are supposedly our actions, since it is inappropriate even to infer anything about them from the fact that our thoughts, wills and actions succeed one another. The occasionalists explain the concurrence of spiritual and bodily movements by the activity of the Creator—for it is He, whose command over the spiritual—as it were—occasions His command over the bodily. For example: "God has willed that my arm shall be set in motion at the instant that I will it myself (given the necessary conditions). His will is efficacious, His will is immutable, it alone is the source of my power and faculties. He has willed that I should experience certain feelings, certain emotions, whenever there are present in my brain certain traces, or whenever a certain disturbance takes place therein. In a word, He has willed—He wills incessantly—that the modifications of the mind and those of the body shall be reciprocal."[21]

In the works of Malebranche, we find a number of arguments in support of the thesis that neither the mind influences the body, nor the body the mind. Man is not an actor in the theatre of the world, but a puppet, used by God like a mere thing for the realisation of His plan. Firstly, the true cause of events must know their nature, have an in-depth understanding of how reality operates, and not—as man does—infer causal connections from the simple succession of events. Malebranche anticipated Hume's *Treatise of Human Nature* in stating that we credit ourselves with knowledge that man cannot possibly fathom. From the fact that we want to do something it does not necessarily follow that we can do it or have done it.[22] Secondly, this ignorance of the processes that take place inside our body makes us powerless to control the latter, and thus equally powerless to control objects through it. Is it not true that in order to do something we must know *how* to do it? Finally, it is unlikely for thought to be able to control bodies, since it is so dissimilar to them. The philosophical origin of occasionalism in this respect is the Cartesian view on the nature of

---

[19] N. Malebranche, *Dialogues on Metaphysics and on Religion*, transl. M. Ginsberg, London 1923, p. 185.
[20] *Ibid.*, p. 190.
[21] *Ibid.*, p. 136.
[22] S. Nadler, *Malebranche on Causation*, in: *Cambridge Companion to Malebranche*, ed. S. Nadler, New York 2000, p. 117.

souls and bodies. The first — unextended — can have nothing in common with the second — extended and material. The idea of a soul controlling a body is just as absurd as that of a body controlling a soul.

Malebranche's argumentation, proclaiming Divine omnipotence and human powerlessness, went hand in hand with the belief that this order, created and continuously sustained by the Divine will, was the best match for the Divine attributes of perfection and its consequence, simplicity of action. Would a world in which everything had its own part in the shaping of reality not be much more complicated and less perfect than one in which the Creator was at the helm of all things? Let us imagine an order, where in the absence of universal laws every element did whatever it wanted to. Would it still be an order, or would we have to call it anarchy? Would it not contradict the idea of Divine wisdom? After all, "A God who is infinitely wise cannot will anything which is, so to speak, unworthy of being willed; He cannot love anything which is not lovable."[23]

This view had a direct impact on the issue of general will. Since God created and continues to sustain the world according to the simplest and immutable laws, then even though He desires to save all people, He will not do so.[24] The world is all too often the scene of suffering, temptation of every kind and the moral downfall of man — presaging his eternal damnation. And although God could intervene whenever His commandments are violated and bring sinners back onto the path of righteousness to shield them from damnation, He will not do so because "God loves mankind [...] but God loves his wisdom infinitely more."[25] This wisdom finds its fullest reflection in the simple and universal laws that the world is subject to. It is they that constitute the Divine *volontés générales*.

> God being obliged to act always in a way worthy of him, through simple, general, constant, and uniform means — in a word means conformed to the idea that we have of a general cause whose wisdom has no limits — he had to establish certain laws in the order of grace, as I have proved him to have done in the order of nature. Now these laws, because of their simplicity, necessarily have unhappy consequences with respect to us: but these consequences do not make it necessary for God to change these laws into more complicated ones. For these laws have a greater proportion of wisdom and of fruitfulness to the work that they produce, than all those which he could establish for the same plan, since he always acts in the wisest and most perfect way. It is true that

---

[23] *Ibid.*, p. 187.
[24] P. Riley, *The General Will Before Rousseau*, p. 28.
[25] N. Malebranche, *Traité de la nature et de la grace, Eclaircissements*, III, XXIII, in: N. Malebranche, *Oeuvres complètes de Malebranche*, Vol. 2, Paris 1837, p. 356.

> God could remedy these unhappy consequences through an infinite number of particular wills: but order will not have it so. The effect which would be produced by each of his particular wills would not be worth the action which would produce it. And in consequence God is not to be blamed for not disturbing the order and the simplicity of his laws by miracles which would be quite convenient to our needs, but quite opposed to the wisdom of God, whom it is not permitted to tempt.[26]

God "must act by general wills, and so settle a constant and regular order, by which He foresees, through the infinite comprehension of His wisdom, that a work so admirable as His must needs be formed".[27] General wills, the unchanging laws of nature, are binding for all of God's creatures — man, animals and things. They include the law of gravitation as well as the law of life and death, which all living beings are subject to. God has given distinct ways of feeding and reproducing themselves to different species; their behaviour follows suitable psychological and physiological laws. "I say that God acts by general wills, when he acts in consequence of general laws which he has established. For example, I say that God acts in me by general wills when he makes me feel pain at the time I am pricked."[28] Is there a universal way of telling when we are dealing with a general, and when with a particular, will? When do we witness a universal law, and when an intervention that violates it? How are we to treat events that leave us uncertain as to the universal or particular nature of their causality? In such cases, writes Malebranche, "we must judge that an effect is produced by a general will, when it is obvious that the cause has proposed no particular end to himself."[29] When rain falls onto a single meadow, we have grounds to suppose that God wants to help its owner through His particular will. But when it also rains on all the surrounding meadows, then we may be sure that the general will is speaking through the unchanging laws of nature.

The *volontés particulières* are thus Divine interventions in the established order, perturbing the ordinary course of events and ignoring the laws that govern them; they are the miracles that protect people from suffering, both temporal and eternal — born of their moral downfall.[30] Believing firmly in the wisdom and omnipotence of God, Malebranche

---

[26] N. Malebranche, *Treatise on Nature and Grace*, transl. P. Riley, Oxford 1992, I, XLIII, pp. 128–129.
[27] *Ibid.*, I, XXXVIII, p. 27.
[28] *Ibid.*, Illustration I, p. 195.
[29] *Ibid.*, VI, p. 198.
[30] Cf. S. Brown, *The Critical Reception of Malebranche*, in: *Cambridge Companion to Malebranche*, pp. 270–272.

could not conceive that God uses miracles to violate his own laws. Hence he rejected even the mere idea of Divine intervention. What should we then think of the miracles described in the Bible? Are we to pass over them in silence, pretending that they never happened, thereby discrediting the authority of Scripture? No, was Malebranche's answer. It is simply that what to us appears a miracle, a violation of the laws governing the world, an exceptional intervention by God, correcting the imperfections in the order of the world, is no such thing. It of course looks like that from our perspective, but we should have the humility to admit that since we do not have perfect knowledge of the laws governing creation, we cannot accurately tell the difference between their operation and their suspension.[31]

This was the bone of contention between Malebranche and Arnauld (as expounded by the latter in *Neuf lettres de M. Arnauld contre R.P. Malebranche* and *Réflexions philosophiques et théologiques sur le nouveau système de la nature et de la grâce*). Their differing opinions on the generality/particularity of will and Divine laws found an outlet in the debate on grace and miracles. On the first issue, Arnauld maintained that if God had wanted to save only the elect, He would have to use His particular will to do so, since people cannot be differentiated when subjected to a universal, simple and inflexible law of salvation. Malebranche on the other hand saw such a possibility, arguing that the same universal grace accorded to all can permanently transform some into men of virtue, while having no such effect on others. For it also falls upon hearts that are corrupt beyond moral repair.[32]

On the second issue—the possibility of Divine intervention—Arnauld accuses his adversary of a dual offence.[33] Firstly, that Malebranche has questioned events confirmed by the Holy Scripture, which in itself merits condemnation. Secondly, that he has attempted an illegitimate redefinition of the concept of God, replacing the merciful Father with a soulless tormentor, in love with himself rather than his children, who would sooner observe the suffering and death of multitudes than admit that his laws do not make the world the best of all possible places. Malebranche's cardinal error, and the source of all his subsequent sins, was the unjustified equation of universal laws with the general will. Having established the former, why should God not desire to act in the particular? Why should He refuse Himself the right

---

[31] N. Malebranche, *Treatise of Nature and Grace*, I, LVII, p. 137.
[32] D. Rutherford, *Malebranche's Theodicy*, in: *Cambridge Companion to Malebranche*, p. 178.
[33] See D. Moreau, *The Malebranche–Arnauld Debate*, in: *Cambridge Companion to Malebranche*, pp. 100–102.

to intervene in the established order? The generality of God's will may both signify its general conformity with universal laws and its direction towards particular objects.[34]

Summing up, it should be noted that in the *Traité de la nature et de la grâce*, the subject of the general will appears within a novel context where it is no longer related to the posthumous fate of people. Malebranche understands it not as the goal, but as the nature of Divine action. It is no longer the salvation of all versus the salvation of a few that provides the measure of generality, but the means God employs to carry out His intent. In this way, as Riley correctly pointed out, the theological concept is placed within a legal context.[35] God acts through universal laws, thereby expressing His wisdom and omnipotence. From here, there is but a single step to the political postulate of limiting the number of positive rights. It follows that a wise ruler, similar to God, will contribute more effectively to the good of his subjects with one good law than with hundreds of interventions aiming to redress the damage caused by a bad one.[36]

1.1.3. Jacques-Bénigne Bossuet, François Fénelon, Pierre Bayle

Malebranche's conception of the general will met with violent resistance from the most eminent minds of seventeenth-century Europe. Bossuet criticised it both in his *Oraison funèbre de Marie-Thérèse d'Autriche* (1683) and later in his introduction to Fénelon's *Réfutation du système du Père Malebranche sur la nature et la grâce*. This question had already preoccupied him earlier, when still a supporter of Jansenism and a defender of its main theses—sometimes in ways virtually indistinguishable from the later conceptions of Rousseau. But it was only in his famous funeral speech, written and delivered on the death of Maria Theresa, that he chose the subject as one of his main themes. Referring directly to Malebranche, he clamoured: "How I despise those philosophers who, making their own intelligence the measure of God's purposes, would regard Him merely as the creator of a certain general order which He then left to develop as best it might. As if, like ours, God's aims were vague and confused generalities, as if His sovereign intelligence were powerless to include in its scheme those individual existences which alone, strictly speaking, can be said to live."[37] There is no greater mistake than to think that God acts solely through universal

---

[34] *Ibid.*, p. 101.
[35] P. Riley, *The General Will Before Rousseau*, p. 17.
[36] N. Malebranche, *Treatise of Nature and Grace*, I, XXXVIII, p. 127.
[37] Cited after: P. Hazard, *The European Mind 1680–1715*, transl. J.L. May, Middlesex 1964, p. 248.

laws. Has He not appointed specific families to rule in specific countries, of which He gives proof in the Holy Scripture?[38] Was it not God who brought Maria Theresa and Louis XIV before the altar, so that she could become queen of the French? Is this not evidence of grace bestowed on those most worthy of it? For by all accounts, grace is nothing but an exception from universal laws, rewarding a specific person or group. A similar tone was employed by Bossuet in a letter to the Marquis d'Allemans, where he stated that by his *Traité de la nature et de la grâce* Malebranche had completely depreciated grace, praising nature in its place.[39]

Bossuet particularly disparaged the Cartesian cast of Malebranche's apotheosis of general laws. For that matter, Malebranche openly voiced his sympathy for the author of the *Discourse on Method*. For is the Cartesian system not more helpful in elucidating God's intentions than a jumble of Moses' words from the Book of Genesis?[40] The allegedly "scientific" analysis of Scripture, made possible by Cartesianism, could not be reconciled with the orthodox outlook of Bossuet the convert. Why reach for philosophical novelties, instead of relying on the authority of the Bible? Is this not how the main heresies were born? *Pulchra, nova, falsa* – these are the words Bossuet added in the margins of his copy of *Traité de la nature et de la grâce*.

But it is not solely in his critical works that Bossuet expresses his views on the nature of Divine will. His whole *Discours sur l'histoire universelle* is an apology of *Providence particulière*. It contains many fragments which clearly suggest that it is "particular Providence (*Providence particulière*) with which he governs human things".[41] Embarking on a history of the chosen people, Bossuet remarks that "Surely, Sir, nothing can be conceived more worthy of God, than to have, first of all, chosen to himself a people, who should be a palpable instance of his eternal providence; a people, whose good or ill fortune should depend upon their piety, and whose condition should bear testimony to the wisdom and justice of Him who governed them."[42] In the subsequent chapters, Bossuet summed up the fate of nations in the following way: "Who would not here admire the divine providence, so manifestly declared upon the Jews and Chaldeans, upon Jerusalem and Babylon? God means to punish both; and that they may not be ignorant, that it is he

---

[38] Ex. 17:6.
[39] P. Riley, *The General Will Before Rousseau*, p. 71.
[40] Cf. P. Riley, *Introduction*, in: J.-B. Bossuet, *Politics Drawn from the Very Words of Holy Scripture*, transl. P. Riley, Cambridge 1990, p. XXIV.
[41] J.-B. Bossuet, *An Universal History from the Creation of the World to the Time of Charlemagne*, London 1810, p. 181.
[42] *Ibid.*, p. 158.

alone who does it, he is pleased to declare it by an hundred prophecies."[43]

A similar position was taken by Bossuet's disciple, Fénelon. Encouraged by his master to confront Malebranche, in the *Réfutation du système du Père Malebranche*, written expressly for this purpose, he reproved the latter for depreciating God's particular will. In light of his inspiration, it is hardly surprising that Fénelon's critique so greatly resembles that of Bossuet. For he wrote that, since the world is full of imperfections, then having made the assumption that God cannot intervene to ensure people's good, one would have to deny Him the attribute of mercy. On the other hand, if He were to intervene too often, He would be neither omniscient nor omnipotent. He would simply have chosen the wrong laws to impose on the world, which might have been made to work more effectively. Malebranche's Cartesianism inevitably leads him to the antipodes of Catholic orthodoxy, if not beyond the pale of Catholicism as such.

Despite their contribution to the development of the idea of *volonté générale*, neither the writings of Bossuet nor those of Fénelon served directly to inspire subsequent secular interpretations of the concept. No straight line can therefore be traced connecting their theories with the conceptions of Montesquieu or Rousseau. Riley saw the link between the theist tradition and the later secular and political one as residing in the writings of Bayle, who both popularised and continued the thought of Malebranche.

Bayle—today remembered mainly for his work on the *Dictionnaire historique et critique* as well as his staunch defence of religious tolerance —saw Descartes and Malebranche as the greatest minds of the seventeenth century. On more than one occasion, he engaged in a fervent defence of the latter's views. He rebutted charges against Malebranche's understanding of the nature of bodies and, in numerous articles and letters, defended his position in the controversy against Arnauld and Fontenelle. Nonetheless, it would be a mistake to infer that he was an uncritical disciple. The evolution of Bayle's views on Malebranche's philosophy can be discerned particularly when we consider his early writings and those published posthumously.

The young Bayle was a zealous champion of occasionalism. On this particular point the convergence of his views with those of Malebranche had a direct impact on the debate concerning the general will. It was precisely in this early period of his work that Bayle wrote the *Pensées diverses sur la comète* (1683). In this book, published as a contribution to the debate about the meaning of the comets that appeared

---

[43] *Ibid.*, p. 235.

in December 1680, he argued — against the supporters of Bossuet — that Divine wisdom presupposes the necessity of keeping to universal laws, established once and for all, and has no need for interventions whose only effect is to preserve superstitions (for what else can we call predictions on future misfortunes based on a falling comet?). "God, as being the disposer of events, and the distributor of good and bad success on earth, has submitted virtue and innocency to general laws, no less than health and riches."[44] In the *Pensées diverses*, quite in the spirit of Malebranche, the author claimed that man,

> [w]retched and frail creature that he is, he can persuade himself that he could not die without troubling the whole of nature and without obliging heaven to put itself to the expense of illuminating his funeral procession. Stupid and ridiculous vanity! [...] We would say with the one who had the most sublime thoughts of all the philosophers of ancient Rome, that in truth the concerns of Providence extend as far as us and that we for our part share in it but that its end is indeed considerably different from our preservation and that while the movements of the heavens bring us things of great utility, this is nevertheless not to say that these vast bodies are moved by love of the earth.[45]

God does not intervene in the order of the world to satisfy man's sense of justice or his curiosity of future events. Even were He to intervene, His action would doubtless not be so unclear as to occasion a debate on whether it is one or not. After all, wanting to convey His message to humanity, he had sent Christ, whose divinity was indisputable, although He could have sent hundreds of comets or other equally easily interpreted signs. Let us therefore not overestimate the meaning of God's particular will, of whose operation in nature we have so little proof. Nor should we question's God's authority as lawgiver, since we are apt to mock and scorn even earthly rulers, who too frequently issue commands in order to reverse the damage accomplished by earlier unjust edicts, and ridicule the gravity of their office. Would God, intervening by means of falling comets, not merit even greater disdain — He to whom we ascribe omniscience and omnipotence?

It is easy to detect a repetition of Malebranche's theses in the above argument. Still, as we noted earlier, Bayle was not entirely uncritical of the teachings of his master. He had difficulty in accepting Malebranche's soulless vision of the world — with no place for either human freedom or Divine mercy. On the first issue, Bayle was aware that the freedom, which the heart instinctively demands, cannot with-

---

[44] P. Bayle, *An Historical and Critical Dictionary Selected and Abridged from the Great Work of Peter Bayle,* Vol. III, London 1826, p. 385.

[45] P. Bayle, *Various Notes on the Occasion of a Comet,* transl. Robert C. Bartlett, Albany 2000, p. 104.

stand rational argumentation. The freedom of Luther, Calvin and the Jansenists, founded on the thesis of predestination, is backed by metaphysical deductions and the postulates of reason. Both ethics and theology require freedom based on spontaneous action, the autonomy and liberty of trial and error. If the accountability for human deeds rests not with man but with God, commanding man as He sees fit, then how can one explain the existence of evil? Is it not then inevitably imputable to God, the sole cause of all things?

This argument appears in Bayle's unfinished, posthumously published *Entretiens de Maxime et de Thémiste*. Recognising God as the cause of all things, we must then burden Him with responsibility for suffering. However, such a step gives rise to a number of doubts. Why would He bring misfortune upon people who are merely passive executors of His will? How can He judge and condemn only some, since all are His puppets? If blind adherence to universal laws can lead to evil, which might be avoided if the Creator were to make even the most minute intervention, then why does He not do it? Does Scripture not give examples of greater miracles, though perhaps less spectacular than the one which might have kept Adam and Eve from sin? The fall of the first people, but also the sins of those who followed, show that God has more appreciation for the aesthetic value of a world operating according to fixed laws than for its moral value. Does this not contradict our image of a merciful God? Can such an attribute be ascribed to a God who cherishes the iron steadfastness of His actions above man? Seemingly not.

1.1.4. Montesquieu

The works of Montesquieu are the first example of a systematic consideration of generality and particularity as political categories. This reflection can be said to take two tracks. On the one hand, it exalts the Divine wisdom underlying the eternal, unchanging laws governing the world, and in this it is distinctly Malebranchian. Like the author of the *Traité de la nature et de la grâce*, Montesquieu did not apply this reasoning solely to theological matters, but also to issues relating to state governance. On the other hand, the dichotomy between generality and particularity manifests itself with full force in an issue directly linked to the art of government, although not fully dependent on it, namely the influence that geopolitical conditions (in particular geographical location) have on specific nations.

Montesquieu's use of the concept of *volonté générale*, and especially the marked influence of Malebranche on his understanding of it, are hardly surprising given his education and his immediate circle of friends. Montesquieu was educated by the Oratorians at the Collège de

Juilly, while his friends included figures such as Father Nicolas Demolets, the Oratorians' librarian and editor of some of the thoughts of Pascal, Cardinal Melchior de Polignac, the author of *Anti-Lucrèce*, a work imbued with the ideas of Malebranche, as well as Fontenelle's close associate, Dortous de Mairan.[46] It is therefore highly probable that Montesquieu was not only familiar with Malebranche's works, but also that they significantly shaped his own views. It is hardly difficult to find traces of this influence in his writing. They are present both in the early *Persian Letters* (1721), in the only fragmentarily preserved *Traité des devoirs* (1748), as well as the late *Spirit of the Laws* (1748). In this last work, Montesquieu writes:

> God is related to the universe, as Creator and Preserver; the laws by which He created all things are those by which He preserves them. He acts according to these rules, because He knows them; He knows them, because He made them; and He made them, because they are in relation to His wisdom and power. Since we observe that the world, though formed by the motion of matter, and void of understanding, subsists through so long a succession of ages, its motions must certainly be directed by invariable laws.[47]

Here, Montesquieu is of course referring to Malebranche's thesis regarding the generality and immutability of Divine laws. For their mutability would make the perspicacity of the the Creator's judgments questionable. It is therefore not surprising that in the following fragment of *The Spirit of the Laws* its author effects a positive valorisation of the permanence of the laws of nature: "particular intelligent beings are of a finite nature, and consequently liable to error",[48] "[m]an, as a physical being, is like other bodies governed by invariable laws. As an intelligent being, he incessantly transgresses the laws established by God, and changes those of his own instituting."[49] Montesquieu clearly contrasts Divine wisdom and human pride here. For this is the only term with which to designate the belief that the power of human reason can equal the omnipotence and omniscience of the Creator. One can easily discern an analogy here with the later thought of Rousseau. For although the latter was clearly hostile to Montesquieu's works (especially his *magnum opus*), he nevertheless made the dichotomy between generality and particularity the centre of his political philosophy, criticising particularism and praising the general in a manner reminiscent of Montesquieu.

---

[46] P. Riley, *The General Will Before Rousseau*, pp. 139–140.
[47] Montesquieu, *The Spirit of the Laws*, Book I.I, transl. T. Nugent, New York 1899, p. 1.
[48] *Ibid.*, I, I, p. 2.
[49] *Ibid.*, I, I, p. 3.

This dialectic between generality and particularity also manifests itself in the *Persian Letters*.[50] But the fragment of Montesquieu's writing considered by scholars to contain the most evident proof of the politicisation of the category of *volonté générale* is chapter six of his famous eleventh book of *The Spirit of the Laws*. It is here, describing the dismal state of liberty in the Italian republics, that he writes: "In what a situation must the poor subject be in those republics! The same body of magistrates are possessed, as executors of the laws, of the whole power they have given themselves in quality of legislators. They may plunder the state by their general determinations; and as they have likewise the judiciary power in their hands, every private citizen may be ruined by their particular decisions."[51] The author's intention here is to show that an institutional separation of powers is necessary. In contrast to his earlier theological remarks, in which he voiced his unmistakable disapproval for particularisms, the political dimension of the opposition *générale – particulière* does not incite him to such categorical judgments. Generality and particularity must coexist within the same administrative body — this is a deplorable fact — but it is also what makes it so important for this body not to possess both the power to create and to enforce laws. Montesquieu approached this dichotomy in a more critical, Rousseauian fashion in *Mes Pensées*, giving advice both on how princes should act and on the general order within a community. Regarding the first, he stated that princes should only succumb to the lure of great things, and never to the *affections particulières* tied to particular phenomena (people, events, opinions).[52] As for the second, he emphasised — practically in the style of the *Social Contract* — the necessity of the reign of the general spirit (*esprit général*) in republics, and so the restriction of particularisms. One of the means to this end was to be the limitation of luxury, so that citizens would be ready to pursue the common good even at the expense of personal material losses.

Montesquieu's remarks were in a similar tone in the *Traité des devoirs* (1725). Unfortunately, this work has not survived to our day and we can only deduce information about it from the works of his contemporaries or from his own references to it in the *Pensées*, as well as Book I of *The Spirit of the Laws*. We know that in it Montesquieu referred to Cicero's *De Officiis* and Pufendorf's *De Officio hominis et civilis*, using them to counter Thomas Hobbes' positivism. We also know that he

---

[50] Montesquieu, *The Complete Works of M. de Montesquieu*, London 1777, Vol. 3, *Persian Letters*, XXIV.
[51] Montesquieu, *The Spirit of the Laws*, II, XI, p. 153.
[52] Montesquieu's argument keeps to a similar spirit in *Considérations sur les causes de la grandeur des Romains et de leur décadence*, in: Montesquieu, *Œuvres complètes*, ed. D. Oster, Paris 1964, pp. 453, 462.

came across as a fervent advocate of the theory of natural law, whether in its ancient or modern form. Finally, we know that he wrote about justice as firmly established in the very essence of the coexistence of individuals, and not as dependent on individual opinions. Thus, there is nothing surprising that the nature of his considerations on the general will and the laws of nature was a forerunner of the later thought of Diderot. Montesquieu affirmed that whenever we encounter a conflict between our particular duties (*devoirs particuliers*), deriving from our civic responsibilities, and our responsibilities towards the human race, we should always act to fulfil the latter.

The second context of those mentioned above, in which Montesquieu employed the general–particular dichotomy, is the geopolitical one. Long before Friedrich Ratzel — who founded geopolitics as an academic discipline — and his followers such as Johan Rudolf Kjellén, Montesquieu noted that "[m]ankind are influenced by various causes: by the climate, by the religion, by the laws, by the maxims of government, by precedents, morals and customs; whence is formed a general spirit of nations."[53] Laws "should be in relation to the climate of each country, to the quality of its soil, to its situation and extent, to the principal occupation of the natives".[54] Ample thought has been devoted to this issue in the relevant literature, so we can permit ourselves only a summary presentation of it. Montesquieu's postulate of the particularism of laws is the result of the valorisation of the character of the specific community they are to serve. The latter is determined in part by the views of the inhabitants, their number, and the geographical and historical context of their existence. Hence, although they are common for the citizens of a given state, they cannot be said to have universal applicability. This is why the author of *The Spirit of the Laws* is sometimes thought to be an opponent of the theory of natural law. Our next thinker, Diderot, placed his considerations on the general will within an entirely different and, as suggested earlier, universalist and jusnaturalistic context.

1.1.5. Denis Diderot

The sincere and lively friendship Diderot and Rousseau initially enjoyed can only be measured against the hatred and contempt they had for each other subsequently. It is therefore just as likely that Rousseau heard the main idea of his prize-winning *Discourse on the Arts and Sciences*, the source of his fame, which determined his further philosophical development, from the lips of Diderot, at that time a

---

[53] Montesquieu, *The Spirit of the Laws*, XIX, III, p. 293.
[54] *Ibid.*, I, III, pp. 7–8.

prisoner at the Vincennes fortress, as it is that the latter invented the story to spite his later enemy. A similar shadow of doubt casts itself on the question of the potential influence of the author of the *Letter on the Blind* on Rousseau insofar as the issue of the general will is concerned. It is known that, during the period of their friendship, both published articles concerning *volonté générale* in the same fifth volume of the *Encyclopédie*—Rousseau his *Discourse on Political Economy*, and Diderot his entry on *Droit naturel*. Charles Edwin Vaughan even considered the possibility that it was Diderot who inspired the Rousseauian idea of the general will, although he himself, as with many of his other ideas, did not develop it any further.[55] The reference[56] made by the author of the *Discourse on Political Economy*, Rousseau's first work touching on the problem of the general will, to Diderot's article may be evidence of this.

Nonetheless, the possibility that Rousseau may have drawn his inspiration from Diderot does not alter the fact that, although their conceptions of the general will converge on certain points, they remain irreconcilable. For what precisely did Diderot write in his article? He examined the case of a man explaining his readiness to harm others by the natural desire for his own happiness. "If my happiness demands that I destroy the lives of all those who disturb me, it is also necessary for an individual, whomever he may be, to be able to destroy mine if he is similarly disturbed; reason requires this, and I subscribe to it."[57] We must reject the views of this "violent reasoner", as Diderot calls him. No one may try to resolve issues of natural law, and therefore also of unchanging human needs and the ways in which they can be satisfied, based solely on their own desires. The precepts of nature cannot be discovered by way of introspection, as Rousseau maintained. In that case "where shall we place this great question? Where? Before the entire human race; for only they may decide the issue, since the good of all is the only passion they have, Particular wills are suspect; they can be good or evil, but the general will is always good: it is never wrong, it never will be wrong."[58] The general will is thus an attribute of the entire human race. Diderot did not ascribe it to the political community, as Rousseau later did, or to the legislative power, as Montesquieu

---

[55] C.E. Vaughan, *Droit Naturel*, in: J.J. Rousseau, *The Political Writings of Jean-Jacques Rousseau. In Two Volumes*, ed. C.E. Vaughan, Vol. 1, Cambridge 1915, pp. 425–427.

[56] J.J. Rousseau, *Discourse on Political Economy*, in: J.J. Rousseau, *The Social Contract and Other Political Writings*, ed. V. Gourevitch, Cambridge 1997, pp. 6–7.

[57] D. Diderot, *Denis Diderot's The Encyclopedia: Selections*, ed. S.J. Gendzier, New York 1967, pp. 115–116.

[58] *Ibid.*, pp. 115–116.

did. Humankind is the residuum of precepts that are "always good". "It is to the general will that the individual must address himself to know up to what point he must be a man, a citizen, a subject, a father, a child, and when it is suitable to live or to die. The general will determines the limits of all duties."[59] No individual suppositions or even positive rights determine what is right. This power belongs to all of humanity. "You have the most sacred natural rights in everything that is not contested by the entire species."[60] Where then should we look for an indication of which actions are permissible by this final instance insofar as morality is concerned? "In the principles of law written by all civilised nations; in the social practices of savage and barbaric peoples; in the tacit conventions between enemies of mankind among themselves; and even in the feelings of indignation and resentment, these two passions which nature seems to have placed even in animals to compensate for the deficiency of laws in society and the blemish of public vengeance."[61]

All human communities have hitherto governed themselves according to the precepts of the general will. Not only people, but also other animals (Diderot considered humans as such) follow its prescriptions, although due to a lack of capacity for reasoning it manifests itself in them as instinct. Diderot closes his reflections with a synthetic comparison of eight conclusions regarding the role of the *volonté générale* in the life of political communities and all of mankind: 1) "that the man who listens only to his particular will is the enemy of the human race; 2) [...] the general will in each individual is a pure act of understanding that reasons in the silence of the passions about what man can demand of his fellow man and about what his fellow man can rightfully demand of him";[62] 3) that its rules apply equally to relations between individuals and between societies; 4) "the submission to the general will is the bond of all societies";[63] 5) laws must be general in their object; 6) the goal of legislators should be to put the precepts of the general will into law; 7) the general will, like natural law, remains constant; 8) there is only natural justice, while that which contradicts it is always unjust.

Many of Diderot's theses were later repeated by Rousseau in his work. A comparative analysis of their distinct approaches is not our aim here, but one is tempted to give a general idea of a number of particularly striking similarities and differences. In terms of the former, our

---

[59] Ibid.
[60] Ibid.
[61] Ibid.
[62] Ibid.
[63] Ibid.

attention is drawn to statements by Diderot such as: "what veneration we owe the august mortals whose particular wills reunite both the authority and the infallibility of the general will", or his critique of those who follow only their particular will at the expense of the general good. These statements bring to mind not only Rousseau's glorification of the *volonté générale*, but also the works of Pascal or Montesquieu already cited here. Yet while the similarities between both visions of the general will can be ascribed to a mere stylistic convergence, the differences concern fundamental issues. It is not the human race — Rousseau shall later say — but specific communities that dispose of general wills, and therefore the *volonté générale* does not exist in the natural state, but only within society. For that matter, Rousseau's "noble savage" was only noble because he lacked reason. Meanwhile, Diderot suggested that he too could be credited with "a pure act of understanding [...] in the silence of the passions". And since, according to Rousseau, there is no such thing as a natural general will that determines what is just, there is also no such thing as natural justice.

It is in this manner that a concept whose initial meaning was strictly theological became entirely secularised. Whereas Montesquieu, in a manner practically indistinguishable from the occasionalism of Malebranche, still used it to refer to the general, divinely-established laws governing the world, Diderot used it solely within the context of laws serving to preserve the human race. This understanding was also decidedly closer to that of Rousseau, though he tied it more closely with Montesquieu's contextualism. And although the notion of the general will can be read within a number of other philosophical contexts, while its specific incarnations can be found in the pantheism of Baruch Spinoza, Leibniz's theodicy, not to mention defenders of Malebranche such as Voltaire,[64] the last pre-nineteenth-century thinker to be discussed in this chapter will be the figure who permanently transplanted the subject of the general will into the political arena — Rousseau.

1.2. The general will in the thought of Jean-Jacques Rousseau

For a long time — in fact until the beginning of the twentieth century[65] — Rousseau's thought was considered inconsistent, frequently treating

---

[64] Voltaire, *Grâce*, in: idem, *Dictionnaire philosophique portatif*, London 1764, pp. 212–215.

[65] A pioneering work in this respect was Gustav Lanson's essay *L'Unité de la pensée de Jean-Jacques Rousseau*, "Annales de la société Jean-Jacques Rousseau" 1912, Vol. 8, pp. 1–12. This thesis was later repeated by George Douglas Howard Cole (G.D.H. Cole, *Introduction*, in: J.J. Rousseau, *The Social Contract & Discourses*, London 1913, p. XVII), Ernst Cassirer (E.

the same problems in ways so dissimilar as to make it impossible to extract a single interpretative key allowing the reader to grasp it as a whole, or even an unquestionable leading idea that could be used to class the subjects touched upon by this thinker by order of their importance. An echo of this approach can be found in the theories of the most important contemporary scholars of Rousseauian thought. Some would like to perceive him only[66] as a rationalist, or even a protoplast of Kantianism,[67] assigning the key role in the creation of the ideal personality and social order to reason, and totally depreciating or at least diminishing the part played by emotions. Others focus on the religious dimension of his philosophy, studying the influence on his thought of the Calvinism of his native Geneva, or the place occupied by religious issues in the totality of his output. Others yet emphasise the sentimental quality of his work or explain his entire legacy in the light of his life or psychosomatic condition.

Differences in the appraisal of Rousseau's work are particularly visible in the analysis of his philosophical and political themes. Was he an apostle of the Revolution, his writings offering a theoretical justification of all of its atrocities, an unfavourably interpreted democrat seeking the source of the legitimacy of power in the consent of the people, a methodological individualist, a precursor of conservatism, socialism and Marxism, or is it perhaps that his thought lends itself to each of these interpretations? Scholars have given various answers to these questions, sometimes proposing differing interpretations of the same fragments of Rousseau's writing. In their analyses, some have only considered the *Social Contract* and its project for the constitution of a state governed by the precepts of the general will. Others, taking into account only Rousseau's practical projects—*On the Government of Poland* and the *Constitutional Project for Corsica*—saw their author as the initiator of the concept of the imperative mandate, entirely disregarding the explicit critique of the institutions of representative democracy in his other works. Some, accepting the claim of the irreducible complexity of Rousseau's work, deliberately ignored in their analyses the

---

Cassirer, *L'Unité dans l'œuvre de J.J. Rousseau*, "Bulletin de la société française de philosophie" 1932), Pierre Burgerlin (P. Burgerlin, *La philosophie de l'existence de J.J. Rousseau*, Paris 1952, pp. 505–507), Jean Starobinski (J. Starobinski, *La pensée politique de Jean-Jacques Rousseau*, in: *Jean-Jacques Rousseau*, ed. S. Baud-Bovey, Neuchâtel 1962, p. 86).

[66] R. Derathé, *Le rationalisme de Jean-Jacques Rousseau*, Geneva 1979.
[67] E. Cassirer, *Rousseau, Kant, Goethe*, New York 1965; P. Burgelin, *Kant lecteur de Rousseau*, in: *Jean-Jacques Rousseau et son œuvre. Problèmes et recherches. Commémoration et Colloque de Paris (16–20 octobre 1962)*, Paris 1964, pp. 303–315.

writings they considered as straying from what they saw as the leading ideas of the philosopher's world view.[68]

Rousseau's legacy has been interpreted in nearly all of its aspects. At the same time, the specific nature of his thought has frequently constituted an obstacle to attempts to treat its various elements independently. Rousseau himself is not without fault here. Regardless of whether he can be called a systemic thinker, he certainly cannot be called a systematic one. His own usage of the key concepts of his thought was never precise. Their definition often changed with subsequent works, and sometimes even with subsequent pages of the same work (of which the category of the general will is the best example). From the perspective of a scholar of Rousseau's thought this has both a positive and negative aspect. The former includes the possibility of a constant reinterpretation of his writings. This applies both to new perspectives on the links between their basic categories as well as the emphasis of different aspects of Rousseau's thought. The analytical treatment of the legacy of this thinker provides us with a perfect example of a "hermeneutic circle". This susceptibility to interpretative innovations is also one of the main reasons underlying the interest Rousseau's works sparked among representatives of deconstructionism, with Jacques Derrida[69] and Paul de Man[70] at the forefront. And yet the main advantage of this lack of systematicity also turns out to be one of its greatest flaws. The diversity of potential references and approaches precludes the use of a single interpretative key, the plurality and diversity of the ideas present in Rousseau's work prevent the formulation of a definitive description of their interrelationships, binding for later generations of scholars. And although many of the canonical works by experts in Rousseauian thought have laid foundations for the creation of distinctive schools of interpretation, it is impossible to speak of any dominant reading of his philosophy among them.

---

[68] Raymond Polin considered the *Constitutional Project for Corsica* to be such a work (R. Polin, *La politique de la solitude. Essai sur la philosophie politique de Jean-Jacques Rousseau*, Paris 1971, p. 132). Similarly so with *On the Government of Poland*, which instead of direct democracy, constituting the foundation of the government of the general will in the *Social Contract*, also give raison d'etre to representative organs (cf. O. Krafft, *La politique de Jean-Jacques Rousseau: Aspects Méconnus*, Paris 1958).

[69] See J. Derrida, *Of Grammatology*, tranls. G.C. Spivak, Baltimore, MD 1997, pp. 97–100.

[70] P. de Man, *Allegories of Reading: Figural Language in Rousseau, Nietzsche, Rilke and Proust*, New Haven, CT–London 1979.

1.2.1. The general will. Definition and interpretations

It is fitting to begin the definition of the notion of the general will, both so crucial to Rousseau's thought and so enigmatic, with the remark that the author never explicitly gives one. Which is doubtless why opinions similar to that voiced by Bertrand Russell, who called the Rousseauian general will a doctrine "both important and obscure",[71] have gained such popularity in the relevant literature. The works in which Rousseau indicates the correct understanding of the *volonté générale* are those written after 1754. It was at that time that he began work on the *Discourse on Political Economy*, where the term appears for the first time. The political conceptions expounded therein correspond nearly in their entirety to the content of the *Social Contract*, written eight years later. Hence the second work of key importance to our considerations is the *Social Contract* itself. This is supplemented, though to a small degree, by a chapter of *Emile, or On Education*, in which the author presents a general outline of his philosophy of the state.

Several generations of scholars have investigated the nature of the *volonté générale*, based on the sources mentioned above, defining it in the most varied ways. And so, for instance, Frank Thakurdas writes that "the General Will is a unifying, constructive and integrating principle which alone gives and can give coherency to the body politic in all its diverse aspects";[72] to Franz Haymann it is a maxim which takes the good of all people as a directive;[73] James MacAdam defines it as "will of that which is in the common interest";[74] to Guglielmo Ferrero it is a religious absolute that can only be discovered by a mind in the state of grace;[75] while Émile Durkheim calls it "an impersonal form of the forces of nature".[76] It would be hard to come up with more ambiguous and less congruous definitions. This is hardly surprising, since what their authors attempted was to condense the meaning of a concept, serving so many functions in the thought of Rousseau, and which he himself employed in a variety of contexts, into a single brief formula. These attempts were inevitably bound to produce imprecise definitions or reduce the term to only one of the meanings assigned to it by Rousseau. Let us therefore analyse the designations and functions assigned to the

---

[71] B. Russell, *History of Western Philosophy*, London 1947, p. 724.
[72] F. Thakurdas, *Rousseau and the Concept*, p. 80.
[73] F. Haymann, *J.J. Rousseau Sozialphilosophie*, Leipzig 1899, p. 80.
[74] J. MacAdam, *What Rousseau Meant by the General Will*, in: *Rousseau's Response to Hobbes*, ed. H.R. Cell, J.I. MacAdam, New York 1988, p. 147.
[75] G. Ferrero, *Pouvoir. Les génies invisibles de la cité*, Paris 1943, p. 59.
[76] É. Durkheim, *Le "Contrat Social" de Rousseau*, "Revue de Métaphysique et de Morale" 1918, Vol. 25, p. 23.

volonté générale in his work so that we may avoid the error of reducing its essence to but one of many possible interpretations.

Since Rousseau does not give a clear definition of the general will, we must look for its attributes wherever the concept appears in his writing:

> [E]ach of us puts his person and all his power in common under the supreme direction of the general will, and, in our corporate capacity, we receive each member as an indivisible part of the whole.[77]

> The body politic, therefore, is also a moral being possessed of a will; and this general will, which tends always to the preservation and welfare of the whole and of every part, and is the source of the laws, constitutes for all the members of the State, in their relations to one another and to it, the rule of what is just or unjust.[78]

The body politic, the community, is a "moral being" to which citizens belong like parts to a whole. It has its own will—the general will—deciding what is just and always directed towards the "preservation and welfare of the whole and of every part". This body is indivisible, and so is not a simple aggregation of individuals, but a moral whole irreducible to the sum of its parts.

> [T]he general will is always right and tends to the public advantage.[79]

> [E]ach individual, as a man, may have a particular will contrary or dissimilar to the general will which he has as a citizen. His particular interest may speak to him quite differently from the common interest.[80]

> The first and most important deduction from the principles we have so far laid down is that the general will alone can direct the State according to the object for which it was instituted, *i.e.* the common good.[81]

> There is often a great deal of difference between the will of all and the general will; the latter considers only the common interest, while the former takes private interest into account, and is no more than a sum of particular wills.[82]

The general will—the expression of "public advantage" and "common interest"—has to be differentiated from private will, the expression of particular interest. Although both can coexist in a person, each speak-

---

[77] J.J. Rousseau, *The Social Contract and Discourses*, transl. G.D.H. Cole, London 1923, I, VII, p. 15.
[78] J.J. Rousseau, *Political Economy*, in: J.J. Rousseau, *The Social Contract and Discourses*, p. 253.
[79] J.J. Rousseau, *Social Contract*, II, III, p. 25.
[80] *Ibid.*, I, VII, pp. 17–18.
[81] *Ibid.*, II, I, p. 22.
[82] *Ibid.*, II, III, p. 25.

ing to him in its own way, as a citizen he will only obey the dictates of the general will.

> [T]he general will, to be really such, must be general in its object as well as its essence; [...] it must both come from all and apply to all; [...] it loses its natural rectitude when it is directed to some particular and determinate object, because in such a case we are judging of something foreign to us, and have no true principle of equity to guide us.[83]

> [W]hen the whole people makes a statute applying to the whole people, it considers only itself; and if a relation is formed, it is between the whole object seen from one point of view and the whole object seen from another point of view, without any division of the whole. Then the object applying to which the statute is made is general, and the will which makes the statute is also general.[84]

> Inasmuch as the essence of sovereignty consists in the general will, it is also hard to see how one can be certain that a particular will always will agree with this general will. One ought rather to presume that the particular will will often be contrary to the general will, for private interest always tends to preferences, and the public interest always tends to equality.[85]

The will is general when it comes from all members of a community, at the same time applying to all. It is not directed to a "particular and determinate object".

> The acts of the sovereign can only be acts of general will — that is, laws.[86]

> [W]ill either is, or is not, general; it is the will either of the body of the people, or only of a part of it. In the first case, the will, when declared, is an act of Sovereignty and constitutes law: in the second, it is merely a particular will, or act of magistracy — at the most a decree.[87]

> [T]he social compact gives the body politic absolute power over all its members also; and it is this power which, under the direction of the general will, bear, as I have said, the name of Sovereignty.[88]

It is the source of laws. Losing the attribute of generality, directing itself towards a particular object, being merely the will of a part, and so a private will, it is at most the source of government decrees. As an attribute of the whole community and its lawgiver, it transfers full power over citizens to it.

---

[83] Ibid., II, IV, p. 25.
[84] J.J. Rousseau, *Emile, or On Education*, transl. A. Bloom, New York 1979, p. 462.
[85] Ibid., pp. 462–463.
[86] Ibid., p. 462.
[87] J.J. Rousseau, *The Social Contract and Discourses*, II, II, p. 23.
[88] Ibid., II, IV, p. 29.

> The power of the laws depends still more on their own wisdom than on the severity of their administrators, and the public will derives its greatest weight from the reason which has dictated it.[89]

> [W]hoever refuses to obey the general will shall be compelled to do so by the whole body. This means nothing less than that he will be forced to be free.[90]

> [F]or the particular will tends, by its very nature, to partiality, while the general will tends to equality.[91]

The general will has its source in reason. Citizens should submit to its products—laws. Life in accordance with them is equivalent to freedom.

Based on the above examples, we can extract the main features of the general will. Thus: 1) it is an attribute of political communities; 2) it is the measure of what is just; 3) it "tends always to the preservation and welfare of the whole and of every part", being at all times guided by the common interest; 4) it is the source of laws, its declaration is "an act of Sovereignty" and constitutes law; 5) it is the opposite of particular will (*volonté particulière*) and of the will of all (*volonté de tous*); 6) it can be equated with free will, i.e. a person who is truly free will follow only the precepts of the general will; 7) it is rational; and 8) it always aims to preserve legal equality between citizens. In light of these attributes, we can distinguish three levels on which the term *volonté générale* can be understood: the politico-legal, the ethical and the metaphysical.

In the politico-legal context, the general will should be understood as the belief shared by the members of a community as to the nature of its good, expressed in an appropriately enacted law. The general will is equated here with the result obtained each time an appropriate legislative procedure is followed. It is general both in its content and object, which means that in order for a law to be recognised as the expression of the *volonté générale* it must be voted on by all the members of a community, and its content must be abstract, since decrees concerning individuals are, in Rousseau's view, acts of the executive, not of the legislative power. It is probably this very feature of the *volonté générale* —its generality—that inspired the famous first two sentences of the *Social Contract*: "I mean to inquire if, in the civil order, there can be any sure and legitimate rule of administration, men being taken as they are and laws as they might be. In this inquiry I shall endeavour always to unite what right sanctions with what is prescribed by interest, in order that justice and utility may in no case be divided."[92] Merging the inter-

---

[89] J.J. Rousseau, *Political Economy*, p. 257.
[90] J.J. Rousseau, *Social Contract*, I, VII, p. 18.
[91] *Ibid.*, II, I, p. 23.
[92] *Ibid.*, I, p. 5.

est of individuals, who see the law as a guarantee of their possessions, with the good of the community can be done precisely by virtue of the general will. It is thanks to this philosophico-political construct that the power of the sovereign, although not subject to any formal limits,[93] encounters an actual obstacle in the interests of citizens. The domination of private interests protects the community from all forms of tyranny on the part of the majority. The natural desire to ensure one's own welfare can—given an appropriate ordering of political institutions— make individuals, otherwise prepared to sacrifice the good of their fellow citizens, inclined to treat them as equals. For no one will agree to a law favouring a particular group of citizens, since they cannot be sure that they will never find themselves among those disadvantaged by it. Being unable to foresee their futures, citizens taking part in the legislative process will tend to be impartial rather than attempt to ensure their own gain. This is why Harald Höffding[94] and Leo Strauss maintained that the general will is the social equivalent of *amour de soi* (love of oneself, making the individual desire himself in an unrestrained way[95])—the second, next to *pitié* (pity), motive of human action in the state of nature, while "[l]egislation by the all-inclusive citizen body is therefore the conventional substitute for natural compassion."[96]

The ethical dimension of the general will links it to the categories of the common good and public interest. In light of this interpretation, Rousseau's concern is not merely to order political institutions in such a way as to make people, guided by egotistical interest, mutually restrain one another in the unbridled pursuit of their desires. The point is not that unrestrained desires should lead to the emergence of a spontaneous order, the optimal and inevitable result of *bellum omnium contra omnes*. Such a postulate had already been formulated by Bernard Mandeville, who claimed that human flaws contribute to universal welfare.[97] But this was not the task the author of the *Social Contract* put before legislators when stating that "he who dares to undertake the making of a people's institutions ought to feel himself capable, so to speak, of changing human nature, of transforming each individual, [...] of altering man's constitution for the purpose of strengthening it; and of substituting a partial and moral existence for the physical and independent existence nature has conferred on us all."[98] Rousseau's guiding

---

[93] Ibid., II, IV, p. 29.
[94] H. Höffding, *Rousseau und seine philosophie*, Stuttgart 1897, pp. 135–136.
[95] Cf. G. Besse, *De Jean-Jacques Rousseau à Hegel: Premices d'une Phénoménologie*, "Hegel-Jahrbuch", 1974, pp. 490–495.
[96] Cf. L. Strauss, *Natural Right and History*, Chicago, IL 1953, p. 285.
[97] B. Mandeville, *The Fable of the Bees*, London 1729–1730.
[98] J.J. Rousseau, *Social Contract etc.*, II, VII, p. 35.

light was not that of enlightened egotism, with individuals caring for the common good in spite of their own intentions. He wished to restore them to their natural condition, insofar as this was possible within the limits of social coexistence, and to halt the process of moral depravity wherever it could be.[99] Of course, each nation can establish institutions that impose self-restraint on individuals effectively, but the very idea of organising society in such a manner seems dubious. Would this be sufficient to replace—paraphrasing the title of Jean Starobinski's book[100]—"obstruction with transparency"? The answer is no; changing the legislative system does not in itself bring about a moral renewal. The dominion of the general will is not accomplished in the sphere of institutions, but within citizens. Its purpose is to put an end to that insupportable and destructive state of the human condition, in which individuals perceive one another solely as the means to their own ends. It is on this point that Rousseau's conception is regarded as unique — the first modern attempt to reconcile two divergent traditions: the ancient view of community, with its emphasis on cohesion, unity and harmony among fellow citizens, each prepared to make sacrifices for the common good, and the voluntarist tradition, seeking the origins of human conduct in the possibility, or even inevitability, of individual, autonomous choice, and not in factors heteronomous to the individual. The point is for "the generality—non-individualism, or rather pre-individualism—of Antiquity to be legitimized by consent".[101]

The ethical interpretation of the general will is the most common among scholars of Rousseau's thought. This fact is hardly surprising, since it is based on the thesis of a theoretical continuity in his writing. Rousseau's critique of the social life of eighteenth-century Europe (*Discourse on the Arts and Sciences*) and his subsequent explanation of the genesis of moral downfall (*Discourse on the Origin of Inequality*) precede the political treatise (the *Social Contract*) and the educational treatise (*Emile*) intended as a remedy for ethical ills, in the logical order. Viewed from any other perspective than the ethical, Rousseau's work cannot be grasped as a whole, and inevitably collapses into social, political, educational, descriptive and normative components. Rousseau's description of the ideal community does not then fit his analyses of other forms of government, and more so still the path of self-improvement sketched out in *Emile*.

---

[99] J.J. Rousseau, *The Government of Poland*, transl. W. Kendall, Indianapolis, IN 1985, p. 12.

[100] J. Starobinski, *Jean-Jacques Rousseau. Transparency and Obstruction*, Chicago, IL 1988.

[101] P. Riley, *A Possible Explanation of Rousseau's General Will*, "The American Political Science Review" 1970, Vol. 64, No. 1, p. 87.

Analyses of the moral dimension of the general will have often been accompanied by references to the ethical concepts of Immanuel Kant in the relevant literature.[102] In particular, these parallels were drawn by Ernst Cassirer.[103] However, this approach has many opponents, both among those who consider it unjustified to ascribe Kantian inclinations to Rousseau,[104] as well as those holding that the pre-Kantian tendencies were in this case much weaker than the pre-Hegelian ones. The latter camp often tended to interpret the general will in metaphysical terms.

The metaphysical interpretation is presented by scholars who have found the germ of the nineteenth-century concept of objective idealism in Rousseau's work. According to them, the author of the *Social Contract* ascribed the attribute of existence (understood as an analogon of human existence) to supra-individual entities like the nation or the state.[105] These scholars attach particular weight to Rousseau's description of the state governed by the general will as a "moral and collective body" (*corps moral et collectif*). In the *Social Contract*, we read: "this act of association creates a moral and collective body, composed of as many members as the assembly contains votes, and receiving from this act its unity, its common identity, its life and its will."[106]

The act constituting a political community founded on the prescriptions of the general will is equated here with the creation of a new entity, more spiritual than material, of which it can only be said that it has a will (the general will) and a body[107] (composed of political institutions). It is not merely a "mental construct" erected by the citizens, but manifests an existential independence from their opinions.[108] Whether they act in their own interest or in that of the community, the general will remains unalterable. This can be understood in two ways: firstly, that there is always a position which expresses the community's best interest, even though it is not always shared by the citizens, or, secondly, that the moral subject of which the general will is an attribute exists independently of their views and actions. Scholars adhering to

---

[102] See S. Ellenburg, *Rousseau and Kant: principles of political right*, in: *Rousseau after 200 years. Proceedings of the Cambridge Bicentennial Colloquium*, ed. R.A. Leigh, Cambridge 1982, pp. 3–36; P. Riley, *Will and Political Legitimacy. A Critical Exposition of Social Contract Theory in Hobbes, Locke, Rousseau, Kant, and Hegel*, Cambridge, MA–London 1982, pp. 125–128.

[103] E. Cassirer, *The Question of Jean-Jacques Rousseau*, transl. P. Gay, New York 1956.

[104] See J. MacAdam, *What Rousseau Meant by the General Will*, pp. 149–151.

[105] J.P. Plamenatz, *Consent, Freedom and Political Obligation*, Oxford 1968, p. 31.

[106] J.J. Rousseau, *Social Contract*, I, VI, p. 15.

[107] See J.J. Rousseau, *Social Contract*, III, I, p. 49; cf. J.J. Rousseau, *Political Economy*, pp. 252–253.

[108] J.J. Rousseau, *Social Contract*, IV, I, p. 91.

the metaphysical interpretation of the general will usually lean towards this second interpretation. The community understood in this way is not a simple aggregate of individuals — as the precursors and proponents of classical liberalism supposed. Their atomist-mechanicist visions of society are out of place here. The organicist approach — focusing on the interdependence of members of a community and viewing it as a living body — is more appropriate.[109]

The metaphysical understanding of the general will is the most controversial of those cited above, hence only a relatively small number of scholars mention it. The attribution of such unequivocally pre-Hegelian inclinations to Rousseau compels some to perceive him as an advocate of the absolute power of the state over its citizens and to put him in the same basket as Hegel and Bosanquet, both misconstrued at times. Most scholars view such claims as a complete misunderstanding. Robert Derathé rightly noted[110] that Rousseau could not have disposed of the notion of the state as an entity transcending individuals. The concept of the "moral person", the main argument used by supporters of Rousseau's Hegelianism, appeared long before the publication of the *Social Contract* in the works of Hobbes[111] and Samuel Pufendorf,[112] yet without any transcendental connotations[113] and merely as an abstract designation of the community as an aggregation of individuals. There is no convincing proof that the Rousseauian "moral person" was intended to refer to anything other than a group of people assembled as a political community either. However, let us at once make clear that this does not mean ascribing an atomistic vision of inter-human relations to Rousseau. On the contrary, the community remains a living body, whose members (the citizens) cooperate for the welfare of the whole, fulfilling their assigned duties. The metaphysical nature of the general will may at most signify that the community is a group held together by a special type of bond — belief in the existence of a common

---

[109] J.J. Rousseau, *Political Economy*, p. 252.

[110] Frank Thakurdas indicated (F. Thakurdas, *Rousseau and the Concept of the General Will*, p. 280) that, not long before Derathé, this view was expressed by Otto Friedrich von Gierke in his work devoted to the notion of natural law (O.F. von Gierke, *Natural Law and Theory of Society*, transl. E. Barker, Vol. 1-2, Cambridge 1934).

[111] T. Hobbes, *Leviathan or the Matter, Form and Power of a Commonwealth, Ecclesiastical and Civil*, London 1887, p. 84.

[112] S. Pufendorf, *De Iure Naturae et Gentium Libri Octo*, Londini Scanorum 1672, VII. 2, 13-14, p. 886: "[p]ersona moralis composita, cuius voluntas, ex plurium pactis implicita & unita, pro voluntate omnium habetur." Cf. Q. Skinner, *Liberty Before Liberalism*, Cambridge 1998, p. 4.

[113] R. Derathé, *Jean-Jacques Rousseau et la science politique de son temps*, Paris 1970, pp. 397–410.

good, whose realisation overlaps with the particular interests of citizens.

Of the above ways of conceiving the general will, the metaphysical is thus rightly rejected as replicating the error of anachronism. The remaining two, the politico-legal and the ethical, should be considered in unison as moments of the same phenomenon perceived from different angles.[114] Otherwise, the picture of the place occupied by the *volonté générale* in Rousseau's thought becomes overly simplistic and hence inadequate. Limited to the politico-legal context, the general will appears either as the outcome of every vote taken by the citizens, if cast within the proper institutional setting, or as a means of enslaving particular wills, moulding them into one within the melting pot of the *volonté générale*. This happens similarly for the ethical dimension. Perceived solely as an ideal of social coexistence, independent of the role played by political and *quasi*-political institutions in the life of the community, it can only be applied to analyses of the so-called golden age of humanity—the happiest period in human history, before the positive traits of coexistence were destroyed by the invention of property and specialised production.[115] The later period, following the "second revolution" caused by the discovery of agriculture and metallurgy, is already an endless trail of human suffering. In order to put a term to it, it is indispensable to establish a society governed by the precepts of the general will. This cannot be done without the support of appropriate institutions. "Citizens are made, not born."[116] Rousseau's project is therefore above all pedagogical in nature. Its goal is to produce citizens prepared to subordinate their will to the public interest, so that by reconciling themselves with it they may regain their lost peace of mind.

1.2.2. The general will and natural law

For a complete understanding of the role played by the general will in Rousseau's thought, it is necessary to establish whether it is not merely a modification of previous natural law theories, or—if a novel concept—to determine how it differs from previous accounts of natural law. This matter has already received many interpretations, most of

---

[114] Two types of general will were also distinguished by Faguet (É. Faguet, *Rousseau penseur*, pp. 345–236). These he described as general general will (*volonté générale générale*) and particular general will (*volonté générale particulière*). The attributes of the first include immutability and being directed towards the common good. The second is that which is embodied in correctly enacted legislation.

[115] J.J. Rousseau, *Discourse on the Origin and Foundations of Inequality among Men*, p. 214.

[116] J.W. Chapman, *Rousseau – Totalitarian or Liberal*, New York 1956, p. 60.

which unfortunately amount to a confusion between the general will and natural law. Appropriate treatment of the question will require us to first analyse the meaning Rousseau assigned to the category of nature. It seems that we can here speak of a dual definition—historical and normative—both of nature as such and of natural law.

The historical understanding of nature has a descriptive character, relating to the hypothetical state of nature, the pre-civil period of human existence. Employed in this context, it carries no deontological content. It describes humanity's happy period, which has irrevocably passed. Two main elements form this description: a picture of inter-human relations, and—even more importantly—of individuals as such, including their psychological constitution, with a particular focus on their emotional relation to their surroundings. This understanding of nature is especially present throughout the *Discourse on the Origin of Inequality*.

In contrast to the descriptive understanding of nature, the normative one has a strictly deontological function. Rousseau uses it to express the need for a reform of social relations, establishing the most "natural" possible human existence (this understanding is predominant in the *Social Contract* and the *Discourse on Political Economy*, but we also encounter it in *Emile* and the *New Heloise*) or the appropriate formation of individual personality (*Emile*). Above all, we should consider as normative those descriptions of human nature which—while characteristic of the state of civil coexistence—do not contain a reference to the state of nature.

Rousseau himself did not give a precise account of the relationship between these two views of nature. They often took quite a complicated form, at times complementing each other—as in the case of Rousseau's polemics with Grotius, Hobbes, Spinoza or Locke. Criticising the claim that it is admissible to submit voluntarily to slavery, put forward by Grotius and Hobbes, the author of the *Social Contract* stated that

> To renounce liberty [...] is incompatible with man's nature; to remove all liberty from his will is to remove all morality from his acts. Finally, it is an empty and contradictory convention that sets up, on the one side, absolute authority, and on the other, unlimited obedience.[117]

Our attention is drawn here to the admission that there exists a natural human rationality, precluding transactions in which certain losses exceed presumed gains. An agreement that does not benefit the parties involved is impossible; "the right of slavery is null and void, not only as being illegitimate, but also because it is absurd and meaningless."[118]

---

[117] J.J. Rousseau, *Social Contract*, I, IV, p. 10.
[118] *Ibid.*, I, IV, p. 13.

Rousseau thus suggests that the precepts of man's innate rationality (which, however, does not exist in the state of nature) must prevent him from consciously acting to his own detriment. Or, should he do so, nullify the obligations resulting from such acts.

Despite such an imprecise definition of nature, it seems that at least one of the claims regarding its relationship to the general will finds sufficient support in the works of Rousseau. According to this thesis, it is impossible to extrapolate a normative concept of the institutional structure of a state and society from a hypothetical/historical state of nature: "when we have defined a law of nature, we shall be no nearer the definition of a law of the State."[119] The way people lived in the pre-civil period of peace and innocence does not define how societies should be organised today.[120] It is true that some fragments of Rousseau's writing seem to allow for such an extrapolation, although for a long time most scholars denied it. A change of position on this issue was initiated by the now classical work of Derathé, *Jean-Jacques Rousseau et la science politique de son temps*.[121] He maintained that it is possible to perceive continuity between the presumed state of nature and the state of society. On what grounds, since *l'homme naturel* differed so vastly from civil man? It is in fact the same natural law, initially regulating human action through instincts, which now takes the form of the laws of reason in society.[122] Derathé backed this thesis with citations from the works of Rousseau,[123] including, in particular, *Réponse à une Lettre Anonyme dont le contenu se trouve en Caractère Italique*

---

[119] *Ibid.*, II, VI, p. 32; cf. J.J. Rousseau, *Political Economy*, p. 251.

[120] See J.J. Rousseau, *Letter to D'Alembert on Theatre*, in: J.J. Rousseau, *Letter to D'Alembert on Theatre and Writings for the Theatre*, eds. A. Bloom, Ch. Butterworth, Ch. Kelly, Lebanon, NH 2004, p. 263. J.J. Rousseau, *Lettre de J.-J. Rousseau à M. Philopolis* [MS. Neuchâtel, 1836], in: J.J. Rousseau, *The Political Writings*, Vol. 2, pp. 221–223.

[121] R. Derathé, *Jean-Jacques Rousseau et la science politique*, pp. 155–160. Cf. F. Haymann, *La loi naturelle dans la philosophie politique de J.J. Rousseau*, "Annales" 1943–1945, Vol. 30, pp. 65–109.

[122] Which was the reason for attacking the concept of the state of nature expounded by Hobbes, who erroneously based his image of original man on the citizens of seventeenth-century nations (J.J. Rousseau, *L'etat de la guerre* [MS Neuchâtel, 7856], in: J.J. Rousseau, *The Political Writings*, Vol. 2, pp. 306–307).

[123] J.J. Rousseau, *Social Contract*, II, IV, p. 26–27; J.J. Rousseau, *Emile*, p. 289; J.J. Rousseau, *Moral Letters*, transl. Ch. Kelly in: *Rousseau on Philosophy, Morality, and Religion*, ed. Ch. Kelly, Lebanon, NH 2007, pp. 93, 96; J.J. Rousseau, *The Government of Poland*, pp. 28–29; J.J. Rousseau, *Julie, ou la Nouvelle Héloïse. Lettres de Deux Amants*, Paris 1828, pp. 368–369.

dans cette Réponse,[124] in which, to the question of whether he admits an authority superior to that of the sovereign in the state, Rousseau replies: "I allow only three of them. First, the authority of God, and then that of the natural law that derives from the constitution of man, and then that of honour."[125]

But citations are often one thing (and those corroborating a contrary claim are hardly lacking in Rousseau's work[126]), while cohesive argumentation is another. In order to meet the requirements of the latter, Derathé also cites Rousseau's view of how the social contract was made. The argumentation is simple: Rousseau writes of the constitutive act of the community as an obligation undertaken by all and observed by all, on pain of death for those who would break it. Derathé therefore asks why individuals should feel obliged to obey these rules. For in order for this to be so, prior to entering into the agreement, they would first have to conclude another, in which they would agree to obey the *pacta sunt servanda* principle. Yet does this reasoning not inevitably lead to a *reductio ad infinitum*? An earlier agreement laying the foundation for the next one would always be needed. It is therefore logical that the *pacta sunt servanda* principle should function prior to any other agreements. This is how we arrive at a principle which is universally binding, although no one has expressly agreed to it, which all agree on, although they never pledged to obey it. The necessity of honouring it

---

[124] J.J. Rousseau, *Réponse à une Lettre Anonyme dont le contenu se trouve en Caractère Italique dans cette Réponse*, in: J.J. Rousseau, *Œuvres complètes de J.J. Rousseau avec des notes historiques*, Vol. 3, Paris 1835, p. 179.

[125] J.J. Rousseau, *Letter to D'Alembert and the Writings for the Theatre*, Lebanon, NH 2004, p. 379. Cf. R. Derathé, *Jean-Jacques Rousseau et la science politique*, p. 157. Cf. A. Cobban, *Rousseau*, p. 76. Since the last of these factors plays no essential part in the works of Rousseau, apart from in this sole fragment, interpreters usually focus on the other two: God and nature. The possibility of founding human rights on a belief in God is based on the *Creed of a Savoyard Priest*, where the author clearly suggests that natural law is linked directly to the action of God and the "eternal truths" established by Him. For although Rousseau decidedly pronounced himself against the pantheism of Spinoza, like him, he believed that we discover God through nature, in which He revealed Himself through the intermediary of His laws. Thus, although the Creator Himself is the foundation of natural laws, the distinction Rousseau makes between Him and His laws is without practical significance for the discussion on the relationship between the general will and natural law. Studying the influence of natural law on man, we study Divine actions at the same time. We can, and should in Rousseau's view, confront theological problems through the study of natural law.

[126] J.J. Rousseau, *Lettres écrites de la Montagne*, in: J.J. Rousseau, *The Political Writings*, Vol. 2, p. 219. Cf. J.J. Rousseau, [MS. Neuchâtel, 7840, p. 61], in: J.J. Rousseau, *The Political Writings*, Vol. 1, p. 311.

has to result directly from human nature. This is what makes it tangible proof of the existence of natural laws; the theory of the social contract cannot be reconciled with the negation of natural law, since the latter is the foundation of all agreements.[127] Social coexistence is not only compatible with the theory of natural law—it is hardly even conceivable that it should not be founded upon it; "natural law, in its rational form, can only appear at the same time as social life and the development of reason which results from it",[128] "natural law" or "law of reason" cannot be perceived as anterior to civil laws, yet this does not preclude its being superior to them.[129] "In other words, there are two types of natural law; the first, *secundum motus sensualitis*, is 'natural law in the proper sense' and corresponds to the state of nature. The other, *secundus motus rationis*, or 'rational law of nature', does not appear until after the establishment of civil societies."[130]

But does the admission of the existence of natural laws (understood in the sense of Derathé) really add anything to the debate on the general will? Even if we accept their validity in the social state, what does this change on the deontological level of public order as postulated by Rousseau? Can the law of nature, as a law of reason, legitimate positive legislation, and if so, in what sense? Can natural law justify political revolutions? Can the legislation of nature be reconciled with the legislation of the general will? At least to this last question, a positive answer can be given. This is also Derathé's position. Although one of Rousseau's theses is that an appropriately enacted law always expresses the general will, it is impossible to deduce from this that all of the latter's precepts are purely a matter of convention and have nothing to do with the immutable law of nature. This law of nature may find its *raison d'être* as a force delimiting the scope of civil laws that can be enacted. The fact is, there are some regulations that individuals in their right mind will never agree to. For instance, the previously mentioned renouncement of freedom. Rousseau considers such a step inadmissible, since it contradicts rational human nature. One cannot give away all one possesses in exchange for nothing, or the promise of an uncertain future gain: "[t]o say that a man gives himself gratuitously, is to say what is absurd and inconceivable; such an act is null and illegitimate, from the mere fact that he who does it is out of his mind. To say the same of a whole people is to suppose a people of madmen;

---

[127] Cf. R. Derathé, *Jean-Jacques Rousseau et la science politique*, p. 160; cf. *ibid.*, p. 166.
[128] *Ibid.*, p. 164.
[129] *Ibid.*, p. 165.
[130] *Ibid.*, p. 166.

and madness creates no right."[131] Derathé argues that, through this, Rousseau unites the positivist thought of Hobbes, who ascribed unlimited power to the sovereign, with the jusnaturalism of Jurieu and Jean-Jacques Burlamaqui, who believed that absolute power does not mean unrestrained self-will, being bound by the precepts of nature and God.[132]

Yet there also is no shortage of scholars opposed to this view of the relationship between *volonté générale* and natural law. These include Strauss.[133] The divergence between the views of Derathé and Strauss on this matter is significant. Whereas the first assumes that the precepts of natural law take precedence over the general will, the second recognises no instance superior to it. Strauss considers the general will of the community as the foundation of the Rousseauian political order. Meanwhile, Derathé's position implies the grounding of this order on a foundation independent of it. Where is the source of such differences in interpretation? It lies in Rousseau's relatively carefree mixing of the two meanings of nature — historical and normative. And so the following question emerges: since both positions are equally justified in light of Rousseau's writings, is it possible to reconcile them? Based on previous analyses, the following thesis may be ventured. In the case of a democratic system, natural law (understood in the sense of Derathé) cannot justify a change of the political *status quo*. Being both a necessary condition of the functioning of democracy (since it is ultimately based on an agreement made by the people, and this in turn requires honouring the *pacta sunt servanda* principle) and delimiting the scope of acceptable laws that are compatible with human nature, the postulates of natural law are always reflected in legislation. It can be said that natural law gives no additional power to civil laws. Since the *volonté générale*, reflected in legislation, will never be irrational, it will never be opposed to natural law (a law of reason). In this way, the recognition of the omnipotence of the *volonté générale* is not at odds with the recognition of the primacy, or even superiority, of the precepts of natural law.

Yet we should not confuse the above thesis on the compatibility of natural law (understood in such a particular way) with the general will, with the claim denied here. Namely, that it is possible to project the order, proper to the state of nature, onto modern societies (and so mix

---

[131] J.J. Rousseau, *Social Contract*, I, IV, p. 10.
[132] R. Derathé, *Jean-Jacques Rousseau et la science politique*, pp. 339–341.
[133] L. Strauss, *Natural Right and History*, Chicago, IL 1953, p. 286. A similar view was expressed by George Sabine (G.H. Sabine, *A History of Political Theory*, Hinsdale, IL 1973, p. 587), Vaughan (C.E. Vaughan, *First Draft of Contrat Social*, in: J.J. Rousseau, *The Political Writings*, Vol. 1, pp. 426, 440–442).

the historical and normative understanding of nature). The analogies Rousseau made at various points between the state of the first people and the later state of society should not in fact be treated as such. Even advocates of Rousseau's jusnaturalism, like Derathé and Alfred Cobban,[134] reject the possibility of translating the laws applicable in the state of nature into the rational laws of socialised man. The reason why these two orders should be differentiated is simple: Rousseau doubts the permanence of human nature. The two forms of existence — the pre-civil and the civil — have little to do with each other.[135] The fact that man possessed certain traits in the first does not imply that he also possesses them today. Nor, for that matter, that he will possess them in the future. Natural man was characterised by sentiments proper only to himself: *amour de soi* and *pitié*.[136] In the social world, these have degenerated, their restoration is impossible. And since there has been a change in inter-human relations, it is not even clear what it would have to consist in. Rousseau presents the differences separating the two states in the *Discourse on the Origin of Inequality*, where he notes that in the state of natural happiness, pity prompted men to follow the maxim: "[d]o good to yourself with as little evil as possible to others", while within society, reason ordains: "[d]o to others as you would have them do unto you."[137] The first exhorts us to love ourselves while also taking into account the well-being of others. It provides an outlet for both instincts: love of self and pity. The second is the result of mistrust and caution in the calculation of potential gains.[138] It is thereby also an effect of the action of *amour propre*, self-love, a form of *amour de soi*[139] degenerated by reason.

The question of the establishment of natural equalities and freedoms, postulated by Rousseau, is similar. None of them can be brought back in their original form, and so their fulfilment cannot come through a "return to nature", but through the creation of a real community and citizenship: "[t]here can be no patriotism without liberty, no liberty without virtue, no virtue without citizens."[140] "If we ask in what precisely consists the greatest good of all, which should be the end of every system of legislation, we shall find it reduce itself to two main objects, liberty and equality — liberty, because all particular dependence

---

[134] A. Cobban, *Rousseau and the Modern State*, London 1934, p. 76.
[135] J.J. Rousseau, *Social Contract*, I, VIII, pp. 18–19.
[136] J.J. Rousseau, *Discourse on the Origin*, p. 199; cf. J.J. Rousseau, *Moral Letters*, p. 582.
[137] J.J. Rousseau, *Discourse on the Origin*, p. 200.
[138] Cf. J.J. Rousseau, *Political Economy*, p 257.
[139] J.J. Rousseau, *Discourse on the Origin*, p. 197–199.
[140] Cf. J.J. Rousseau, *Political Economy*, p. 267.

means so much force taken from the body of the State, and equality, because liberty cannot exist without it."[141]

There is another reason Rousseau cannot be seen as an advocate of the supremacy of natural laws reformulated as political postulates: he does not recognise the existence of universal sources of morality and legislation. The only rightful legislator is the sovereign, guided by the precepts of the general will.[142] The latter, as an expression of the common good, is necessarily contingent, dependent on the existential context of communities. Hence, Strauss writes that "the source of the positive law, and of nothing but the positive law, is the general will; a will inherent or immanent in properly constituted society takes the place of the transcendent natural law",[143] it "constitutes for all the members of the State, in their relations to one another and to it, the rule of what is just or unjust",[144] "because, according to the fundamental compact, only the general will can bind the individuals".[145]

This is also why there is no such thing as a general will of mankind. For is there such a thing as a pan-human community with its own *volonté générale*, directed to the attainment of its good? Rousseau at times suggests that since the general will of one nation is bound to be seen as particular by another, then this is possible only thanks to the existence of some kind of higher *volonté générale*, a natural law applicable to the "great city of the world".[146] In the Geneva manuscript of the *Social Contract*, however, he notes that this cosmopolitanism springs from an error of hypostasis, projecting the local understanding of common interest onto humanity.[147] The image of a global community rallying together to pursue a universal common interest is quite beautiful, albeit totally unrealistic.

1.2.3. The general will and the will of all

In order to define the role attributed to the general will by Rousseau, it is not enough to merely list its positive definitions. The nature of the distinction Rousseau makes between *volonté générale* and *volonté de tous* is also of fundamental importance. The relevant literature is plagued with doubts as to the nature of this opposition. The very possibility of

---

[141] J.J. Rousseau, *Social Contract*, II, XI, p. 45.
[142] Cf. A. Cobban, *Rousseau*, pp. 63–65.
[143] L. Strauss, *Three Waves of Modernity*, in: *Political Philosophy. Six Essays by Leo Strauss*, ed. H. Gilden, Indianapolis, IN 1975 p. 91.
[144] J.J. Rousseau, *Political Economy*, p. 253.
[145] J.J. Rousseau, *Social Contract*, II, VII, p. 37; cf. ibid., II, XII, p. 47–48.
[146] J.J. Rousseau, *Political Economy*, p. 253.
[147] J.J. Rousseau, *Contrat social*, first Version, in: J.J. Rousseau, *The Political Writings*, Vol. 1, pp. 452–453.

maintaining it consequently is even sometimes questioned. The matter is crucial to Rousseau's thought, since — as we shall see in the following subsections — adopting one of the possible definitions of this relationship implies the recognition of one of two fundamentally different views of the nature of socio-political relations.

1.2.3.1 *The will of all*

The reader of Rousseau's works will have no major difficulty in defining the will of all. Whereas defining the general will required a multifaceted investigation, there is no need for such extensive and thorough analyses in this case. Yet even here we must begin by citing the positive designations of the *volonté de tous*. From a reading of Rousseau's works it follows that:

> [i]n fact, each individual, as a man, may have a particular will contrary or dissimilar to the general will which he has as a citizen. His particular interest may speak to him quite differently from the common interest: his absolute and naturally independent existence may make him look upon what he owes to the common cause as a gratuitous contribution, the loss of which will do less harm to others than the payment of it is burdensome to himself.[148]

> In reality, if it is not impossible for a particular will to agree on some point with the general will, *it is at least impossible* [Ital.—J.G.] for the agreement to be lasting and constant; for the particular will tends, by its very nature, to partiality, while the general will tends to equality. It is even more impossible to have any guarantee of this agreement; for even if it should always exist, it would be the effect not of art, but of chance.[149]

Rousseau defines the particular will/will of all negatively by contrasting it with the general will. The first is oriented towards the pursuit of personal interest, and characterises the individual not as a citizen, but simply as a person, an "absolute and naturally independent" being. And although "it is not impossible for a particular will to agree on some point with the general will", they are separated by a chasm, since the first always tends towards privileges enabling the realisation of personal interest, while the second always articulates the requirements of the common good.

> [S]uch assessment, in order to be lawful, must be voluntary; it must depend, not indeed on a particular will, as if it were necessary to have

---

[148] J.J. Rousseau, *Social Contract*, I, VII, pp. 17–18.
[149] *Ibid.*, II, I, pp. 22–23.

> the consent of each individual, and that he should give no more than just what he pleased, but on a general will.[150]

> [W]ill either is, or is not, general; it is the will either of the body of the people, or only of a part of it. In the first case, the will, when declared, is an act of Sovereignty and constitutes law: in the second, it is merely a particular will, or act of magistracy — at the most a decree.[151]

> The influence of all these tacit or formal associations causes, by the influence of their will, as many different modifications of the public will. The will of these particular societies has always two relations; for the members of the association, it is a general will; for the great society, it is a particular will.[152]

Private will amounts to self-will. The sense of duty, of being dedicated to something other than its own "I want", is alien to it. It belongs to all associations as a will of all/public will. It is not a desirable source of law, since it lacks a general object. At most, it creates custom, a set of beliefs devoid of rational justification. The general will, on the other hand, is rational, an effect of self-restraint finding its outlet in laws.

The following designations can therefore be attached to the concept of particular will/will of all: 1) it tends to the realisation of personal interest; 2) it may characterise both individuals (this is when we call it particular) and groups (will of all); 3) it is arbitrary and has no foundation except in the subjective judgment of individuals; 4) it characterises people as "absolute and naturally independent" beings, not as citizens; 5) it tends to privilege, regarding the state of equality (also legal) as undesirable; 6) it may occasionally overlap with the general will, to which it is, however, opposed by nature; 7) it does not belong to the sovereign, but to the executive power; it is the *causa sui* of executive acts; 8) it creates custom, not laws.

1.2.3.2 The general will versus the will of all

Four differences can be shown between the general will and the will of all/particular will defined in this manner:

1. Quantitative difference. The general will is one,[153] since it represents the best understanding of the common good. By contrast, the will of all is the sum of the wills of particular individuals pursuing their personal interests.

2. Qualitative difference. The general will can be deemed rational and just, and individuals guided by its precepts can be deemed free. This is

---

[150] J.J. Rousseau, *Political Economy*, p. 278.
[151] J.J. Rousseau, *Social Contract*, II, II, p. 23.
[152] J.J. Rousseau, *Political Economy*, p. 254.
[153] J.J. Rousseau, *Social Contract*, II, IV, pp. 25–26.

not the case with the particular will/will of all, which is irrational and unjust, while those who execute its precepts are slaves to their own passions.

3. Difference in source. The particular will springs from the subjective desires of individuals. The general, from the requirements of the common good, independently of anyone's opinion.

4. Difference in aim. The general will is oriented towards the establishment and maintenance of equality between individuals; the particular tends towards privilege and self-advancement. While the first desires the common good, the second aims for personal good. Both may have an identical effect—political postulates motivated by personal interest can coincide with the interest of the community. But this does not mean they are identical. For this would require unity of motive, not of effects.

Where the general will reigns, the particular is necessarily lacking. And conversely, in a morally corrupt society, where everyone seeks to fulfil their own interest, or that of the group they belong to, there can be no representation of the general will. But does this arrangement really have to resemble a zero-sum game, with a larger number of particular interests translating into a reduced representation of the general will? It seems that there are at least two types of relation that can be distinguished in the opposition *volonté générale–volonté de tous*: a variant of *exclusion* and a variant of *coexistence*. In the first case, both wills inevitably limit one another. The more there is of the general will, the less of the particular, and vice versa. The rule of the *volonté générale* means identifying personal interest with that of the community, thus a complete renunciation of private interest. This variant is a consequence of the acceptance of an ethical interpretation of the general will. Otherwise, a specific sphere of influence is assigned to each will, in which it does not limit the other in any respect. This occurs when we confine the action of the general will to the political sphere, while that of the particular, to the private and economic domain. This means that while we may be egotists, prepared to sacrifice the good of others for the sake of our own goals in our private and economic lives, whenever we vote on a law, our egotism also forces us to establish legal guarantees for equality and the realisation of the common interest. This manner of understanding the *volonté générale* requires recognition of the supremacy of its politico-legal interpretation.

1.2.4. Two visions of community

This dual interpretation of the relationship between the general will and the will of all relates to the issue of Rousseau's alleged utilitarianism. Our concern here, however, is not to find similarities with the thought of Helvetius, since these would doubtless be few. The problem consists rather in Rousseau's inconsequent mixing of two orders. The first is the already mentioned Mandevillian image of community, in which egotistical acts ultimately bring about the good of society. Citizens need not be made virtuous for the social body to improve its condition. If the public sphere is ordered appropriately, private interest can support the common good, and the particular will, the general. The public good is to everyone's advantage, and so everyone, wishing to attain their particular goals, will incidentally be inclined to pursue the common interest as a means of achieving private ends: "[e]ach man, in detaching his interest from the common interest, sees clearly that he cannot entirely separate them; but his share in the public mishaps seems to him negligible beside the exclusive good he aims at making his own. Apart from this particular good, he wills the general good in his own interest, as strongly as anyone else."[154]

A similar view can be found in the later writings of Kant, who describes the functioning of a "race of devils",[155] and in Johan Gottlieb Fichte.[156] Echoes of it are also present in Montesquieu and Locke, in their postulates on the division and balance of powers, which in their natural desire for dominion over each other mutually limit their temptations. Was this type of reasoning shared by Rousseau? There is doubtless reason to think so. Rousseau did admit the possibility of harnessing human passions to form a lawful society. This solution was dictated to him by a lack of belief in the possibility of moral reform of his contemporaries. Virtue will never vanquish the egotism ruling supremely over the nations of eighteent-century Europe. After all, Rousseau begins his *Social Contract* with the statement: "I mean to inquire if, in the civil order, there can be any sure and legitimate rule of administration, men being taken as they are and laws as they might be. In this inquiry I shall endeavour always to unite what right sanctions with what is prescribed by interest, in order that justice and utility may in no case be divided."[157] It is not merely this scepticism that suggests seeing here the signs of the concept of "directing vice to the good".

Similar conclusions can also be drawn from some of the elements of the meticulously crafted edifice of the state in the *Social Contract*. Take, for example, the plus/minus principle: "[t]here is often a great deal of difference between the will of all and the general will; the latter considers only the common interest, while the former takes private interest

---

[154] J.J. Rousseau, *Social Contract*, IV, I, p. 91.
[155] I. Kant, *Perpetual Peace*, New York 2007, p. 37.
[156] J.G. Fichte, *The Vocation of Man*, transl. W. Smith, Chicago, IL 1931, III, III, pp. 129-131.
[157] J.J. Rousseau, *Social Contract*, I, I, p. 5.

into account, and is no more than a sum of particular wills: but take away from these same wills the pluses and minuses that cancel one another, and the general will remains as the sum of the differences."[158] What exactly is this principle, interpreted in ways that have obscured rather than illuminated its essence? From the fragment cited, it follows that it is an infallible way of discovering the verdicts of the general will, indicating the views that advance the public interest. To the potential legislator, Rousseau seems to say: eliminate associations, for they have wills that are particular from the point of view of society, and then the personal wills of individuals will cancel one another out, while the remaining votes will express the general will.

Nonetheless, at least two charges can be brought against this interpretation. Firstly, its practical uselessness, and this for two reasons. 1) Voting usually consists less in expressing one's own view than in taking a positive or negative stance on the content of the proposed law. This is also how Rousseau himself understood it, stating in the *Social Contract* that the role of the citizens is not to propose laws, but to vote on them.[159] In such a case, one can only speak of the percentage of voices "for" to those "against", and not of the cancelling out of extreme opinions. 2) Even presupposing a plurality of opinions, from which those compatible with the general will must be extracted, establishing equivalence between votes cancelling one another out would require a criterion, according to which individual votes would be valorised, making it possible to make any comparisons. Rousseau's work is silent on the question of such a criterion.

The second charge pertains to the annihilation of the ethical component of the general will. For if we admit that indicating its desiderata requires the extraction of a "golden mean" from among the available opinions by rejecting extreme postulates, then the very purpose of cultivating a civil ethics is put into question. The ethical dimension of the general will becomes redundant the moment the moral reform of citizens becomes unnecessary for the discovery of the content of its prescriptions.

Apart from concepts suggesting the necessity of constituting a community based on an institutional dam, transforming the Hobbesian state of *bellum omnium contra omnes* into voluntary cooperation within the framework of a democratic legal order, there is yet another tendency to be found in Rousseau's writings. This is expressed in the image of the perfect community, in which the citizens equate their private interest with the public one. An example of this is the community of

---

[158] J.J. Rousseau, *Social Contract*, II, III, p. 25.
[159] *Ibid.*, II, VII, p. 37; cf. *ibid.*, IV, I, p. 91–92.

Clarens in the *New Heloise*. It boasts no public institutions in the strict sense, which are unnecessary because good people do not squabble over prerogatives and do not desire to increase their freedom at the expense of others. Since they are without egotisms, it is not necessary for these to cancel one another out. Everyone fulfils their duties towards the common good, perceiving no coercion in this, and without feeling that their own liberty has been curbed. In such a community, the general will is devoid of the institutional component and limited to the purely ethical dimension.

That such a reading of Rousseau's political legacy is correct is proven for example by his conception of the legislator, who is to educate citizens *sensu proprio*, spontaneously equating their own good with that of the community. Had Rousseau's only intention been to order political relations within the state so as to oblige everyone who desires to follow the promptings of their will to support similar pursuits in others, incidentally providing for the good of the community, the legislator would be redundant. Similarly with civil religion, intended to bind individuals emotionally to the community. If skilful use of egotisms enriched with a rational calculation of profits and losses were sufficient for the establishment of a government of the general will, why would Rousseau introduce an emotional component? Besides, even if the citizens failed to note that the welfare of the community is in their interest, the plus/minus principle would permit the extraction of the precepts of the general will.

There are thus ample grounds to believe that Rousseau presents two ways of realising the precepts of the general will: arranging political institutions so as to ensure "that justice and utility may in no case be divided", as well as shaping citizens in such a way that they internalise the precepts of the general will, equating the common interest with their own. Scholars of Rousseau's thought who tend to focus too much on the first of these points, usually perceiving Rousseau as the spiritual father of modern democracy, inevitably disregard his postulates on moral reform, so important within the context of the whole of this thinker's legacy. On the other hand, those who place an excessive emphasis on the acceptance of the ethical solution have a tendency to view Rousseau as a sentimental recluse concerned with the condition of "noble souls" lost in modernity, rather than a political pragmatist and visionary.

Chapter Two

The Community in the Idealist Perspective

Although British idealism had many proponents over the course of nearly half a century of its academic dominance in the British Isles, it is to three of them — on account of the influence exerted by their writing — that special attention should be devoted. They are Thomas Hill Green, Bernard Bosanquet and Francis Herbert Bradley. It is these three who made the greatest contribution to the political conceptions belonging to the tradition we are discussing here, although their influence extended much further. Their works also inspired the leaders and advocates of New Liberalism (J.A. Hobson, L.T. Hobhouse, W.H. Beveridge, Ch. Masterman, D.G. Ritchie, A. Toynbee, H. Jones, J.H. Muirhead, J.S. MacKenzie), socialists with ties to the Fabian Society (S. Webb, B. Webb) and the Labour Party (R.H. Tawney, R.B. Haldane), hierarchs of the Anglican Church, theologians and activists of the Christian Social Union (H.S. Holland, Ch. Gore), those engaged in the operation of the liberal Toynbee Hall and the Workers' Educational Association, conservatives as well as those harbouring conservative sympathies (T.S. Eliot, M. Oakeshott).

Let us now present the figures who will occupy us in the remainder of this work. Green (1836–1882) was the *de facto* founder of the idealist movement,[1] the one who laid its theoretical foundations and defined

---

1   Although it would be an exaggeration to say that the published works of Thomas Hill Green were the first British publications modelled on the writings of Immanuel Kant, Georg Wilhelm Friedrich Hegel and Johann Gottlieb Fichte. He was preceded, amongst others, by James Hutchison Stirling (*The Secret of Hegel*, 1865), Edward Caird (*Account of the Philosophy of Kant*, 1877, and *Hegel*, 1883) and finally also by Francis Herbert Bradley (*Ethical Studies*, 1876). German idealism had already been drawn on by writers such as Samuel Taylor Coleridge (1772–1834) and Thomas Carlyle (1795–1881). Thus, when we speak of Green as the founder of the idealist tradition, we are referring to the popularising impact of his teaching, its

the directions of its development. He is doubtless the most important figure in the movement—not merely its initiator, but also its "spiritual father". At the same time, his role was not limited to the transplantation of speculative thought to Britain, but above all, to the laying of permanent theoretical foundations for the work of its later apologists. Subsequent generations of idealists never abandoned the intuitions present throughout Green's social and political writings, regardless of the stance they took on the other elements of his thought. Developing his original ideas, they at most modified them—either by adding new problems or by adapting them to current trends in the humanities and the natural sciences. Our two remaining protagonists are a case in point. Bradley remained a faithful disciple of Green[2] until the very end. As it turned out after the publication of Green's lectures,[3] Bradley had to a large extent repeated his master's most important theses in his *Ethical Studies*. In this respect, the work of Bosanquet, whose development of Green's thought, especially in its political aspect, went much further than Bradley's, appears somewhat different. Bosanquet's best known work is *The Philosophical Theory of the State*—a consistent and coherent presentation of the idealist position on the issues of the state, civil rights and relations between central administration and all types of social cells, from the family to society as a whole. It is also the work offering the fullest exposition of the intellectual debt owed by the British to thinkers like Aristotle, Rousseau, Kant, Fichte and Hegel.

As the founder of the British idealist tradition, Green employed the terminology and premises developed in Germany to challenge empiricism, realism, utilitarianism, individualism and classical liberalism, predominant in Britain until then. His achievements in political philosophy were particularly significant. His modification of Kant and Hegel's conceptions paved the way for a number of profoundly original ideas. The history of political philosophy has few heroes who allowed themselves such originality that it is difficult even to classify them. Here, this is true of the entire tradition. Subsequent generations of idealists inherited the ambiguities of Green's thought, which makes it equally difficult to situate any of them within a particular political doctrine, especially if we orient ourselves by such theoretical concepts

---

pioneering character insofar as political philosophy is concerned, as well as his skill in combining the concepts of various German idealists.

[2] At least insofar as ethics and politics are concerned. Despite the fundamental convergence of their paradigms, the uniqueness of Bradley's thought in epistemology and ontology is often cited in the relevant literature (see H. Haldar, *Neo-Hegelianism*, London 1927, pp. 247-249).

[3] *Prolegomena to Ethics*, the record of his Oxford lectures from 1880–1882 and *Lectures on the Principles of Political Obligation*—lectures from 1879–1880.

as liberalism, conservatism or socialism (since the idealists were usually believed to belong to one of these frameworks). This is particularly evident with Green, who viewed himself as a liberal who condemned socialism, but also, implicitly, conservative traditionalism, while at the same time criticising classical liberalism, both from socialist and conservative positions, and in doing so, frequently resorting to theological arguments.

The second thinker we will discuss, Francis Herbert Bradley (1846–1924), was a continuator of Green's legacy. Although often involved in polemics with his master, his reflection on social issues followed a pattern similar to Green's,[4] and involved a critique of individualism, subjectivism, apriorism and utilitarianism, which he proposed to replace with holism, objectivism, contextualism and teleologism. The inquisitive reader might be curious as to why Bradley is considered one of the pillars of the tradition rather than merely a less influential interpreter of Green's thought. That answer must include a reminder that it was in fact Bradley who published the first systematic exposition of the idealists' ethical views in Britain. Green published little in his lifetime —his two major works appeared posthumously. With his *Ethical Studies* (1876), Bradley thus launched this school's writing on morality and the role of the community in the lives of individuals. But the importance of Bradley's conceptions within the idealist tradition is not only due to this work. The best known, and still considered the most important, of his books is *Appearance and Reality*, published in 1893. Critics and commentators alike agree that it is the most eloquent, engaging, original and inspiring work of British idealist thought. It is this work, and especially its clear explication of the paradoxes inherent in the opposition between the phenomenal and the real world, that earned its author the title of a modern Eleatic. A somewhat lesser impression was made upon commentators by *The Principles of Logic* (1883), published a decade earlier, and the *Essays on Truth and Reality* (1914), which appeared two decades later. Nevertheless, these publications eclipsed the reflections contained in the earlier works on logic by Green and Edward Caird. In *The Principles of Logic*, the author portrayed logic as a branch of philosophy that studies the structure of knowledge (without resorting to mathematical and formal proofs—in this, his investigations differed significantly from those of today's logicians). Enquiring, for example, into the nature of judgment, inference, truth and the problem of concrete universals. Some of these issues, especially the relationship between truth and reality, were developed in the *Essays on Truth and*

---

[4] J.H. Muirhead, *Recent Criticism of the Idealist Theory of the General Will (II.)*, "Mind" 1924, Vol. 33, pp. 170–172.

Reality, where — in a Hegelian spirit — he saw error in "the division of truth from knowledge and of knowledge from reality. The moment that truth, knowledge and reality are taken as separate there is no way in which consistently they can come or be forced together".[5]

Bradley's first book, *Ethical Studies* — a work Bosanquet called an "epoch-making event" — faded into obscurity within a relatively short time. Although it represented the first systematic British idealist examination of morality, politics and religion, its argumentation lacked precision and comprehensiveness. In spite of this, it is impossible to be indifferent to it, even today. Each of the themes recurring continuously in the works of later idealists found its first formulation in the *Ethical Studies*. Their reader encounters the author's determined opposition to the empirical tradition in epistemology, and utilitarianism and hedonism in ethics. Bradley's position with respect to politics raises the greatest number of doubts. Like Green, he seems not to have opted for any particular political doctrine, vacillating instead between the conservative and liberal perspectives. The final outcome of his deliberations provides no grounds for placing him within any particular political world view. Although his opposition to the atomistic-mechanicist view of society proper to liberalism is clear enough, as is his hostility to the rationalism of the Enlightenment, there are many reasons as to why he should not be deemed a conservative. One of the most frequently cited proofs of the conservative and static nature of his thought, his conception of "my station and its duties", which we shall discuss later, was openly and vehemently criticised by Bradley himself.

Bernard Bosanquet (1848–1923) was the last continuator of Green's thought of comparable stature to Bradley. Of the thinkers discussed here, he is also the figure to have sparked the most controversy in his time, while today he is the most forgotten. An Oxford University professor who left his academic tenure to move to London and implement the ideals of charity he preached (through his activity in the Charity Organisation Society and the London Ethical Society), he is today largely absent from works devoted to English-language political philosophy. While such an omission may be understandable in the case of Bradley, who did not develop his political theses to a sufficient degree to indisputably justify a systematisation of his legacy in this regard, it seems at the very least puzzling in Bosanquet's case. After all, according to numerous scholars, it is in *The Philosophical Theory of the State* that the political philosophy of idealism attained its fullest expression. Why then, in light of the revival enjoyed today by the legacy of Green

---

[5] F.H. Bradley, *Essays on Truth and Reality*, Oxford 1914, p. 110.

(whose authority is still often referenced by adherents of social-liberalism), has nearly all of Bosanquet's work sunk into obscurity?

According to Geoffrey Thomas, the fact that Bosanquet has been forgotten is due to at least four factors: firstly, a general conviction that his thought coincides with that of Bradley, and is therefore merely its restatement; secondly, the attacks of critics who, especially during the inter-war period, attributed totalitarian implications to *The Philosophical Theory of the State*; thirdly, the equally prevalent view that Bosanquet's thought is based upon a "static view of politics" and is of no use for the analysis of socio-political processes; and fourthly, his ideological opposition to the idea of the welfare state conjoined to a recognition of the importance of charitable institutions[6] gave rise to the belief that his postulates for reform were utopian, or at least wishful. Weighing up each of these factors, the principal reason for Bosanquet's meagre popularity would probably be the second listed — the criticism directed towards *The Philosophical Theory of the State*. Its consequence in the relevant literature is the abnormally frequent diagnosis of a fundamental divergence between the political perspectives of Green and Bosanquet. Critics usually view the first as a liberal and the second as a conservative at best, and often as an outright supporter of totalitarianism. Voices diagnosing the falsity of such an opposition, though already heard at the beginning of the twentieth century, did not gain in strength until recent decades.

The opposition between Bosanquet and Green was habitually the result of attributing fundamentally different inspirations to each thinker. While Green's conceptions were often seen as stemming from the Kantian project of "perpetual peace", unequivocally pro-Hegelian inclinations were ascribed to Bosanquet.[7] Although it is highly incorrect to posit similarities between the thought of Bosanquet and a conservative reading of Hegel,[8] this is ultimately what made the former the target of a mass attack by liberals (Hobhouse, A.D. Lindsay,[9] C.E.M. Joad[10]),

---

[6] G. Thomas, *Philosophy and Ideology in Bernard Bosanquet's Political Theory*, in: *Anglo-American Idealism, 1865–1927*, ed. W.J. Mander, London 2000, p. 106.

[7] H. Marcuse, *Reason and Revolution. Hegel and the Rise of Social Theory*, London 1955.

[8] See W. Sweet, *Was Bosanquet a Hegelian?*, pp. 39–60.

[9] A.D. Lindsay, *Bosanquet's Theory of the General Will*, "Proceedings of Aristotelian Society" 1928, Vol. 8; A.D. Lindsay, *The Modern Democratic State*, London–New York 1943, pp. 21–24.

[10] C.E.M. Joad, *Guide to the Philosophy of Morale and Politics*, London 1938.

socialists (G.D.H. Cole,[11] H.J. Laski[12]), as well as a certain number of academics (R.M. MacIver,[13] M. Ginsberg[14]). Most of them, regardless of political orientation, objected to the alleged conservatism of *The Philosophical Theory of the State*, seen as manifest in the already mentioned static nature of Bosanquet's thought — in addition to the absolutisation of the state and the recognition of the primacy of communal over individual interests.

The fate of Bosanquet's thought following his death proved symptomatic of two types of change. Firstly, its critique marked the factual end of idealism in the British Isles. Few later thinkers attempted to refute the charges brought against idealism, not only by liberals, but also by positivists and analytical philosophers. Secondly, from the point of view of the fate of the entirety of twentieth-century political philosophy, this opposition marked an important break. It is not without reason that Peter Laslett once[15] referred to the tradition stretching "from Hobbes to Bosanquet".[16] For the attack on the latter gave the signal for a final assault, not only on the conceptions of British and German idealism, but on all philosophies founded upon metaphysical premises. Doing away with Bosanquet meant the end of a certain paradigm of thinking about politics, in which thinkers set themselves the maximalist goal of finding the ultimate grounding of politics, and above all, the universal sources of the legitimacy of public order. The positivist programme of minimal philosophy and politics, which can today be called the "politics of life" after Anthony Giddens, geared towards the promotion and distribution of prosperity, agnostic on the issue of the true nature of social relationships and sensitised to the threat of totalitarianism, was to reign supreme in political philosophy until the 1970s and the resurrection — perhaps not of metaphysics as

---

[11] G.D.H. Cole, *Conflicting Social Obligations*, "Proceedings of the Aristotelian Society" 1914–1915, Vol. 16; G.D.H. Cole, *Social Theory*, London 1920; G.D.H. Cole, *Essays in Social Theory*, London 1950.

[12] H.J. Laski, *Bosanquet's Theory of General Will*, "Proceedings of the Aristotelian Society. Supplement" 1928, Vol. 8; H.J. Laski, *The State in Theory and Practice*, New York 1935.

[13] R.M. MacIver, *The Modern State*, Oxford 1926; R.M. MacIver, *Community. A Sociological Study*, London 1917, Appendix B: *A Criticism of the Neo-Hegelian Identification of Society and the State*, pp. 425–433.

[14] M. Ginsberg, *Is There a General Will?*, "Proceedings of the Aristotelian Society" 1920, Vol. 20.

[15] P. Laslett, *Introduction*, in: *Philosophy, Politics and Society. A Collection*, ed. P. Laslett, Oxford 1956, p. vii.

[16] Cf. G. Thomas, *Philosophy and Ideology in Bernard Bosanquet's Political Theory*, p. 106.

such, but of political universalism — brought about by the works of John Rawls and Robert Nozick.

In later parts of this chapter, we shall give a general overview of British idealist thought, focusing particularly on its social and political aspects, yet without entirely avoiding references to ethical or metaphysical issues. In particular, we will be occupied with a dual — both positive and negative — definition of the political views of the idealists. We shall first present their critiques of selected thinkers of the past, especially advocates of *a priori* and individualistic theories, contractualists and modern natural law theorists. We shall then review the principal theses and conceptions of the idealists: Bradley's "my station and its duties", Bosanquet's community of ideas and Green's view of the relationship between moral duties and legal obligations, as well as the teleological understanding of reality common to all of them.

2.1. Beyond the abstractions of reason

Both possible manners of philosophical self-definition — positive and negative — played an equally important role in the writings of the idealists, whose world view was to a large extent forged in battles against their philosophical predecessors and contemporaries, at times consciously trying to develop their theories while attempting to avoid their mistakes. This fight, however, was not always uniform. We can distinguish two different types of critiques attempted by the idealists — either the condemnation of a given philosophical current (or its specific representatives), or the use of it as a scaffolding for their own theories, in the belief that its remains can be combined with the other theories absorbed as part of the specific British idealist *Weltanschauung*. In the case of Bradley, Green and Bosanquet, at least with respect to their socio-political views, the dominant role in this theoretical mixture was played by the writings of Hegel. Although each took a different position on the works of the "sage of Berlin" (Bosanquet admired them openly and almost uncritically, Green decisively stated the necessity of modifying them, while Bradley admitted that he had never fully grasped them), Hegelian contextualism, historicism and organicism point to Hegel as the principal source of their inspiration.

Another example — this time of a much more critical and selective absorption — is the idealist approach to the Rousseauian general will. Although judged in a thoroughly negative light without exception, after an appropriate modification (at times resulting in a near total forsaking of the intuitions of the author of the *Social Contract*), it was admitted into the ranks of idealist conceptions. As we shall see in the next subsections, the idealists applied a similarly moderate criticism to the thought of Kant and John Austin, amongst others.

Meanwhile, their treatment of thinkers whose reflections they perceived to be entirely wrong or without use for ethical or socio-political analysis was entirely different. Modifying their theories was out of the question, absolute condemnation the sole option. This was the position of the British philosophers discussed here with respect to declared methodological individualists. Their criticism of their theoretical assumptions was unconditional, their divorce from representatives of this "effete tradition" complete.

In the following subsections we shall examine the idealists' critique of their philosophical predecessors. We shall introduce the thinkers most representative of the tradition discussed here; the originality of Bradley, Green and Bosanquet's interpretation of them having permanently added the latter to the canon of speculative thought. We shall therefore focus, in succession, on the reasons for Bradley's scepticism as to the practical and theoretical value of Kantianism, Bosanquet's critique of liberal individualism, and Green's charges of inconsistency, levelled against representatives of the modern natural law and contractual tradition.

2.1.1. The rejection of apriorism

The idealist critique of apriorism accords perfectly with the tradition — rightly identified as conservative — of refuting post-Enlightenment, rationalist political conceptions. It is based on the belief that theory cannot capture the complexity of social relations, especially if one explicitly abstracts from the existential circumstances of specific communities. Such endeavours can produce nothing else than a philosophical fiction, devoid of any cognitive value. It is therefore hardly surprising that on this point the idealists made Kant the principal target of their attack. In this respect, the greatest accomplishments of the British idealist tradition are owed to Bradley, who first arranged the most important elements of Kant's theory into the concept of "duty for duty's sake", in order to then subject it to a fierce critique. This theory is founded on the well known thesis that "[n]othing can possibly be conceived in the world, or even out of it, which can be called good, without qualification, except a good will."[17] It is precisely in the nature of this "good will" that Bradley saw the greatest defects of Kantian theory. For here it is perceived as: 1) universal — i.e. applicable to all people, regardless of personality, nationality or experience, therefore not the will of a particular man, but rather of man as such; 2) free — not conditioned by anything other than itself, "it exists because of itself and

---

[17] I. Kant, *Groundwork for the Metaphysics of Morals*, transl. T.K. Abbott, Broadview Editions 2005, p. 55.

for the sake of itself",[18] it is not the means to any end, but is an end unto itself; 3) autonomous—it is both universal and free; its autonomy consists in being independent from any authority other than its own; 4) formal—abstracting from specific circumstances, it is both immutable and without material content;[19] offering no direct solutions to specific ethical problems, it is a form that only hints at the correct conduct in each case.

Bradley summarised the concept of "duty for duty's sake" in a single sentence: "I am autonomous only because I am free, free only because I am universal, universal only because not particular, and not particular only when formal."[20] Although it would be a mistake to deny this conception any value, it is unacceptable in this form. The author of the *Ethical Studies* formulated three succinct objections against it. All of them relate to what has been recognised as a universal in it. The problem consists in the fact that it is:

1. Abstract—moral principles formulated in abstraction from real existential conditions, designed to apply to "man in general", cannot have a precise content; in order to follow them in life, it is necessary to apply personal discretion, being *de facto* deprived of any criteria for identifying the correct course of action.
2. Subjective—these principles have no grounding other than in individuals; they are dictated neither by the law of the community nor any moral system, and are merely "an inner notion in moral persons";[21] there is also no instance capable of resolving conflict between individuals in cases where each, believing themselves to be following these principles, would accept the need to act differently.
3. "It leaves a certain part of us outside ourselves"—this conception dictates moral ideals that cannot be attained; its rigorism demands that we ignore our weaknesses and limitations, abjure a considerable part of ourselves; therefore it generates a permanent tension between ideal and reality and divides man's personality into an "ideal self" and a "real self", holding the latter in contempt.

There are thus three reasons why the concept of "duty for duty's sake" and its various embodiments cannot be considered helpful in choosing between possible courses of action. Based on them, the individual 1) "cannot look on his subjective self as the realised moral law"; 2) "cannot look on the objective world as the realisation of the

---

[18] F.H. Bradley, *Ethical Studies*, p. 144.
[19] *Ibid.*, p. 299.
[20] *Ibid.*, p. 145.
[21] F.H. Bradley, *Ethical Studies*, p. 175.

moral law"; 3) "cannot realise the moral law at all, because it is defined as that which has no particular content, and therefore no reality".[22]

2.1.2. Against individualism. Theories of the first look

A priori conceptions are not the only ones to contain defects that render them useless for explaining ethical and socio-political issues. The empiricist and individualist perspectives are also founded on erroneous premises. On this issue, Bradley's critique followed paths belonging to the broadly understood communitarian tradition in political philosophy. Its main theses state that individuals are not capable of abstracting from the community in which they were brought up and educated,[23] and that there can be no individuals without there first being a community, in which they can grow and to which they would owe their identity. The Aristotelian thesis that man is a *zoon politikon* expresses the eternal truth that man "is what he is because he is a born and educated social being, and a member of an individual social organism".[24]

Is it possible to speak of an individual independently of the community? Can he "develop his 'individuality', his self which is not the same as other selves? Where is it? What is it? Where can he find it?",[25] Bradley asked, and immediately rejoined that there is no self apart from the community. For the latter precedes, by order of logic, every dimension of human existence. Individuals, conceived as an absolute beginning, unlimited by their past and the collective experience of the community, are nothing. People never formulate their own moral truths, nor do they ever make a fully rational, sober judgment and choose one of the many existing moral traditions. We always unwittingly become exponents of the morality of the community.[26]

Bradley was not alone to hold this view. He doubtless heard of his master's paeans to the Aristotelian thesis of the *zoon politikon*. In *Prolegomena to Ethics* Green claimed that:

> social life is to personality what language is to thought. Language presupposes thought as a capacity, but in us the capacity of thought is only actualised in language. So human society presupposes persons in capacity — subjects capable each of conceiving himself and the bettering of his life as an end to himself — but it is only in the intercourse of men,

---

[22] Ibid., p. 159; P.P. Nicholson, *The Political Philosophy*, pp. 20–21.
[23] F.H. Bradley, *Ethical Studies*, p. 166.
[24] Ibid.; cf. ibid., p. 168.
[25] Ibid., p. 172.
[26] Ibid., pp. 172–173.

each recognised by each as an end, not merely as a means, and thus as having reciprocal claims, that the capacity is actualized.[27]

Society, as "language to thought", constitutes a reservoir of the individual's possible desires. Apart from the purely biological need to sustain the processes of life and to satisfy sexual desires, all of man's other needs are social in nature. The same thing can be said of the chief motor of human action—the desire for self-realisation. Its most perfect form, the only potential source of a lasting sense of fulfilment, is moral improvement. This in turn is born of contact with other people[28] and can only be achieved within the community.[29] To be good always means to be good to somebody else.

The criticism of methodological individualism was frequently accompanied in the works of the idealists by an open attack on liberal doctrine. In this battle, special merit is rightly attributed to Bosanquet. In *The Philosophical Theory of the State*, he formulated a coherent critique of the liberal paradigm, while the phrase "theories of the first look" coined in it found a permanent place in the vocabulary of subsequent generations of idealists. Just what did Bosanquet chastise the liberals for? First of all, for their tendency to treat individuals as atoms within a social void. From the liberal point of view, inter-human relationships amount to nothing more than the reciprocal limitation of freedom. A similar situation exists with regard to the relationship between individuals and state institutions, against whose coercion the former are practically helpless. This perspective, Bosanquet claimed, is at the root of the liberal impotence to solve the paradox of self-government. Rousseau had already recognised that the greatest challenge facing political philosophy was to make individuals perceive submission to authority, not as a restriction of their freedom, but as an expansion of its scope. This problem, which Rousseau compared to squaring the circle, was to be the central theme of Bosanquet's *magnum opus*. Following in the footsteps of Rousseau, Bosanquet not only traced the limits of his field of interest, but also indicated ways of exploring it. Similarly to

---

[27] T.H. Green, *Prolegomena to Ethics*, in: T.H. Green, *Collected Works of T.H. Green*, ed. P. Nicholson, Bristol 1997, p. 192 (§ 183); cf. T.H. Green, *Lectures on the Principles of Political Obligation*, in: T.H. Green, *Lectures on the Principles of Political Obligation and Other Writings*, ed. P. Harris, J. Morrow, Cambridge 1986, p. 91 (§ 114); C. Tyler, *Contesting the Common Good. T.H. Green and Contemporary Republicanism*, in: *T.H. Green. Ethics, Metaphysics*, pp. 269–270.

[28] T.H. Green, *Prolegomena to Ethics*, pp. 199–200 (§ 190).

[29] See T.H. Green, *Lectures on the Principles*, p. 112 (§ 143); T.H. Green, *Prolegomena to Ethics*, p. 248 (§ 232).

the author of the *Social Contract*, he perceived self-government as the only legitimate source of political power.

There is a paradox at the heart of the concept of self-government, insurmountable on the basis of some political doctrines. Depending on the plane used to examine it, it can take two forms: that of the paradox of ethical obligation (when referring to the individual) or the paradox of political obligation (when the relation of the individual to the community is examined). The first concerns the possibility of self-control, and is founded on the assumption that it is impossible to exercise coercion over oneself. Accordingly, autonomy is not gained in an inner struggle, since the metaphor of coercion is borrowed from relations belonging to the external world, while the terms "internal coercion" and "internal obligation" are self-contradictory.

The paradox of political obligation touches upon a similar issue, this time projected onto the field of the relation of the state to the individual. Like Rousseau, Bosanquet asked how it could be possible for the same person to be at the same time the source and the object of political coercion. Faced with this question, liberals diagnose it as an internal contradiction. They claim that coercion (both political and legal) is always tantamount to limitation of freedom. However, they fail to see that the form of self-determination they promote also has the same paradoxical character at its basis. It is to the political variant of the paradox of self-government that Bosanquet attached the most weight. His study of whether it is possible to justify coercion for the sake of freedom, the famous Rousseauian notion of being forced to be free, proceeded through the analysis of the positions explaining this apparent contradiction. Within this context, he embarked upon a critique of the theories of Jeremy Bentham, John Stuart Mill and Herbert Spencer. He began with Bentham, for it is in his writings that the claim of the original antagonism between law and freedom was first so clearly and emphatically formulated in the modern period. On this issue, Bentham was also the most consequent of the liberals. In the opinion of the author of *An Introduction to the Principles of Morals and Legislation*, it is theoretically impossible, and still less practically so, to reconcile coercion and freedom, law and liberties, government and citizens. The relationship between them resembles a zero-sum game — the more prerogatives a government has, the less freedom its citizens have; the more freedom, the less government. Every law is contrary to liberty. For it implies duty, while liberty is freedom of action. As a utilitarian, Bentham wanted — at all costs — to maximise pleasure at the expense of pain, identified with physical discomfort. And since any limitation of the freedom to act produces this feeling, happiness calls for its elimination.

This, however, does not mean that every law is an absolute evil. The anarchistic eradication of authority still does not establish a kingdom of freedom. Although law is an evil, it sometimes turns out to be a necessary one. If social coexistence were not systemically regulated, the calculus of pleasure and pain would become unpredictable. Although legislation limits freedom, causing pain, it is also a condition of the systematic realisation of pleasure, a stable politics of maximising hedonistic gains.

Admitting Bentham's anthropological paradigm, it is impossible to reject his ethical and political views. The moment one accepts that the goal of life is the pleasure of individuals and that people are differentiated by their preferences, one must also admit that the intervention of government will never guarantee the optimal fulfilment of desires. This can only be achieved through the unrestrained activity of individuals. It is hardly surprising, then, that liberty took a negative form in Bentham's works.[30] The fulfilment of desires should not encounter unnecessary obstacles. Law is also only binding insofar as its absence would prevent fulfilment, while its purpose should be to support individual initiative and spontaneity, acting against their limitation. This reasoning was unacceptable to Bosanquet. He found fault both with its premises and the conclusions that must inevitably flow from them.[31]

The thought of Mill presents a similar case, although it is true that many of his conceptions can be seen to modify or even break with utilitarian tradition. Evidence of these changes is especially visible in the ethical and political domain. After all, Mill was a supporter of moderate state interventionism and of the view that self-realisation was the principal value of human life. It is of little surprise, then, that his works are sometimes perceived as a catalyst for key changes in the liberal world view — the shift from the anthropology of classical liberalism to New Liberalism.[32] For although Mill belonged to the tradition of utilitarian thinking, the fact that he defined the good in a manner different from Bentham engendered equally different political postulates in his work. This appeared most clearly in Mill's attempts to justify state intervention in the lives of citizens. The liberty to do anything one wills, the foundation of Bentham's version of utilitarian liberalism, is

---

[30] J. Bentham, *Letter to Simon Snyder*, No. 4 (July 1814), in: J. Bentham, *Works of Jeremy Bentham, Part. IV*, Edinburgh 1838, p. 471.

[31] B. Bosanquet, *The Philosophical Theory of the State*, London 1910, p. 55.

[32] M. Freeden, *The New Liberalism. An Ideology of Social Reform*, Oxford 1978, p. 12.

opposed here to "true freedom", whose realisation sometimes requires the limitation of "apparent freedom".[33]

Although it is possible to perceive a fundamental difference with respect to the radically liberal utilitarianism of Bentham above, the core of Mill's argumentation remains the same as that of *An Introduction to the Principles of Morals*. Liberty requires protection from social pressure, it is therefore necessary to erect defences protecting individuals from the claims of their fellow citizens, only infringing upon their self-will in exceptional circumstances when their good is threatened. Liberty is the possibility of spontaneous, non-conformist and original action; it is not submitting to social norms of conduct when these inhibit our development. Lack of restraint is equated here with the absence of both conventional social constraints and legal regulations. Coercion and obligation are evils – this is the general principle. That they can sometimes be useful for the realisation of life plans is merely a modification of it.[34]

Bosanquet identified similar conclusions in the works of Spencer, although given their anthropological premises he found a surprisingly large number of accurate statements. No one had previously so distinctly exposed the harmfulness and stupidity of collectivist politics, which ultimately harms the state in a measure far surpassing any profit that might accrue from it.[35] However, Spencer's perspicacity in exploring the theoretical implications of the radical individualist and contractualist perspective is even more surprising. He notes that "[i]t is ridiculous [...] to think of a people as creating rights, which it had not before, by the process of creating a government in order to create them. It is absurd to treat an individual as having a share of rights *qua* member of the people, while in his private capacity he has no rights at all."[36] The fundamental claims of the contractualists are false, since laws had existed long before the constitutions of the states. It is precisely here, in the opposition to the individualistic exegesis of law and state, that we find the discrepancy between Spencer and Bentham. But does this substantiate viewing their thought as fundamentally different? In Bosanquet's opinion, no. Since even correct intuitions did not prevent Spencer from embracing a negative concept of liberty and of the state. In spite of having a different point of departure than the philosophical radicals – evolutionism and social Darwinism, the idea of the "social struggle for survival", from which the best emerged victorious – their

---

[33] J.S. Mill, *On Liberty*, in: J.S. Mill, *On Liberty and Other Writings*, ed. S. Collini, Cambridge 1989, pp. 96–97.
[34] B. Bosanquet, *The Philosophical Theory*, pp. 57–58.
[35] Ibid., p. 65.
[36] Ibid., p. 66.

point of arrival was the same. Despite a different view of the purpose of state institutions (for Bentham, the maximisation of happiness; for Spencer, facilitating the survival of the fittest), they postulated similar means for their attainment. This consisted in the project of the state as an arena for the practice of unrestrained freedom (understood as independence from heteronomous influences). On this point, the philosophy of the author of *The Man versus the State* laid itself open to charges similar to those levelled against earlier theories, in particular the charge of being unable to overcome the paradox of self-government. For any attempt to do so must inevitably result in the annihilation of one of its terms—either government, leading to an apotheosis of the unrestrained self, or the freedom of the self, abrogated in the name of the absolute supremacy of government. *Tertio non datur.* Not on the ground of individualism.

The thinkers criticised by Bosanquet shared a tendency towards strict differentiation between the individual and the community. In the opinion of Bentham, Mill and Spencer, individuals are relatively autonomous, their interest can be separated from that of the community, while the sphere of liberty is readily separable from that of constraint. This is untrue. It is possible, as Mill did, to strictly divide the sphere of law (which we enter when we harm another), from that of morality (when the suspicion arises that harm has been done) and that of liberty (anything that does not belong to the previous cases).[37] It is nonetheless impossible to strictly define in which of these spheres the expression of individualism plays a dominant part, and in which we are determined by the community.[38]

Liberties and rights, individuals and communities, are not fundamentally opposed to one another. It is true that law may limit freedom—but this is not its essence. It is not necessary to annihilate either element of self-government, i.e. neither self nor government. Together they form a single whole, mutually conditioning their existence. The term "individual" can be understood in two ways. Individuals can be viewed as atoms within a social void, alienated from all that surrounds them, colliding with it and being constrained by it in their movements. This is precisely how exponents of "theories of the first look" or "*prima facie* theories"[39] perceive the individual. These theories are a result of the failure to grasp the nature of social existence, of a lack of discernment leading to a view of society as that which it appears to be at first

---

[37] Ibid., p. 59.
[38] Ibid., p. 60; cf. B. Bosanquet, *Life and Finite Individuality. Two Symposia*, London 1918, pp. 89–90.
[39] B. Bosanquet, *The Philosophical Theory*, p. 75.

glance[40] – a collection of individuals pursuing goals they have set themselves, which others continually interfere with (as does the government, through legal regulations). Individuals perceived this way are supposedly relatively autonomous – who they are depends largely on themselves. This perspective, in Bosanquet's view, is particular not only to Bentham, Mill and Spencer, but also to Rousseau.

The second manner in which the individual can be perceived, opposed to the one just described, demands viewing individuality as reflecting the fact that "however full and great his nature, it is so thoroughly one, so vital and so true to itself, that, like a work of art, the whole of his being cannot be separated into parts without ceasing to be what it essentially is."[41] This is how Bosanquet understood the term, applying it not just to individual people, but also to communities. Autonomous people, as portrayed by radical individualists, have never existed. Everyone carries within them a part of the community they grew up in and whose baggage will accompany them until the end of their days. The physical creature called the human being never has a corresponding analogous mental being, different from its surroundings, capable at any given moment of leaving them behind in order to establish itself elsewhere. Hence there are no wholly unique people. Everyone is an embodiment of ideas developed by past generations of ancestors, to which a small amount of personal experience is added.

2.1.3. Against contractualism and modern natural law theory

In Green's main political work, the *Lectures on the Principles of Political Obligation*, the terms *jus naturae* and *natural law* appear quite frequently. Green himself would even have called himself a natural law theorist, although his specific understanding of the term makes his inclusion among modern theorists of natural law questionable. For Green sought signs of the naturalistic fallacy in their works, in its original, Humean meaning.[42] "Political or civil rights, then, are not to be explained by derivation from natural rights, but in regard to both political and natural rights, in any sense in which there can be truly said to be natural rights, the question has to be asked, how it is that certain powers are recognised by men [...] as powers that *should be* exercised,

---

[40] Ibid., p. 77; cf. B. Bosanquet, *The Antithesis Between Individualism and Socialism Philosophically Considered*, in: B. Bosanquet, *Civilization of Christendom*, New York 1893, pp. 308–309, 316–318; B. Bosanquet, *Liberty and Legislation*, in: B. Bosanquet, *Civilization*, pp. 260–262, 365–367.
[41] B. Bosanquet, *The Philosophical Theory*, p. 74.
[42] See W.K. Frankena, *The Naturalistic Fallacy*, "Mind. New Series" 1939, Vol. 48, pp. 464–477.

or of which the possible exercise *should be* secured."[43] Even if we were to admit the existence of primordial laws governing human nature — or even if human relations could be ordered according to such laws — their postulate would demand a justification other than the strictly genetic. The mere fact that such laws exist does not imply that they should be viewed as the foundation of legislation. Existence does not justify itself; *there is* never implies there *ought to be*. This does not mean that deontology does not emanate from ontology,[44] only that this consequence is not *direct*, or more precisely, that the order of argumentation adopted by modern natural law theorists must be reversed.

Green was a supporter of the pre-modern way of justifying the state and law, of emphasising their teleological nature after the manner of the ancients, especially Aristotle. After all, rejecting the theses of the moderns requires no specific metaphysical assumptions. It is sufficient to indicate the internal contradictions in their works. The anthropology they espouse cannot be reconciled with contractualist theory, equally fundamental to them. "'Natural right,' as = right in a state of nature which is not a state of society, is a contradiction. There can be no right without a consciousness of common interest on the part of members of a society."[45] The writings of Baruch Spinoza and of Thomas Hobbes are particularly susceptible to this charge. The error of the former lay in accepting that *jus naturae* is mere *potential*,[46] or power,[47] and in ignoring the consequences entailed by this step. Spinoza should have denied that *jus naturae* "was 'jus' at all".[48]

Green's argumentation is simple. Spinozan ethics considers it natural that people are primarily motivated in their actions by fear of death and by the desire to gratify their lusts.[49] Since these sensations are common to all mankind (*nota bene*, making man at best "the most crafty of the animals"[50]), they are precisely what constitutes the law of nature.

---

[43] T.H. Green, *Lectures on the Principles*, p. 25 (§ 24); cf. *ibid.*, p. 16 (§ 7).

[44] It is in metaphysical reflection that Green ultimately found the justification of his philosophico-political desiderata, as argued by Richter (M. Richter, *The Politics of Conscience. T.H. Green and His Age*, Cambridge 1964) and Jean Pucelle (J. Pucelle, *La Nature et l'Esprit dans la Philosophie de T.H. Green. La Renaissance de l'Idéalisme en Angleterre au XIXe siècle.[é] I. Métaphysique-Morale*, Paris 1960).

[45] T.H. Green, *Lectures on the Principles*, p. 29 (§ 31).

[46] B. Spinoza, *Theological-Political Treatise*, in: B. Spinoza, *Complete Works*, transl. S. Shirley, ed. M.L. Morgan, Indianapolis, IN–Cambridge 2002, XVI, p. 527.

[47] T.H. Green, *Lectures on the Principles*, p. 29 (§ 32).

[48] *Ibid.*

[49] B. Spinoza, *Political Treatise*, in: B. Spinoza, *Complete Works*, I, 4, p. 681.

[50] T.H. Green, *Lectures on the Principles*, p. 30 (§ 32).

"[W]hatever any man does after the laws (*ex legibus*) of his nature, he does by the highest natural right (*summo naturae jure*), and he has as much right (*habet juris*) over nature as he has power."[51] If Spinoza had not admitted an untenable distinction between natural and positive law, if he had not acknowledged the transition from the state of nature to the civil state (*status civilis*) as obvious and unproblematic,[52] he would certainly have avoided this contradiction. For it is impossible for even the mere idea of community to emerge from a group of people guided only by their desires, from the ceaseless conflict of *naturales potentiae*. The passage from the pre-civil state to the civil, the mere possibility of recognising others as kin, requires the mutual recognition of political subjectivity, and so also the existence of a certain kind of community.[53] If this mutual recognition had already been attainable in the state of nature, there would have been no need to create society. It would necessarily already exist. In order for the transition from the *status naturalis*, which Spinoza sees as a state "of pure individualism, of simple detachment of man from man",[54] to be possible, the existence of distinctly social instincts[55] must already be presupposed in it. "Pure individualism" cannot lead to recognising the rights of others, and yet such a recognition is a necessary precondition of all agreements, including the social contract. In sum, for society to be created, there must already exist a morality, although the latter can only come into being within society. But since the natural state lacks "both the natural and the rational principles of social development",[56] it is separated from the state of society by a gulf, which neither Spinoza nor the modern natural law theorists seem to have noticed.

It would be worth changing Spinoza's groundless distinction between *jus naturae* and *jus civile* into a permanent division into *jus* and *potentia*. This for two reasons. Firstly, Spinozan natural law and positive law are essentially alike, for "man, alike in the natural and in the civil state, acts according to the laws of his own nature, and consults his own interest."[57] Secondly, positive law cannot derive from natural law understood in this sense. No ethico-political desiderata can be deduced from the *status naturalis* and the laws that govern it. Duty as the foundation of morality is a social phenomenon — it regulates relations

---

[51] B. Spinoza, *Political Treatise*, II, 4, p. 683; por. *Ibid.*, II, 23, p. 689.
[52] *Ibid.*, III, 3, p. 690.
[53] T.H. Green, *Lectures on the Principles*, p. 34 (§ 36); cf. T.H. Green, *Prolegomena to Ethics*, pp. 200–201 (§ 190).
[54] T.H. Green, *Lectures on the Principles*, p. 35 (§ 37).
[55] *Ibid.*, pp. 91–92 (§ 116).
[56] *Ibid.*, p. 35 (§ 37).
[57] B. Spinoza, *Political Treatise*, III, 3, p. 690.

between people who recognise each other as subjects. For morality is not only made up of rights, but also of duties: respecting the subjectivity of others, their right to acquire and possess goods. Spinoza's reasoning inevitably leads to the conclusion that the state of nature is also the civil state, which can be seen as absurd, given the definition of each. It is precisely this inconsistency that should be treated as the root cause of such awkward passages of the *Political Treatise* as those proclaiming that "the natural right which is special to the human race, can hardly be conceived, except where men have general rights."[58]

Hobbes had already made mistakes similar to Spinoza's, further intensifying them by emphasising the fundamental difference between natural and civil laws. Hobbes "supposes his sovereign power to have an absolute right to the submission of all his subjects, singly or collectively, irrespective of the question of its actual power against them".[59] In light of Green's earlier criticism of Spinoza, charges against this manner of reasoning seem evident. Since apart from force, the Spinozan *potentia*, no other sources of law exist in the state of nature, these cannot exist in the civil state either. If force is the only source of a sovereign's power, it should also be the sole basis for its legitimacy. Once the sovereign's power has ceased, it is impossible for any other obligations to bind individuals. Talk of the supposed morality of the civil state reveals the internal inconsistency of this thinking, since in the civil state understood this way, there is no morality outside of legality.[60] Hobbes was therefore wrong to posit a distinction between the state of nature and the civil state. Although the natural war of all against all ceases in the *status civilis*, there is no change in rules compared to the state of nature, only a difference in the way communal life is organised. In Green's view, Hobbes' conception of the social pact does not justify the thesis that the creation of a social union is accompanied by the birth of morality. The civil state portrayed in the *Leviathan* is nothing other than a limited state of war. Both Hobbes and Spinoza can therefore only understand the term "law" as natural power — not *jus*, but *potentia*. The emergence of law requires the mutual recognition of claims, as well as the agreement that all should have access to a certain category of goods in addition to the guarantee of their possession. This in turn, apart from the recognition of these rights as valid, also implies the necessity of assigning the duty of respecting the rights of others to individuals. The conceptions of the modern jusnaturalists entirely disregarded the issue of duty. If by "law" Spinoza and Hobbes mean only power, then they

---

[58] *Ibid.*, II, 15, p. 687.
[59] T.H. Green, *Lectures on the Principles*, p. 39 (§ 42).
[60] *Ibid.*, p. 42 (§ 47).

are wrong. Law always has two components: the right to something and the duty to respect this right by others. The notion of power, on the other hand, is defined as the right to possess that which one is capable of appropriating. It does not require acceptance on the part of others, but only their fear of force. Power does not imply duty, since the latter presupposes voluntary action or refrainment from action.

Not only Spinoza and Hobbes were "apt to make an absolute opposition between the state of nature and the political state, and to represent men as having suddenly contracted themselves out of one into the other".[61] This was true for all the major modern contractualist theories — in this respect, Richard Hooker, Grotius, Hobbes, John Locke and Rousseau differed only in their application of the same principle.[62] Locke was somewhat of an exception here, and this in two ways. Firstly, by making a distinction between the social contract and the appointment of government in *Two Treatises of Government*,[63] he seems to have avoided the charge of an unwarranted transition from the state of nature to the state of political obligation. *De facto*, however, he did not avoid the errors of his predecessors. Distinguishing two types of contract does not solve the problem of the impossibility of passing from the natural to the civil stage of human existence.[64]

But it was another aspect of Locke's thought that Green was intrigued by more. According to the author of the *Two Treatises*, all natural rights are an extension of the fundamental right to property. This is so in the case of the right to life, to work and its fruits as well as the ensuant right to protect these goods.[65] Here, "right" no longer corresponds to the Spinozan *potentia* or Hobbesian power. These were devoid of moral quality and did not depend on the moral disposition of individuals. Things are entirely different in the state of nature as described by Locke. Here the transition to the state of society does not involve any essential change in interpersonal relations. Individuals are already capable of recognising each other's claims in the state of nature. Within the state of nature, man is therefore not only characterised by desire and its natural extension, right, but also by a sense of duty and obligation.[66] As in the case of Hobbes and Spinoza, the conclusion of a social contract does not revolutionise inter-human relations. Society

---

[61] Ibid., p. 46 (§ 52); cf. A.C. Cacoullos, *Thomas Hill Green. Philosopher of Rights*, New York 1974, pp. 77–80.
[62] T.H. Green, *Lectures on the Principles*, p. 45 (§ 51).
[63] J. Locke, *Two Treatises of Government*, London 1821, pp. 370–372 (§ 211–212).
[64] T.H. Green, *Lectures on the Principles*, pp. 48–50 (§ 55–58).
[65] J. Locke, *Two Treatises of Government*, pp. 28–33 (§ 27–30).
[66] R. Martin, *Green on Natural Rights in Hobbes, Spinoza and Locke*, pp. 111–112, 115.

and government are nothing more than instruments designed to curtail the indignities of the pre-civil state. Avoiding one mistake, Locke inevitably fell prey to another, attributing traits appertaining exclusively to the civil state to the state of nature. Although he was right to deny the existence of pre-moral laws, the root of the naturalistic fallacy of other natural law theorists, he repeated their errors by maintaining the opposition between the state of nature and the civil state. Locke's lack of consistency was thus reminiscent of the contradictions present in Hobbes and Spinoza. Admitting the existence of moral precepts within the state of nature, he also allowed strictly social phenomena to exist therein.

Despite being the most developed within the whole of the British idealist tradition, Green's critique of the theory of the social contract was not unique. Recognising the basic defects of the individualist perspective, Bradley also found himself forced to attack contractualism.[67] Societies did not emerge through the association of asocial, indeterminate individuals, since such beings never existed. Or even if they did, they could hardly have been called human. Humanity is not something given at birth, but a developed ethical sensibility. Although historically morality undoubtedly does not precede humanity, where morality is lacking, humanity can assuredly be said not to exist. The supposition that people in the state of nature could have produced morality is utterly absurd. Moral systems have existed as long as people have existed.

The recognition of the social nature of human personality led Bradley to accept a similar genesis of moral norms.[68] Morality is first and foremost an attribute of the community. The good person obeys the precepts derived from the commonly acknowledged hierarchy of values; the evil one violates them. There are no other indicators of rightness. Both the rationalist view of individuals as indeterminate, and that of the alleged human rights that belong to them (a set of abstract rights detached from the social functions particular people perform), are wrong. Rejecting the existence of man-in-himself, Bradley could not consent to the ascription of attributes in the form of rights and duties to such a being. This reasoning, in fact, applies to all conceptions of natural rights. Basing political or ethical desiderata on these rights, placing an excessive emphasis on what is common to people, while ignoring the differences separating them—this is the hallmark of a disdainful simplification of reality, bypassing the richness of its various manifestations.

---

[67] F.H. Bradley, *Ethical Studies*, p. 174; cf. *ibid.*, p. 209.
[68] *Ibid.*, p. 179.

2.2. The social sources of identity. Towards contextualism

Opposition to abstract ethical codes, these stemming from attempts to rationally defend a universal morality, is a recurrent theme in the writings of the thinkers discussed here. It must be remembered that their main inspiration came from the German idealists, in whose works they sought ways to challenge the dominant position of individualism, empiricism and utilitarianism in Great Britain. The German tradition, however, was not sufficiently uniform for an equal part to be drawn from the works of all its representatives. Next to the rationalism of Kant, we can cite the voluntarism of Fichte and the irrationalism of Schelling; in the domain of ethics, the universalism of *The Critique of Pure Reason* contrasted with the historicism of *Elements of the Philosophy of Right*. The British were aware of these inconsistencies. They were inspired in particular by the Fichtean and Hegelian critique of Kantianism. In it, they found an argumentation that fitted remarkably well with the theses of another thinker, whose authority was uncontested by nearly every representative of the idealist tradition — Aristotle. And although the Stagirite was an inspiration in many areas, his influence is most distinct in ethics and politics. The fundamental role the idealists ascribed to theses positing the social and teleological nature of man deserves special attention. Neither appeared in its pure form in Kant, while both were an integral element of Hegelianism.

This is why the author of the *Critiques*, of all the classical German philosophers, played a relatively small role in the British Isles. The universalism of his fundamental ethical theses, his opposition to consequentialism and teleologism, could not be reconciled with the works of the Greeks, skilfully combining anthropological essentialism and cultural contextualism. This is why the designation "neo-Hegelians" is often used to refer to the British idealists, never "neo-Kantians". It is the thought of the author of *The Phenomenology of Spirit* that shaped the British tradition to a much greater degree than Kant. A distinctly Hegelian strain was seen to run through the theories of Bradley, Bosanquet, Ritchie, William Wallace, John Caird, Haldane, Andrew Seth Pringle-Pattison. The relatively few thinkers to combine Kantianism with Hegelianism included Green, John Watson and Edward Caird. There were, however, none who based their reflections solely on Kant.

It is precisely the omnipresence of Hegel that makes it possible to speak of the convergence of British idealist thought. These similarities, however, did not occur with the same intensity in every field. The greatest divergence seems to have existed in epistemology and ontology. The critique of the real nature of time formulated by John

McTaggart Ellis McTaggart, Bradley's proofs of the contradictions inherent in discursive thinking, Haldane's idealist theory of relativity, Ritchie's Hegelian Darwinism, James Ward's spiritualist monism, are all positions so original as to be impossible to reconcile. A different picture emerges in the field of ethics and politics. Here, the scholar encounters a striking convergence of views. An overwhelming number of idealists made self-realisation the goal of existence, all rejected the liberals' utilitarianism and atomistic individualism. If they put forward political postulates, these were usually democratic. When they proposed economic reforms, their tone was usually social-liberal or socialist. This is why the works of Bradley, Green and Bosanquet had such a crucial importance for the British idealist tradition. For it is in them that the socio-political world view of idealism crystallised. Its later representatives predominantly restated the theses previously expounded in the works of their masters. This can be seen in the writings of Herbert Albert Laurence Fisher,[69] Watson,[70] Wallace,[71] Reinhold Friedrich Alfred Hoernlé,[72] Alexander Lindsay,[73] Ernest Barker,[74] Hector James Wright Hetherington and John Henry Muirhead,[75] John Stuart MacKenzie,[76] as well as Henry Jones.[77] All were permeated by the same mental paradigm, founded on the premise of man's social nature and concentrating on his relation to the communal universe as well as his moral calling, impossible to fulfil without the support of others. In the following subsections, we shall focus on the bonds connecting the individual to the community, presenting the key conceptions of our three protagonists: "my station and its duties" expounded in the *Ethical Studies*, the community of ideas portrayed in *The Philosophical Theory of the State*, and the relationship between morality and legality presented in Green's lectures.

2.2.1. My station and its duties (Francis Herbert Bradley)

> Goethe has said: 'Be a whole or join a whole', but to that we must answer, 'You cannot be a whole, unless you join a whole'. – F.H. Bradley, Ethical Studies

---

[69] H.A.L. Fisher, *The Common Weal*, Oxford 1924.
[70] J. Watson, *The State in Peace and War*, Glasgow 1919.
[71] W. Wallace, *Lectures and Essays on Natural Theology and Ethics*, Oxford 1898.
[72] R.F.A. Hoernlé, *Idealism as a Philosophical Doctrine*, London 1924.
[73] A.D. Lindsay, *The Modern Democratic State*, London 1943.
[74] E. Barker, *Political Thought in England 1848 to 1914*, London 1928.
[75] H.J.W. Hetherington, J.H. Muirhead, *The Social Purpose*, London 1918.
[76] J.S. MacKenzie, *Introduction to Social Philosophy*, Glasgow 1895.
[77] H. Jones, *The Principles of Citizenship*, London 1919.

A critique of rationalist apriorism and empiricist individualism was not a goal in itself for the idealists. It provided a framework upon which they formulated their own views, without the defects attributed to their predecessors. A presentation of this critique may therefore constitute an important — albeit only introductory — stage in the delineation of idealist thought. Its most important theoretical elements were often expressed in concepts-symbols, later criticised as inseparable from the idealist view of reality. Bradley's conception of "my station and its duties" is most often cited within this context. Its essence, which is quite straightforward, consists in the glorification of the duties which the community imposes on its members. To be moral is to be aware of these duties; to be good is to fulfil them in an appropriate manner.[78] There are no other indicators of conduct apart from the precepts of the community. We usually do not even view them as precepts, for what is common — morality — is internalised. What to a member of another community might seem subjective and accidental, the citizen perceives as objectively right. Hence Bradley's ideal of citizenship is φρόνιμος (*phronimos*) — "the man who has identified his will with the moral spirit of the community, and judges accordingly."[79] Since it is impossible rationally to justify moral judgments[80] (rationalism, carried to its full conclusion, leads to universalism, the admission of which would question the primacy of the community in the constitution of the identity of its members), in their conduct, the *phronimoi* are guided by intuition. Their minds are not "full of reflections and theories"[81] (since intuitions are much less fallible than rational deliberations). Their hearts yield to precepts which reason does not have to grasp.

Bradley combined the conception of "my station" with the anthropological thesis that the goal of life is participation in something transcending human imperfections. From a finite part, man wishes to transform himself into an infinite whole, and since this is impossible, the only option is to break free of this sense of finitude by participating in such a whole. This whole is the community — both political and religious. It is here that the true source of *apetitus societas* is to be found. It is not the craving for contact with others, altruism or an instrumental rationality that drive him to band into groups. It is the desire to exceed ourselves, and the faith that this can be accomplished by means of the community, that compel us to cooperate towards its good. In the idealist tradition, such a whole has come to be termed the "concrete univer-

---

[78] F.H. Bradley, *Ethical Studies*, p. 180.
[79] *Ibid.*, p. 196; cf. *ibid.*, pp. 199, 206.
[80] *Ibid.*, p. 194.
[81] *Ibid.*, p. 199; cf. *ibid.*, p. 233.

sal". Its universality is expressed in the fact of its irreducibility to the sum of its parts. This argument already appeared in the critique of contractualism—the community constitutes an inseparable element of the personality, no individual is thus devoid of a communal component. The community shapes the personality of its citizens, determines the nature of their needs, life goals and the means of achieving them. But it is also something concrete. As there are no individuals without the community, so there is no community without individuals.[82] This thesis can be understood in a physical sense—it then amounts to a banal observation that a collective has to have component parts—and in a psychological one—although shaped by the processes of socialisation, citizens are not completely determined. The community directs their way of thinking by providing, amongst other things, a reservoir of possible self-interpretations, without definitively determining their life choices.

Bradley intended his conception of "my station" to transcend the limitations of Kantian ethics. For it considers the universal as:

1. Concrete—related to the life of a specific community; it can serve as an indicator of conduct in every human situation because its precepts are clearly and comprehensibly formulated, their meaning does not have to be discovered by way of complex argumentation.

2. Objective—it allows a "real identity of subject and object", the subjective and the objective; for there are two sides to the moral world: its body, namely "systems and institutions, from the family to the nation",[83] and the soul, without which "the body goes to pieces"; the objective (political institutions and moral systems) remains in harmony with the subjective (the will of the citizens, "the reflection of the objective moral world"[84]).

3. "It leaves nothing of us outside it"—the conception of "my station" eliminates contradiction between the empirical self (the individual, member of a community) and its duties; but here precepts impossible to fulfil, at best producing a feeling of alienation, are no longer incumbent upon the individual.[85]

Individuals are what they are thanks to the community. This is evidenced by the fact that they inevitably perceive themselves from its perspective: "the self-consciousness of himself is the self-consciousness of the whole in him."[86]

---

[82] Ibid., p. 162.
[83] Ibid., p. 177.
[84] Ibid., p. 179.
[85] Ibid., p. 182.
[86] Ibid., p. 183.

2.2.2. The community of ideas (Bernard Bosanquet)

Bosanquet also advocated the ethical placement of individuals within social structures. His political conceptions visibly drew on the works of Bradley — an inspiration the author of *The Philosophical Theory of the State* never denied. According to Bosanquet, the community is a whole, delimiting the bounds of individuality and originality, defining the boundaries of ethical self-knowledge by indicating the values its members may attempt to realise. No one creates their own morality. In any attempt at self-definition, all points of reference in the form of moral systems, types of hierarchies of values as well as lifestyles are derived from the surroundings in which individuals have lived and are living. The choice of the way we live our lives is free only to a certain extent. Bosanquet's opposition to the Cartesian notion of the subject as capable of distancing himself from present and past events[87] is therefore hardly surprising. The community and its members form an indivisible whole.[88] It is of course possible to separate them in theory, as evidenced by the "theories of the first look". These, however, are founded on the error of abstraction and are the result of an academic detachment from reality.[89]

This much we had already learned from a reading of Bradley's *Ethical Studies*. Were Bonsanquet's conceptions limited to the replication of Bradley's schema, or did they introduce something novel into the idealist reflection on social questions? The concept of the community of ideas, formulated in *The Philosophical Theory of the State*, is without doubt Bosanquet's original contribution. According to this theory, the community's expectations towards its members take the form of a system of ideas inculcated to them through the process of socialisation. The fact that functioning within the same institutions, we share the same ideas, and so also systems of values and views of social order, results in the convergence of our interests with both our fellow citizens and those of the community as a whole. Bosanquet held that if we were to ask a methodological individualist how it is possible for society to function without disruption, although people are independent and unconditioned in their choices, he would not be able to give an answer. The functioning of any institution requires a system of unspoken yet common knowledge about expectations, duties and rights, both our own and those of others, a knowledge incommunicable during short

---

[87] B. Bosanquet, *Life and Finite*, pp. 79–84, 91–94.
[88] B. Bosanquet, *The Philosophical Theory*, p. 143.
[89] B. Bosanquet, *Introduction to the Second Edition*, in: B. Bosanquet, *The Philosophical Theory*, p. LVI; see B. Pfannenstill, *Bernard Bosanquet's Philosophy of the State*, p. 186.

acts of social interaction, yet presumed obvious. Only it allows to coordinate goals so that their fulfilment does not cause cooperation to devolve into conflict.

Bosanquet illustrated this issue by comparing two types of coexistence: association, as exemplified by a crowd, and organisation, as exemplified by an army. The crowd is made up of random individuals, and so may be regarded as an artificial entity. It is true that its members influence one another, while individuals in a crowd are not what they would be outside it. A crowd may give the impression of a unity of purpose, which it attempts to achieve, but can never attain a state of true unity.[90] It is a mass in which all individuals are the same. Even if they think differently, they act alike. Their actions are uncoordinated. A crowd may "flow" from place to place, but it cannot distribute functions among its members, should this be necessary to increase its effectiveness. It is precisely as a crowd that exponents of the "theories of the first look" perceive society, seeing in it no more than a mere collection of individuals. It is true that they have similar goals, perform acts of cooperation at times, if this facilitates their achievement, and enter into conflict with one another when all of them cannot be attained. Such cooperation, however, is sporadic and unsystematic. Were it to become permanent, the crowd would transform into an entirely different type of coexistence, governed in a manner more typical of a society.

Society is a much more complex entity than a crowd. It is like an army. It too is made up of units and, like a crowd, has a single purpose. But there is a fundamental difference between them.[91] The army is an organised whole, in which each part has a strictly defined place, where everyone has a precisely defined function in addition to the duties and rights indispensable for its performance. And although all its members share a single purpose, each of them, often quite unwittingly, focuses on the performance of lesser tasks.[92] This is why the metaphor of a machine,[93] next to that of an organism, provides the most adequate description of society. Exponents of the "theories of the first look" failed to see that which was most important in a community—the system of ideas binding its members, the absence of which would render communication on key issues such as mutual expectations, goals and ways of attaining them impossible. They failed to notice that these ideas are also embodied in socio-political institutions, each of which has a concrete

---

[90] B. Bosanquet, *The Philosphical Theory*, p. 150.
[91] *Ibid.*
[92] *Ibid.*, p. 151.
[93] B. Bosanquet, *The Reality of the General Will*, in: *Aspects of the Social Problem*, ed. B. Bosanquet, London 1895, p. 325.

purpose — to realise a given value judged as important from the viewpoint of social coexistence.

The organism and the machine were not the only metaphors through which Bosanquet sought to illustrate the nature of social processes. The comparison to the human mind also proved useful.[94] "The State is, as Plato told us, the individual mind writ large."[95] In support of this view, Bosanquet formulated three successive theses:

1. The form of collective life reflects the system of ideas particular to the minds of its members — take for example a school: it is not a system of buildings and persons, but a set of inter-human relations; it forms when one group of people recognises that they owe obedience and attention to others, while another, that their purpose is to transmit knowledge to the former; it is something immaterial — a system of ideas present in the minds of those involved in its operation.

2. "Every individual mind is a system of such systems corresponding to the totality of social groups as seen from a particular position";[96] the mind of the individual taking part in social life reflects the complexity of its relations; "each individual mind, if we consider it as a whole, is an expression or reflection of society as a whole from a point of view which is distinctive and unique."[97]

3. "The social whole, though implied in every mind, only has reality in the totality of minds in a given community considered as an identical working system";[98] the community exists through individual minds.

Coexisting individuals dispose of the same conceptual apparatus, the same system of ideas, hence "there is no abrupt division between our conscious mind and the social system of suggestion, custom, and force, which supports and extends and amends it."[99] It is only in communities that individuals can find fulfilment and happiness.[100] Thanks to them, they develop talents they could not otherwise have acquired. It is only coexistence that creates the possibility for moral improvement, the

---

[94] B. Bosanquet, *The Philosophical Theory*, p. 158; ibid., pp. 143, 160, 165; B. Bosanquet, *The Function of the State in Promoting the Unity of Mankind*, in: B. Bosanquet, *Social and International Ideals. Being Studies in Patriotism*, New York 1967, p. 278.

[95] B. Bosanquet, *The Philosophical Theory*, p. 143; cf. B. Bosanquet, *Hegel's Theory of the Political Organism*, "Mind" 1898, Vol. 7, p. 9.

[96] B. Bosanquet, *The Philosophical Theory*, p. 159.

[97] Ibid.

[98] Ibid.; cf. B. Bosanquet, *Life and Finite*, pp. 95–96, 99–102; B. Bosanquet, *Science and Philosophy*, in: B. Bosanquet, *Science and Philosophy and Other Essays by the Late Bernard Bosanquet*, ed. J.H. Muirhead, R.C. Bosanquet, London 1927, p. 13; B. Bosanquet, *The Function of the State*, pp. 284–285.

[99] B. Bosanquet, *The Philosophical Theory*, p. 143.

[100] B. Bosanquet, *Life and Finite*, p. 94.

achievement of a developed and harmonious personality. The exchange of ideas and services occurring within this context gives rise to the greatest possible abundance of social functions, and so to the most complete range of potential forms of self-realisation: "in a social community all the private minds, especially those which serve as organs for public functions, supplement each other, the same needs and capacities being present in each, but developed in very various proportions."[101]

Although the metaphor of an organism is not entirely fitting (in the community, not only does the part exist within the whole, but also the whole in the parts[102]), certain resemblances may be found between society and living organisms. Its various cells (individuals) and organs (institutions) cannot function without the cardiovascular and nervous systems (system of ideas). And since every community, conditioned by a history and geopolitical location proper only to itself, is a unique whole with its own distinctive system of ideas, then it is the only judge of the rightness of its internal order. The nation state — since this is the community cited most frequently by Bosanquet — is the only arbiter of moral and political issues.[103]

2.2.3. Moral duties and legal obligations (Thomas Hill Green)

> In contrast to laws of nature, these laws of freedom are called *moral* laws. As directed merely to external actions and their conformity to law they are called *juridical* laws; but if they also require that they (the laws) themselves be the determining grounds of actions, they are *ethical* laws, and then one says that conformity with juridical laws is the *legality* of an action and conformity with ethical laws is its *morality*.[104]

The above quote from Kant's *Metaphysics of Morals* is perfect evidence of the debt Green[105] incurred from its author on the subject of the relationship between legality and morality. The difference between that which is external to the individual, and that which is internal, between what is prescribed and what internalised, is the basis for contrasting legal obligations with moral duties. The relationship between these two categories is an excellent illustration of the idealist renouncement of universalism in favour of ethical, political and legal contextualism.

---

[101] B. Bosanquet, *The State and the Individual*, "Mind" 1919, Vol. 28, p. 75.
[102] B. Bosanquet, *The Philosophical Theory*, p. 163.
[103] B. Bosanquet, *The Philosophical Theory*, p. 274; cf. ibid., pp. 174-175; B. Bosanquet, *The Communication of Moral Ideas as a Function of an Ethical Society*, in: B. Bosanquet, *Civilization*, pp. 166-167, 169-170, 177-178.
[104] I. Kant, *Metaphysics of Morals*, transl. M. Gregor, Cambridge 1991, p. 42.
[105] Green could certainly have drawn the same conclusions from a reading of Spinoza's *Political Treatise* (B. Spinoza, *Political Treatise*, III, 8-9).

The two orders, that of moral normativism and legislation, should be clearly separated. Moral duties are characterised by: 1) the fact that they cannot be compulsory, but must be voluntary; 2) their fulfilment is possible only after the individual has reached an adequate level of practical reason; 3) being related to self-constraint, they are the expression of true obligation. They are therefore the effect of autonomous and unforced self-discipline on the part of citizens. They also reflect their beliefs regarding the values which they should (in their own opinion) pursue. The *sine qua non* condition for the emergence of such duties is freedom (understood as independence from the decisions of others and the capacity for self-definition) and rationality (since self-control requires the subjugation of irrational inclinations). By contrast, legal obligations: 1) involve external coercion; 2) bind all people to the same degree, and 3) rely on fear of punishment. They regulate the lives of individuals as physical beings.[106] Their aim is not to alter dispositions, but to prevent acts that are undesirable from the social point of view.

The relationship between these two categories is quite complicated. For although they pertain to different spheres of life,[107] in practice they are subject to mutual influences. Every member of a community has certain beliefs as to the value or lack of value of certain goods. The egotistical desire to possess some of them leads to their pursuit at the expense of fellow citizens, who for that matter have analogous desires. When an awareness of the intersubjectivity of needs emerges during conflict on these issues, citizens gradually begin to accept each other's pursuits, agreeing to the establishment of a general framework for the acquisition of commonly desired goods. Take for example the right to property. Everyone has a system of values which to a certain degree is proper only to themselves, as a result of which they desire and seek certain goods more and more often than others. This is the source of their desire for a guarantee for the unrestrained pursuit of these goods. Since the quantity of material goods is necessarily limited, conflict erupts over them with others. Seeing that it is impossible to possess goods permanently without the consent of fellow citizens, individuals discern the need for a social contract regulating ways in which goods are acquired and possessed, consequently also recognising the ethical and legal subjectivity of others, thus attributing to them the same desires and legitimacy of satisfying them as to themselves. When these beliefs are shared by a majority of citizens, a right to property, respected on pain of punishment, is established, regulating issues pertaining to the acquisition, disposal and exchange of property. In this way,

---

[106] T.H. Green, *Lectures on the Principles*, p. 17 (§ 10).
[107] Ibid., p. 17, § 10.

the recognition of the universality of desire leads to the recognition of the legitimacy of the guarantee of its realisation, as a result of which laws guaranteeing the freedom to acquire goods are enacted. The aim of legislation is thus to guarantee the realisation of the hierarchy of goods and values accepted in a given community. Green's remark that the sovereign does not create laws, but only shapes state institutions according to them, becomes understandable in this context. Legislation derives its public legitimacy from moral duties, commonly accepted beliefs as to the desired shape of public order. Both categories, morality and legislation, are thus strictly connected, "It cannot be said that the most elementary consciousness of right is prior to [institutions], or they to it. They are the expression in which it becomes real."[108] Thus, as the views of citizens as to the nature of the desired goods evolve, as the socially accepted hierarchy of values become reordered, so legislation is also subject to the same changes. The role of the law becomes securing the moral gains of the citizens, protecting a certain vision of the public good against the action of amoral individuals. The existence of such a stable legislative foundation enables the development of moral ideals.

2.3. Teleologism, historicism, moral ideal. Towards objective values

As time went by, the British idealist tradition underwent significant transformations. The theories of its main exponents differed from generation to generation. What is most striking is the divergence of views regarding the relation of the general (the Absolute, society, the state) to the particular (the individual). These discrepancies in opinion led to the emergence of two varieties of idealism: the absolute and the personal. The most important representatives of the latter are thought to include Pringle-Pattison and his brother James Seth, McTaggart, Ward, Borden Parker Brown and Clement C.J. Webb.[109] The main claim underlying their theories was that the general exists solely on account of and through the specific. The Absolute could not exist without individual persons, society without individuals, the state without citizens. From this, the personal idealists refuted the legitimacy of sacrificing individuals for the sake of the social whole and their interests for the sake of the good of community. Since the latter could not exist without citizens, the thesis legitimising the sacrifice of their good on the altar of abstract entities (such as the community) is an absurdity.

---

[108] T.H. Green, *Lectures on the Principles*, p. 91 (§ 115).
[109] See J.O. Bengtsson, *The Worldview of Personalism. Origins and Early Development*, Oxford 2006, pp. 177–202.

Green, Bradley and Bosanquet represented the position regarded as absolute. They shared the belief that reality was ultimately spiritual. Nature and the human world exist only thanks to and by virtue of the spiritual principle, the Absolute. But each of them depicted this being in a different way. Green called it "eternal consciousness", seeing the sense of all transformations occurring in the world in its progress towards self-knowledge. Just as in Hegelianism, so here too the Absolute was thought to use material and spiritual reality for the acquisition of self-knowledge. And since its nature is spiritual, this process must take the form of an evolution of moral ideas and take place within the history of human thought.

From the thesis positing the existence of the Absolute, Bradley also inferred that the process by which it realises itself stands for the moral improvement of humanity. His demonstration of the contradictions inherent in discursive thinking indicated the need for cognitive methods other than the logical or empirical. As a result of progressing along the path of science and rational thought, the world appears as a set of phenomena capable of being isolated and analysed. But in reality these are all components of an Absolute, knowable only through intuition.

It was similar for Bosanquet. If we were to seek a keyword, permeating all the elements of his thought, it would certainly be "wholeness".[110] In Bosanquet's epistemology, this concept stood for a fundamental unity of thought, will and action, combining to form the indivisible totality of the real. In his ontology, it gave rise to the concept of the Absolute — a spiritual principle running through all things, of which William Mander writes that "for Bosanquet the Absolute is not a mind, and and it is not God — although it bears many of the marks of both."[111] Applied to ethics, this whole determined the teleologism and perfectionism of Bosanquet's thought, in politics it denoted the political community, whose citizens are imperfect parts of a totality transcending them, while the general will embodied in them assigns them to their places and functions in the communal infrastructure.

Each of these thinkers recognised that the theory of the Absolute has to have weighty consequence for socio-political reflection. Theses on the fundamental desire to participate in a limitless whole, our role as miniature reproductions of the spiritual principle upon which reality is founded, and of the moral nature of our self-realisation all spring from idealist metaphysics. *"The world judges in me, though from my point of*

---

[110] A. Vincent, *The Individual In Hegelian Thought*, "Idealistic Studies" 1982, Vol. 12, pp. 158–162.

[111] W. Mander, *British Idealism*, p. 337.

view" — Bosanquet wrote, summarising this world view.[112] It is precisely in the metaphysical elements of idealist thought that we should seek the source of the idealists' ultimate opposition to the concept of "my station and its duties".

2.3.1. The moral ideal

The concept of "my station", in spite of its superior standing with respect to the positions of "duty for duty's sake" and methodological individualism, criticised by Bradley, also has its limitations. The most serious charge that can be brought against it is founded on the claim that it has proven impossible to overcome the dichotomy between "is" and "ought". Although its aim was to avoid the errors proper to the individualist paradigm, it also failed, without giving any satisfactory explanation as to the sources of morality.[113] The problem of dividing "is" from "ought", also known as the naturalistic fallacy, transposed into philosophico-political language, takes the following form: if "is" — the current state of awareness of the members of a community as well as the institutional *status quo* — were the sole indicator of what "ought to be", then, although the contradiction between the "true self" (the socially created ideal of human personality and institutions) and the "actual self" would be overcome, its removal would entail that of the purpose and possibility of social development (if the *status quo* is the only available ideal, then it is impossible to transcend the current state of affairs), the possibility of a genetic explanation of moral beliefs as well as the purpose of morality itself (since it is based on a distinction between the factual and the desired state[114]).

Apart from these theoretical charges, Bradley also levelled a number of practical ones, by indicating the facts of social life which stand in contradiction to the concept of "my station". The attempt to eradicate the contradiction between "is" and "ought" proved susceptible to a triple falsification in this case. In the first instance, this is expressed in the observation that it is impossible to identify the "particular self" with the "communal self", man as a private person with the citizen-patriot, in such a way as to eliminate this dichotomy. Just as ideal types belong to pure theory, so too the ideal community is impossible to implement. There will always be those who distinguish their interest from that of the community,[115] while the already mentioned *phronimoi*,

---

[112] B. Bosanquet, *Life and Finite Individuality. Two Symposia*, London 1918, p. 98.
[113] F.H. Bradley, *Ethical Studies*, pp. 203–204.
[114] *Ibid.*, p. 178.
[115] *Ibid.*, pp. 182, 226–228, 234, 308.

if they do exist, are few. There are doubtless too few of them to form a society.[116]

The second practical charge is based on the observation that it is intuitively possible to judge some communities as degenerate, potentially including our own, which would not be possible if communal morality were the only criterion for judgment. Identification with our station in the community is not always desirable. The *phronimoi* will not be good in every situation. Their actions, though they may conform to the community ethos, may contrast with the moral intuitions of their brethren, raised to respect the same ethical principles.

The third and last charge involves duties irreducible to "my station", and so those whose source lies beyond the community. From the latter's perspective, they are purely supererogatory, if not entirely indifferent. Bradley described two such cases. The first are duties towards mankind. Why should morality be limited to particular communities? The desire to be a part of a greater whole, the main motivation for communal life as presupposed by Bradley, might just as well result in loyalty to mankind. The second case are extra-social values. These are also deprived of significance from the social point of view, yet people feel a moral duty to realise them, as in the case of searching for truth or experiencing beauty. They cannot be reduced to "my station", and may sometimes even conflict with it. It is perhaps more fitting to call them "universal duties".[117] "To say, without society science and art could not have arisen, is true. To say, apart from society the life of an artist or man of science can not be carried on, is also true; but neither truth goes to show that society is the ultimate end [...] Man is not man at all unless social, but man is not much above the beasts unless more than social."[118]

The above critique of the radical placement of the individual within the community, considered irrefutable by Bradley himself, demonstrates the need of adapting his earlier views. Their defects were to be overcome by the concept of the "moral ideal",[119] above all constituting a response to the charge that it is possible to challenge communal moral

---

[116] See P.P. Nicholson, *The Political Philosophy*, p. 32.
[117] F.H. Bradley, *Ethical Studies*, p. 205.
[118] *Ibid.*, p. 223.
[119] Bradley's unequivocal inclusion within the conservative tradition is usually a simple consequence of failing to take this very part of his philosophy into account (*Moral Ideal* — the sixth essay in the *Ethical Studies*). A typical example of this approach is the work of George Santayana (G. Santayana, *Fifty Years of British Idealism*, in: idem, *Some Turns of Thought in Modern Philosophy. Five Essays*, New York 1933, pp. 53–55) and Dorothy Krook-Gilead (D. Krook-Gilead, *Three Traditions of Moral Thought*, Cambridge 1959).

systems as well as the existence of extra- and supra-social goods and values. Within its framework, Bradley distinguished a triple source of morality:

1. "The objective world of 'my station and its duties'" — the source of regulations defining our relation to other members of the community; although Bradley abandoned the idea of radical determination, he continued to recognise the important influence of communities on their members.

2. "The ideal of social perfection" — the factor that prevents us from being satisfied with the current state of development of commonly accepted moral ideals, compelling us to continually search for defects in them; it also has a social variety — the "ideal of perfect social relations" which explains the occurrence of socio-political transformations; whereas the effect of (1) is the glorification of a certain factual state ("is"), (2) admits the possibility of presenting desirable states ("ought to be"), thereby making it possible to avoid theoretical charges against the conception of "my station".

3. "The ideal of extra-social perfection" — a factor unrelated to inter-human relations, pertaining to values which do not have direct bearing on the welfare of the community.[120]

The last two ideals clearly show that the community is not the only source of norms and values. They explain the phenomenon of change within the *status quo* as well as the possibility of realising oneself through extra-social activity. Conduct can thus be viewed as right both as a result of obeying and transgressing communal norms.[121]

But how to describe the relations connecting these three sources of morality? Will they not conflict with one another, as when being a good artist requires being a bad father or citizen? Can reformers ignore their "station and its duties" in the name of the perfection of social relations? These are questions about potential conflicts between values and ways of resolving them. Bradley's response to them is permeated with anthropological pessimism. Conflicts are inevitable,[122] they are an inseparable part of social life. Anticipating the later position of Oakeshott, Bradley criticised the liberal belief in the possibility of conciliating the claims of community members. If it were not enough that conflicts cannot be prevented, there is not even a way of creating a universal hierarchy of values, allowing the recognition of some values as worthy of protection, and others as possible to sacrifice. It cannot be determined whether precedence should be given to the ideals of our

---

[120] F.H. Bradley, *Ethical Studies*, p. 220.
[121] P.P. Nicholson, *Bradley as Political Philosopher*, pp. 123–124.
[122] F.H. Bradley, *Ethical Studies*, pp. 225–226.

community, those transcending it, or those that are extra-social. There is only one rule that should always be respected — maintaining public order. Criticism of institutions can only be limited. Attempts to destabilise order are justified only in exceptional circumstances, in the name of "overpowering moral necessity".[123] Freedom of action or incitement to action is not an unconditional value. The *sine qua non* condition for the realisation of goods is the existence of the community, whose undisrupted functioning is a superior good.

2.3.2. Teleologism, historicism. The moral goals of the community and mankind

Bradley's conception of the "moral ideal" produces certain difficulties which had previously led its author to reject Kant's theories. It fails to establish a practical criterion for resolving moral disputes and enabling the hierarchisation of goods and values. Is the idealism of the author of the *Ethical Studies* therefore doomed to relativism? Since there are no universal values, why see virtue in the fulfilment of duties associated with "my station"? Were Bradley to accept relativism, would he not also have to renounce the deontological part of his philosophy? Accepting relativism, is it possible to also accept the existence of universal criteria for judging moral systems? In Bradley's view, ethical teleologism is the perspective which reconciles these positions.[124] It is true that communities differ in their moral views. They have different expectations towards their members, recognising no superior instances capable of challenging their exclusive right to enforce obedience. However, this does not mean that they have equal rights to their claims. For there are criteria for valuating particular moral systems. Although people remain loyal to various hierarchies of values, which are often impossible to reconcile, they have a common *telos* every community should strive towards. Cultural relativists are thus right to claim that communities should not be judged according to a universal morality. The claim that there is a single correct and ideal way of life is unjustified. Nevertheless, thinkers referred to as postmodern today are also wrong in thinking that human existence has no strictly defined purpose. Such a purpose exists, Bradley claimed, and it is self-realisation.[125] What was his understanding of it? It may take various forms, such as hedonism or perfectionism. Does this amount to their being equal? No, since not all of its forms are legitimate. Protagoras' *homo mensura* principle failed to gain Bradley's assent. Not all man wants is in line with his nature.

---

[123] *Ibid.*, p. 227.
[124] *Ibid.*, pp. 65–66.
[125] *Ibid.*, p. 118.

There is an immutable essence of humanity and a goal of existence implied by it.

Communities can achieve this goal in various ways. Since they exist within different geopolitical contexts and each has a different history behind it, it is no surprise that the differences between them are at times so deep that what is good for one can be fatal to another. So although the *telos* of existence is one, individuals and communities are forced to achieve it in different ways. These may differ in terms of the path chosen or the temporal order of its stages.[126] Teleologism was united in Bradley's thought with historicism, expressed in the thesis on the evolution of world views towards the emergence of the "true idea of man";[127] it enabled Bradley to combine essentialism with contextualism, to accept the existence of an unchanging human nature, while appreciating the factual diversity of its manifestations. Each stage in the evolution of morality can be regarded as objectively, though not absolutely, true. Morality surpasses the subjectivism of individuals, reflects beliefs pertaining to the *bonum publicum* that are common to members of a given community, although this does not mean that an equal value can be attributed to each and every system of beliefs: "[m]orality is 'relative', but none the less real."[128]

The reader of Green's works will come upon similar views. Here too, the Absolute, the foundation of reality, strives towards self-realisation. Everything that exists derives the reason for its existence from the role it plays in this process. A special function is attributed to man within this context. Since the evolution of the Absolute is of an immaterial nature, its self-realisation must be based on the development of finite, imperfect human selves (the development of the material world is here merely a means of perfecting the spirit). From the spiritual character of this process, Green inferred that it is also moral, identifying the perfecting of the Absolute with the evolution of moral ideals in the socio-cultural sphere. If ideals develop within the public sphere, then it is not so much individuals, with their specific views on moral issues, as whole societies that are a handy, since relatively constant, tool of development. The evolution of individuals, of societies and of the Absolute are here inextricably welded together, private interest permanently linked with the communal, while ethical development

---

[126] *Ibid.*, p. 192. Cf. P.P. Nicholson, *The Political Philosophy*, p. 30.
[127] F.H. Bradley, *Ethical Studies*, p. 190.
[128] *Ibid.*

implies the postulate of the realisation of an analogon of the Kantian ideal of the kingdom of ends.[129]

Belief in the inevitability of the process of self-realisation of the Absolute was accompanied, in the works of Green, by theses similar to those of Kant's "asocial sociability"[130] and Hegel's "cunning of reason".[131] In spite of the willingness or opposition of individuals, communities always strive towards moral perfection. The Absolute often exploits the ignorance of individuals, turning their evil deeds into good, using their egotistical interests for the moral improvement of whole societies.[132] Let us consider Napoleon as proof. Although motivated by his desire for personal glory, he could not have achieved it without contributing to the moral advancement of mankind.[133]

On the subject of the relationship between the individual and the community, of all the British idealists, Bosanquet was undoubtedly the one to antagonise liberals the most. This is hardly surprising since already on a very basic level this author appeared to strike at the very foundations of liberal thought. His fascination with ancient philosophy led, amongst other things, to the abandonment of a strict distinction between state and society. It is true that Bosanquet considered the possibility of collision between legislation and custom, although he seems not to have attached too much weight to this issue. In his view, both the state and society are permeated by the same system of ideas, coordinating the actions of citizens. Both have the same function and the same goal: "assuredly good life or the excellence of souls."[134] The influence society has upon individuals differs from that exercised by the state only in its form.[135] The pressure exerted by social institutions is usually imperceptible, while the state's use of force, or threat thereof, makes us tend to perceive it as existing only in a sphere that is external to individuals. But the political and social spheres cannot be separated. The state encompasses not just political institutions but also the "entire hierarchy of institutions by which life is determined, from the family to

---

[129] See A. Simhony, *Rights that Bind: T.H. Green on Rights and Community*, in: *T.H. Green. Ethics, Metaphysics*, p. 250.

[130] I. Kant, *Idea for a Universal History with a Cosmopolitan Purpose*, in: *Kant. Political Writings*, ed. H.S. Reiss, Cambridge 1991, p. 44.

[131] G.W.F. Hegel, *Lectures on the Philosophy of History*, transl. J. Sibree, London 1861, p. 34.

[132] T.H. Green, *Four Lectures on the English Revolution*, in: T.H. Green, *Works of Thomas Hill Green*, Vol. 3, p. 278.

[133] T.H. Green em, *Lectures on the Principles*, p. 101 (§ 128–129).

[134] B. Bosanquet, *Introduction to the Second Edition*, p. XXXIX; cf. B. Bosanquet, *The Philosophical Theory*, p. 173.

[135] *Ibid.*, p. 172; cf. B. Bosnaquet, *The Function of the State*, p. 273.

the trade, and from the trade to the Church and the University".[136] Hence the conclusion that it is "above all things, not a number of persons, but a working conception of life".[137]

However, the recognition of the immanence of the state to human existence is not an exhaustive appraisal of its functions. For the state also operates within a space that is external to individuals. Not only does it impact their motivations, but it also enables the coordination of their actions, safeguarding them from the unforeseeable consequences of unfortunate events, and should these occur, alleviating their effects. The purpose of both society and the state is to promote the "best life" of citizens. The means by which this is achieved is primarily the harmonisation of their actions, enabling moral improvement. Hence the secondary task of the state is to "hinder the hindrances" to the development of its citizens.[138] "The State, it might be said, is thus conceived as the operative criticism of all institutions — the modification and adjustment by which they are capable of playing a rational part in the object of human will. And criticism, in this sense, is the life of institutions."[139] Whenever these cease to remove the obstacles to the development of citizens, they receive from them a suitable signal in the form of criticism and postulates to change the unacceptable *status quo*. If order is to be maintained, they must remain attuned to these charges and realise the desiderata contained therein.

Bosanquet's belief in the importance of criticism in the life of the state emanated directly from his scepticism as to the possibility of creating an ideal community. This is also one of the main reasons why he pronounced himself in favour of political and legal contextualism. Since no state is ideal, authorities will always be exposed to criticism from the governed. And if it is equally difficult to expect that the needs of communities, on account of their different existential circumstances, will be the same, it cannot be thought likely that there will be an overlap in the expectations of their citizens. As consequence of this, the universalist apology of a single political system or set of legal regulations, devised in abstraction from specific communities, is necessarily unsatisfactory.[140]

---

[136] B. Bosanquet, *The Philosophical Theory*, p. 140.
[137] *Ibid.*, pp. 140–141.
[138] *Ibid.*, pp. 178, 184–185.
[139] *Ibid.*, p. 140.
[140] *Ibid.*, p. 141.

2.4. "The duties of citizenship"
(Bernard Bosanquet and Francis Herbert Bradley)

Some scholars[141] of idealism diagnose a gulf between the conceptions of Bradley and those of Bosanquet, casting doubt on whether they can be examined jointly as embodiments of the same philosophical paradigm. By his interpretation of the individual's relation to society and the state, Bosanquet is sometimes thought to overcome the limitations of Bradley's theory, especially on the issue of the sources of morality. Having examined the conception of "my station" from the angle of potential charges, the author of the *Ethical Studies* recognised the need to supplement it with the conception of the "moral ideal". *My station and its duties* did not answer the question concerning the origin of extra-social values, nor did it explain how social criticism was possible (in other words the provenance of the ideal of social perfection). *Ideal morality*, intended to fill these gaps, proved highly unsatisfactory as a theory, since it failed to reveal the foundations of morality, only implying an enigmatic form of moral intuitionism in which the subject, unable to identify the precise source and content of moral precepts, was doomed to act in accordance with what was merely an indefinite sense of duty. Bradley's moral theory—suspended between the world of everyday duties and the world of indistinctly sensed ideals—had no chance of erecting a practical code of ethical conduct. Bosanquet, persistently abiding by "my station and its duties", aware that stepping beyond this conception must inevitably lead to fatal theoretical difficulties, was supposed to overcome the contradictions gnawing at Bradley's theories.

If the above thesis were confirmed, it would require a reassessment of the current appraisal of British idealist thought. After all, the attempt to ease the tension between the universal and the specific, to reconcile personal interest with the ethical reality of the community, is thought to be one of its essential elements. Had Bosanquet reduced ethics and politics to the narrow horizons of "my station and its duties", he would have *de facto* abandoned the sphere of transcendental truths, and placed upon a pedestal a profane and earthly God—the community, whose rulings in matters of morality and politics would be unappealable. Many fragments of Bosanquet's works seem to speak in favour of such an interpretation.[142] When in *The Philosophical Theory of the State* we read that "[d]uties are relative to positions; I may not and must not do what

---

[141] B. Pfannenstill, *Bernard Bosanquet's Philosophy of the State*, pp. 256-257; G. Thomas, *The Moral Philosophy of T.H. Green*, Oxford 1987, p. 107; J. Robinson, *Bradley and Bosanquet*, "Idealistic Studies" 2000, Vol. 6, p. 162.

[142] B. Bosanquet, *The Duties of Citizenship*, in: *Aspects of the Social*, pp. 4-5.

you must and may",[143] that "everyone who has a fair judgement of what his own place demands from him, has, at his own angle, so to speak, a working insight into the end of the State",[144] the analogies with Bradley's conception of "my station" impose themselves at once. In fact, in the radicalism of his claims, Bosanquet sometimes seems even to exceed Bradley's position, since the latter had after all explicitly acknowledged the need to modify this conception in light of its limitations. This consciousness seems to be lacking in Bosanquet, who unequivocally suggests that even if sources of morality and legislation other than the communal could be found somewhere, the precepts generated by socio-political institutions would always take precedence.[145] It is not moral intuition pointing to some abstract social ideal, nor the belief in the need to realise the good and the beautiful, but duty, inextricably linked with social function, that is the supreme indicator of conduct. Finally, when Bosanquet defines moral evil as the inability to adapt to one's social position,[146] it is difficult to conceive that he could have bypassed the charge of absolutising the institutions of public life in addition to utterly depreciating individual liberty.

If the issue discussed here had appeared in precisely this manner in the works of Bosanquet, it would be hard to reconcile the apotheosis of common interest with the recognition of criticism as the basis of the "life of institutions" and the postulate of their reform in the wake of public criticism. However, it seems that Bosanquet did not succeed in grounding the conception of "my station" convincingly. The same intuition which had driven Bradley to formulate the "moral ideal" (unsatisfactory as it may have been), in Bosanquet's case resulted in tacit concessions towards an acceptance of supra- and extra-social criteria for judging morality and legislation. Certain scholars are therefore wrong to look for a fundamental discrepancy between the ethical and political perspectives of these thinkers. The claim that Bosanquet definitely overcame the internal contradictions of Bradley's theory is equally unjustified.

Although there are many passages in Bosanquet that clearly suggest the collectivist hue of his socio-political ideal, we can also find therein a glorification of the "ideal of social perfection". After all, social order can or even should be criticised, while the mere admission of such a possibility suggests the existence of sources of morality other than the

---

[143] B. Bosanquet, *Introduction to the Second Edition*, p. LIII.
[144] B. Bosanquet, *The Philosophical Theory*, p. 141; cf. *ibid.*, p. 292.
[145] *Ibid.*, p. 191.
[146] *Ibid.*, p. 294.

communal. *The Philosophical Theory of the State* gives at least two examples of this type of criticism:

1. Intra-communal — brought forth by individual members of a given society, called by Bosanquet the "life of institutions". Criticism of institutions is necessary if they are to realise changing visions of "the best life"; it is a signal to them, indicating that citizens' expectations, with respect to the politico-legal conditions of their lives, diverge from what institutions are prepared to offer them.[147]

2. Extra-communal — this brings to mind Bosanquet's criticism of militarily expansive communities; their designation as "sick" as opposed to "healthy" (those with a peaceful attitude) in *The Philosophical Theory of the State* points to the existence of criteria for an ethical and political assessment of countries from a point beyond communal morality.

The first type of criticism suggests the existence of a non-social criterion for evaluating intra-communal order, namely the degree to which it realises human potential. Since individuals find deficiencies in the conditions of communal life, they require an ideal of social perfection. The second type of criticism, the extra-communal, plays a lesser role in Bosanquet's philosophy. Nonetheless, evaluating states based on the level of their militarisation also points to extra- and supra-social criteria for judging political order. Stopping at the concept of "my station", Bosanquet would have had to reject the existence of supra-national authorities, recognising the stigmatisation of one community, based on the moral system embodied in the institutions of another, as particularly unjustified. Both forms of the criticism admitted by Bosanquet unequivocally show that he did not restrict himself to "my station". Both Bradley and Bosanquet succumbed to the temptation of founding their conceptions on an indefinite universal morality. The difference between them lies only in the fact that, whereas the first consciously recognised the failure of "my station", the second was wholly convinced that his theories were free of these contradictions.

---

[147] See C. Tyler, *Idealist Political Philosophy. Pluralism and Conflict in the Absolute Idealist Tradition*, London–New York 2006, pp. 184–185.

Chapter Three

Idealist Interpretations of the General Will

The critique of Jean-Jacques Rousseau's thought as effected by the British idealists was not without precedent. They pointed to its excessive individualism as the main problem. This perception may strike the modern reader as at least somewhat unorthodox. The last century was altogether more inclined to accuse Rousseau of collectivism, the readiness to sacrifice the individual for the good of an abstract moral entity — the community. One of the first readings of the *Social Contract* of this type is quite rightly attributed to Benjamin Constant. The principle of unlimited state power, of denying the people the right to oppose regulations that stifle them, and above all, the general will, lying at the base of these perversions and described so cryptically and confusingly as to make it impossible to ascertain its precepts or indicate the limits of its power — all this conspired to make Rousseau an enemy of freedom, a harbinger of revolutionary terror.

Alongside this collectivist interpretation, prevalent in scholarly literature as recently as the second half of the twentieth century, another form of critique was also present, accusing Rousseau of the opposite — an individualism blown out of all proportion. The author of the *Social Contract* was not regarded as an exceptional thinker in this respect. He was listed alongside other contractualists — John Locke, Thomas Hobbes or Baruch Spinoza — since it is necessary to be an individualist to believe in the consensual genesis of communities. Already the first counter-revolutionaries had pointed this out. In the *Étude sur la souveraineté*, Joseph de Maistre wrote that societies did not emerge based on the consensus of individuals. The latter would simply not have existed without the former. In a similar vein, other counter-revolutionaries did not spare the concept of the state of nature either: Louis de Bonald and Antoine de Rivarol mocked it, Antoine Sabatier de Castres pointed out its insufficiencies as compared to the civil state.

For their criticism, French thinkers often drew upon the works of Edmund Burke, who railed against the contractualists for their theses on the existence of a state of nature, especially those proclaiming natural man the most virtuous of creatures, calling for the abolition of the bonds of tradition, either in the form of customs detrimental to man, or that of institutions limiting and alienating him from his brethren. It is not only contractualism that merits criticism here, but also the democratism that often accompanies it, especially in its radicalised form as found in the *Social Contract*.[1]

However, the counter-revolutionary attack on contractualism was seldom aimed at Rousseau himself, who was after all but one of many proponents of the concept of a social contract. If he was treated as an exception, it was on the basis of the role ascribed to his works during the French Revolution. This is why the criticism of the British idealists, thorough and concentrating on the concept of the *volonté générale*, is chiefly foreshadowed by the writings of Georg Wilhelm Friedrich Hegel. It is known that in his youth the "sage of Berlin", along with most of the German bourgeois intelligentsia of the time, was under the overpowering influence of Rousseau. That which most attracted the Germans to the *Social Contract* and *Emile* was the attempt to revitalise the ancient ideal of community and to overcome the particularisms of eighteenth-century societies, presaging Romantic thought. Therefore, the admiration shown to the author of the *Social Contract*, in Hegel's early works while still at Jena, is hardly surprising. The more mature Hegelianism exhibits a much more critical evaluation of Rousseau's works, born mainly of an evaluation of revolutionary events. It is most visible in the *Phenomenology of Spirit* and the *Elements of the Philosophy of Right*. In the first work, Rousseau was but a silent hero of one of its fragments. In the second, Hegel referred to him directly, his analyses following in the footsteps of conservative critics of the Revolution, attacking the contractualism and abstractionism of the individualistic conception of liberty presented in the *Social Contract*, attempting to find a foreshadowing of and theoretical basis for Jacobin terror in the words of its author.[2] Despite this, there is no lack of a certain ambivalence in its evaluation of the *Social Contract*. For Hegel also included the positives of Rousseau's position, who

> is to be ascribed the merit of discovering and presenting a principle, which comes up to the standard of the thought, and is indeed thinking itself, not only in its form, such as would be a social impulse or divine

---

[1] E. Burke, *Reflections on the French Revolution*, London–New York 1910, p. 57.
[2] P. Méthais, *Contrat et volonté générale selon Hegel et Rousseau*, in: *Hegel et le siècle des Lumières*, ed. J. d'Hondt, Paris 1974, pp. 103–104.

authority, but in its very essence. But he conceives of the will only in the limited form of the individual will, as did also Fichte afterwards, and regards the universal will not as the absolutely reasonable will, but only as the common will, proceeding out of the individual will as conscious. Thus the union of individuals in a state becomes a contract, which is based upon caprice, opinion, and optional, explicit consent.[3]

This is the greatest error made by Rousseau — an individualism encouraging him to seek the genesis of political communities in the agreement of their members. For it is simply impossible for such entities to be anything other than a compromise between egotistical individuals. Societies born in this fashion are not ethical bodies, but communities of interest, linked not by spiritual bonds, but by the desire for individual benefits. There is therefore no place in Rousseauian thought for communal spirit, the identification of individual well-being with the good of a moral entity. There is also no place for a true general will, only a multiplicity of particular wills, at times converging, yet conflicted by their very nature.[4]

This same path, conservative and Hegelian, criticising Rousseau for errors inherent in all contractualist and individualist conceptions, yet also appreciating his input into the development of the idea of community and of will as its basis, was trodden by the British idealists.

3.1. Novelty and limitations of the thought of Jean-Jacques Rousseau

We have already noted that it is perfectly justified to speak of British idealism as a philosophical phenomenon in its own right. After more than a century of domination by the empiricist tradition, George Berkeley's nominalism, David Hume's positivism, Locke's empiricism and Jeremy Bentham's utilitarianism, British universities allowed themselves to be seduced by the speculative thought originating in early nineteenth-century Germany. That which, from the perspective of continental Europe, may appear as a renaissance of idealism within the British context bears closer resemblance to an unexpected break in the uniform empiricist tendency of conducting studies based on experience above all. What in this context is applicable to Immanuel Kant or Hegel can also be stated of Rousseau. The author of the *Social Contract*, roundly criticised on the continent, was also rarely a positive inspiration for the British thinkers. If we are to seek a chain of inspiration, then it would be easy to see that it led rather from London to Les Charmettes and L'Ermitage, than the other way round. The balance of

---

[3] G.W.F. Hegel, *The Elements of the Philosophy of Right*, transl. H.B. Nisbet, ed. A.W. Wood, Cambridge 2001, p. 277 (§ 258).
[4] *Ibid.*, p. 58 (§ 29).

borrowings is definitely to Rousseau's disadvantage. In pedagogical matters, he built on Locke's *Some Thoughts Concerning Education*; in ethics, he owed a great deal to Shaftesbury, for instance; British theists influenced his thinking in religious matters, Alexander Pope delighted him with his providentialism. Yet it would be hard to list the English-speaking authors who publicly acquiesce to a debt of gratitude towards the author of the *Social Contract*. There is therefore no option but to agree with Bertil Pfannenstill, who claimed that British idealists spread not only German speculative thought in the Isles, but also Rousseau's philosophy. Let us examine in detail the opinions which the representatives of this movement had of the Swiss philosopher.

3.1.1. From the utopia of atomism to the utopia of community

Let us start with Green, on whom Rousseau's thought had a twofold effect—firstly, a direct influence, mostly as a reaction to the *Social Contract*. Despite the fact that Green's works often display proof of his knowledge of both *Emile* and the *Confessions*, the weight he attributes to these works unequivocally suggests that he considered the *Social Contract* to be the only valid expression of Rousseau's political philosophy. He did not analyse the practical examples of the general will presented in the *New Heloise*, *Considerations on the Government of Poland* or the *Constitutional Project for Corsica*. Instead, he presented the thought of the Swiss philosopher in a near-encyclopaedic manner, making him the subject of his lectures.

The second type of effect Rousseau had on Green was his "inherited" influence, through the German idealist tradition. In light of the gaps in his reading of the author of the *Confessions*, it would appear that precisely this reading of the *Social Contract* or *Emile* by Kant and Hegel was much more instrumental to the form the general will took in Green's writing. Particularly Kant, reforging Rousseau's ideas, not as ethical theories, but as a political vision of a republican state, laid the foundations for a vision of a community of people rationally recognising their rights, which in turn shape legislation and the institutional order.

There is a substantial evolution apparent in Green's relationship to Rousseau. The two works in which he discusses the thought of the author of the *Social Contract*, the article *Popular Philosophy in its Relation to Life* (1868) and the *Lectures on the Principles of Political Obligation* (lectures 1879–1880), demonstrate that the intervening decade led to a more thorough analysis of Rousseauian political philosophy, the differences in his perception of it being substantial. The first source clearly shows that still at the end of the 1860s Green did not consider Rousseau's philosophy to be anything exceptional against the backdrop of the Enlightenment. *Popular Philosophy* does not contain an analysis of the philosophy of the Genevan thinker as such, but of the whole tradition of thinking about social issues, the members of which are treated here as a more or less coherent school. As its representatives, apart from Locke, its founder, Green noted Hume, Joseph Butler, Joseph Priestley and Rousseau. What connected all of them was an epistemological sensualism and ethical sentimentalism, the propensity to seek the motivations for people's actions in their passions.[5] A closer analysis of Green's essay reveals that, contrary to the other thinkers discussed in it, Rousseau's works created the greatest difficulties for him. On the one hand, the author of the *Social Contract* undoubtedly proceeded from the same premises as the other preachers of "popular philosophy". On the other, the conclusions he reached visibly diverge from those of the others. Rousseau's uniqueness as compared to them lies in the observation that the consciousness of being ruled by the affects automatically leads to the conviction that one ought to control, not flatter, them. This thesis forms the nucleus of Rousseau's three *Discourses*, in particular the *Discourse on the Sciences and the Arts*. Criticising submission to unnatural passions, the author betrays a conviction that it is possible to distance oneself from them. In this manner, the "philosophy of feeling became the food of a spirit"[6] in Rousseau's writings. The possibility of distancing oneself from the affects is the first step towards resisting them. This is the main reason why Rousseau's writing could not meet with the understanding and approval of the eighteenth-century *philosophes*. The birth of self-consciousness, as observed on the pages of the *Discourses*, already belonged to a different era, directly influencing the formulation of Kant's key theses.[7]

However, the differences separating Rousseau from the other representatives of the Enlightenment were not a determining factor for Green on the issue of his intellectual affiliations. They did not concern the key questions of "popular philosophy". Rousseau was unable to avoid the fundamental error of all its representatives—reducing the genesis of the human psyche to the affective level. It is therefore hardly surprising that in his thinking on society and politics he turned out to be a representative (though not an advocate) of the individualist paradigm.[8] It is true he stopped midway, going beyond the sentimentalism of his predecessors to a certain extent, but since the semi-rational

---

[5] T.H. Green, *Popular Philosophy in Its Relation to Life*, in: T.H. Green, *Works of Thomas Hill Green*, Vol. 3: *Miscellanies and Memoir*, ed. R.L. Nettleship, London 1889, p. 97.
[6] Ibid., p. 113.
[7] Ibid.
[8] Ibid., p. 116.

individualism that can be found in his writings was not based on enduring, objective foundations, it could only result in political Jacobinism. The self-consciousness presented in Rousseau's writing inevitably had to result in hostility towards anything alien, external and mysterious to the individual.[9] It is only later, in the interpretations of nineteenth-century scholars of Rousseauian thought, that this alleged Jacobinism was transformed into a "soft liberalism", expressing not only its anarchic but also its constructive implications.[10]

The category of the general will itself was not the subject of analysis in *Popular Philosophy*. Also, the philosophical assumptions attributed to Rousseau here fail to suggest any of its possible interpretations. It is true that if we were to view the classification of Rousseau within a single tradition with Locke and Hume as such a suggestion, the conclusion would be self-evident. Understood as a manifesto of individualism and utilitarianism, the *Social Contract* would demand that its author be seen as the foremost representative of liberalism. It is hard to say if that is precisely the manner in which Green viewed Rousseau's thought. In the end, he also searched for the roots of Jacobinism in the *Social Contract*, attempting to find a particular manifesto of the plasticity of the human psyche in its pages, sometimes correctly read as an announcement of positivism and unrestrained socio-political constructivism. Regardless of which of these interpretations was preferred by Green, both imply an image of Rousseau as an individualist.

When reading the second source, *Lectures on the Principles*, one is struck by the difference with respect to Green's earlier interpretation of Rousseau's works. In the *Lectures*, Green claims that the legacy of Rousseau often met with great misunderstanding. This is the only explanation for why his works were regarded as one of the first, programmatic expositions of legal positivism. The absolutism of the general will, its function as a last instance, provoked claims that it was tyrannical — claims which Green considered to be utterly wrong. Its fundamental positive definitions were completely ignored. Concentrating on identifying the general will with the sovereign, commentators ignored one of its main features: the "attribute of pure disinterestedness".[11] The consequence was "a vague exaltation of the prerogatives of the sovereign people, without any corresponding limitation of the conditions under which an act is to be deemed that of the sovereign

---

[9] *Ibid.*
[10] *Ibid.*, p. 117.
[11] T.H. Green, *Lectures on the Principles of Political Obligation*, in: T.H. Green, *Lectures on the Principles of Political Obligation and Other Writings*, ed. P. Harris, J. Morrow, Cambridge 1986, p. 57 (§ 68).

people".[12] The general will was considered independently of the conditions of its appearance, as if the manner in which law was enacted did not directly influence its content.

Green's position in his lectures evidences a change from his earlier interpretation of Rousseau's thought, still present in *Popular Philosophy*. He now presents Rousseau as an advocate of the idea of the common good, finding virtue in obedience to the precepts of the general will. The earlier, individualist, reading could find no place for the positive valuation of communal existence. Placed in the same line as Hume and Locke, Rousseau was very nearly added to the list of reductionist utilitarians. Green's later analyses are in this respect vastly different. The introduction of a distinction between *volonté générale* and *volonté de tous*[13] in the *Social Contract* precludes the attribution of a radically individualist anthropology to its author. The fact that we may be guided by the interest of the community in our actions, often even at the price of personal losses, demonstrates the possibility of an ethical disposition, a civic or patriotic attitude, absent from the liberal-utilitarian view of the state.

Yet Green still considered Rousseau's thought unsatisfactory, and for two reasons. Firstly, the individualist perspective characteristic of the *Social Contract* drew its author into the difficulties inherent to all contractualist theories and linked to the explanation of the genesis of the social contract.[14] As we have already mentioned, the objections raised by Green to the theories of Spinoza and Hobbes clearly demonstrate that it is an insurmountable difficulty. The hypothetical state of nature and the social contract, through which asocial yet at the same time moral individuals decide to form a community, are contradictory. In this respect, Rousseau's thought presents nothing particular as compared to the era. Its uniqueness is solely in its acceptance of the general will as the sovereign and foundation of the legitimacy of political order.

The second weakness of Rousseau's thought is his concept of sovereignty. In the *Social Contract*, sovereignty is identified with compliance with the precepts of the general will. A nation governed according to the *volonté de tous* is a nation that is not sovereign. The problem lies in the fact that Rousseau was too rigorous in his formulation of the conditions for the emergence of the *volonté générale*, and so of the conditions for sovereignty. The assumption that direct democracy is inseparable from it, that citizens should not contact each other while voting, that the existence of factions dividing the community into ideological

---

[12] *Ibid.*, p. 57 (§ 69).
[13] *Ibid.*, p. 59 (§ 71).
[14] *Ibid.*, p. 91 (§ 116).

camps which—though guided by the general will with regard to their members—follow the particular will with regard to the whole political body—all this makes the *volonté générale* part of a political utopia. It is therefore hardly surprising that of all contemporary nations, Rousseau was ready to recognise as sovereign only the Swiss, the Poles and the Corsicans.[15]

Yet Rousseau's errors can be avoided, according to Green, even without having to abandon the concept of the general will. For it can be interpreted in a way which makes it possible to ascribe the attribute of sovereignty to every community. Green found the key to the Rousseauian aporiae in the writings of the Genevan philosopher himself. Namely, he employed the distinction found in the *Social Contract* between *de jure* and *de facto* sovereignty, of which Rousseau wrote: "[i]f finally the prince should come to have a particular will more active than the will of the Sovereign, and should employ the public force in his hands in obedience to this particular will, there would be, so to speak, two Sovereigns, one rightful and the other actual, the social union would evaporate instantly and the body politic would be dissolved."[16] There is only one sovereign in every community governed according to the precepts of the general will—the general will, expressed in the votes of the people. The mediating agent between their decisions and themselves (no longer considered as the sovereign, but as the subjects of a superior) is the executive power—the ruling individual or government. Yet it happens that this individual or group of people at the helm of power use their privileged position to further their own interests, thereby following their particular will. In such a case, Rousseau diagnosed the existence of two sovereigns: the rightful, that is the people expressing the general will through their votes, and the actual, a ruler or government guided by a particular will. This division stems from the acceptance of the thesis that the general will never disappears; at most, it is not expressed. And by the same token, when the will of a people cannot be fulfilled, neither the *volonté générale* nor true sovereignty ceases to exist.

Green's critique of Rousseau will be discussed at length elsewhere in this work, along with his views on the general will as outlined in the *Lectures on the Principles*. We will now examine the shortcomings which Bosanquet saw in the thought of the author of the *Social Contract*.

---

[15] *Ibid.*, p. 64 (§ 78).
[16] J.J. Rousseau, *The Social Contract and Discourses*, pp. 52–53.

3.1.2. Ancient intentions, modern failures

Bosanquet's views on the *Social Contract* can already be guessed from his inclusion of the conceptions of its author on the list of the "theories of the first look", along with the philosophies of Bentham, Mill and Spencer. Bosanquet did note significant differences separating these philosophers from Rousseau, and recognised the novel nature of the latter's thought. "For it is Rousseau who stands midway between Hobbes and Locke on the one hand, and Kant and Hegel on the other, and in whose writings the actual revival of the full idea of human nature may be watched from paragraph to paragraph as it struggles to throw off the husk of an effete tradition."[17] This "effete tradition" is of course individualist liberalism with its attendant conviction that political communities are founded on the "liberty of the moderns", to use the category coined by Benjamin Constant, freedom from participation in public life, from making decisions that are key for the community, and at the same time, self-will, the full freedom to give in to the realisation of one's desires. How Rousseau's thought contrasts with this tradition. Though he had predecessors in Vico and Montesquieu, he placed more emphasis than they did on the necessity of resurrecting the order proper to the ancient *poleis* and the idea of the social nature of man. "And he bequeathed to his successors the task of substituting for the mere words and fictions of contract, nature, and original freedom, the idea of the common life of an essentially social being, expressing and sustaining the human will at its best."[18]

The novel nature of the *Social Contract* is primarily evidenced by the definition of the community as an indivisible moral entity disposing of its own will, different from a simple aggregation of individuals.[19] This had an essential significance for the further development of political philosophy. Firstly, it was the first step on the road to the theoretical reconciliation of fellow citizens, instead of the previous understanding of them as competitors. Secondly, in this approach to the problem "the negative relation of the self to law and government begins to disappear in the idea of a law which expresses our real will, as opposed to our trivial and rebellious moods. The whole notion of man as one among others tends to break down; and we begin to see something in the one

---

[17] B. Bosanquet, *The Philosophical Theory of the State*, London 1910, p. 12; cf. *ibid.*, pp. 38–39.
[18] *Ibid.*, p. 12.
[19] B. Bosanquet, *Les idées politiques de Rousseau*, "Revue de métaphysique et de morale" 1912, Vol. 20, pp. 323, 329; cf. W. Sweet, *Bernard Bosanquet and the Development of Rousseau's Idea of the General Will*, "Man and Nature/ L'homme et la nature" 1991, Vol. 10, p. 179.

which actually identifies him with the others, and at the same time tends to make him what he admits that he ought to be."[20]

Rousseau lacked consequence, however. He left his thought suspended between two worlds: the ancient community, in which individualism had not yet been born, and the rationalism of the Enlightenment, where it was the dominant anthropological view. Thus, though the path he chose to overcome the "paradox of self-government" was inherently correct, he lacked the attention, or perhaps the courage, to follow it to its end. Because of this, his conceptions are incomplete, inconsistent and in general unsatisfactory. "On almost every page there is relapse and vacillation. The fictions which are being cast aside continually reassert themselves; the embodiment of the principle which the author's genius has discerned is sought for in expedients essentially opposite to its nature, while the instruments which it has developed for itself are contemptuously rejected."[21]

But Rousseau's position also sometimes deserves praise, as when he attributes an essentially social nature to man. Did he not finally state that true freedom is the moral freedom born only within society? Natural freedom, if it ever actually existed, must have belonged to a being that cannot *sensu proprio* be called man. It therefore must have been of a much lower nature than social and moral freedom.[22] This wholly correct intuition, incorrectly developed, led Rousseau's thought into internal contradictions. The hypothesis of the contract itself, through which the passage from the state of nature to the civil state, from natural liberty to social liberty, would have been accomplished, demonstrates the hesitancy of the author between a radically individualist perspective, in which individuals, through a collective decision, constitute a "moral self", and the acceptance of a communal perspective, in which they are the product of a society that always precedes their existence. This type of "language of compromise" between individualism and collectivism is unacceptable. Rousseau's "constant failure, entire or partial, to free himself from the language of 'first appearance theories' [...] is just what makes him so instructive, in view of the similar inclination which besets us all".[23]

Rousseau's attraction to the contractualist rhetoric, resulting in his acceptance of the individualist paradigm, also directly impacted his view of the general will. This is evident, for example, in those fragments of the *Social Contract* where he confidently states that the legis-

---

[20] B. Bosanquet, *The Philosophical Theory*, p. 95.
[21] *Ibid.*, p. 79.
[22] *Ibid.*, p. 84.
[23] *Ibid.*, p. 85.

lative body composed of the members of a community cannot desire its own harm, necessarily implementing the precepts of the general will.[24] This is not the end, however. Rousseau, despite the correct attribution of a moral being to the community, and the equally correct statement that the "real will" and "real liberty" of individuals resides in its will, interests and precepts, simultaneously maintained that each person can be defined by both the particular (when they are simply considered as an individual) and the general will (when perceived as a citizen).[25] Each person may simultaneously be an egotist, depraved by their own interest, and a patriot, prepared to serve the community — it is hard to find better illustration of the inconsistency of the *Social Contract*.

Signs of the same error are visible in Rousseau's attempts to define the precepts of the general will. In this respect, Bosanquet drew attention to the plus-minus principle in particular.[26] Rousseau should have come to a decision: either remain an advocate of individualism and accept that the term "general will" is contradictory (since only individual wills exist), and that there is little purpose to attempting to list its precepts, or embrace the ethical or collectivist position, maintaining that individuals are linked by moral ties hidden beneath the surface of everyday activities, yet incessantly, through their actions, express the general will. Then the determination of its precepts, if not entirely unnecessary, would certainly not be achieved through the counting of votes.[27] And so, despite the intrinsically correct distinction between the will of all and the general will, and the no less apt definition of their interrelations, Rousseau *de facto* equated these categories, bringing the nobler *volonté générale* down to the level of the nefarious *volonté de tous*. In spite of his intention, the *Social Contract* is in fact an apology of the will of all. Rousseau "has affirmed the absolute supremacy of the popular will in the very sense against which his conception of the Will of All is a protest".[28]

The main source of Rousseau's failure, the reason for all his back-breaking efforts to solve the "paradox of self-government", and his defeat in revitalising the ideal of the ancient *polis*,[29] were his philos-

---

[24] *Ibid.*, pp. 88–89.
[25] J.J. Rousseau, *Social Contract*, I, VII, p. 22.
[26] *Ibid.*, II, III, p. 29.
[27] B. Bosanquet, *The Philosophical Theory*, p. 109; B. Bosanquet, *The Reality of the General Will*, in: *Aspects of the Social Problem*, ed. B. Bosanquet, New York 1895, p. 320.
[28] B. Bosanquet, *The Philosophical Theory*, p. 109; cf. P.P. Nicholson, *The Political Philosophy of the British Idealists. Selected Studies*, Cambridge 1990, pp. 200–201.
[29] B. Bosanquet, *The Philosophical Theory*, pp. 123–125; cf. *ibid.*, pp. 139–140.

ophical inspirations. Although he often spoke disparagingly of the thinkers today seen to belong to the classical liberal tradition, it is precisely in his polemic with them that he constructed his own vocabulary, the use of which necessarily led to errors in his argumentation. This is why Rousseau used a terminology which today suggests pro-communal leanings, while at the same time most of his claims have an individualist foundation. The similarities between the paradigms of Rousseau, Hobbes and Locke are evidenced by the conception of the *volonté générale* sketched out in the *Social Contract*. Hobbes "insisted that sovereignty must lie in a will and that this will must be real and must be taken as representing or standing for the will of the community [...] he in fact *substituted* the will (taking the word in its ordinary sense) of a certain individual or certain individuals *for* the will of the community or moral person as such".[30] Locke, for his part, identified the will of the community with the decisions of a government universally chosen by the citizens. Moulding together the conceptions of Hobbes and Locke, Rousseau wanted to give a theoretical outline of a will that was both real and general.[31] Yet he was doomed to failure from the outset. His predecessors never managed to elaborate a real notion of community, always seeing the latter as a mere aggregation of individuals. It is therefore hardly surprising that Rousseau, modelling his work on theirs, was also unsuccessful.

3.2. The general will as...

The idealists' critique of Rousseau gave them the impulse to formulate their own perspectives on the general will, allegedly free of the individualist and utopian tendencies imputed to the *Social Contract*. Let us now examine these theoretical constructs and consider their practical and political implications. The following subsections will concern themselves with successive idealist incarnations of the *volonté générale*, which first took the form of Bradley's universal will as set down in the pages of the *Ethical Studies*. Later, Green identified it as the "congeries of the hopes and fears of a people bound together by common interests and sympathy". Finally, Bosanquet saw it as a system of ideas embodied both in the minds of individuals and in the shape of socio-political institutions.

---

[30] *Ibid.*, p. 97.
[31] *Ibid.*, pp. 98–99, cf. B. Pfannenstill, *Bernard Bosanquet's Philosophy of the State*, pp. 64–65.

3.2.1. ...universal will (Francis Herbert Bradley)

Although Bradley never explicitly referred to the general will, his *Ethical Studies* never once referencing Rousseau's theses, certain facts suggest that it is justified to examine his thought in the light of the distinctions proposed by the author of the *Social Contract*. Firstly, the main aims of both Rousseau's and Bradley's works: the establishment of a "third way" between the extremes of autonomy and heteronomy, the attempt to reconcile liberty with duty towards the community, and so the problem of the sources of political obligation, indicate a similarity in the subjects considered by both of these thinkers.[32] Secondly, and this is by far the more important reason for making the comparison, in the place of Rousseau's opposition of the general will to the particular will, Bradley employed the dichotomy universal will–particular will, seeing the first as an attribute of the community, and the second of individuals.

What did Bradley mean when he stated that the general will is an attribute of the community? For the citizens, the community represents the universe of objective moral precepts, the set of which can be seen as its will—the universal will. This will can take two forms:
1. That of custom—as the will of society it manifests itself as custom, observance of which is sanctioned either by social approval or disapproval.
2. A politico-legal form—as an attribute of political institutions, the universal will takes the form of precepts formed into positive laws—a set of strictly defined rules and sanctions for their violation.

The particular will is the will of individual citizens. Already here we can discern a fundamental difference between the dichotomies of will presented by Bradley and Rousseau. In the *Social Contract*, both wills—the particular and the general—were in strict opposition. They were assigned a similar subjective scope, but a different objective character. *Volonté générale* and *volonté particulière* could coexist in the same person or institution. The first was directed towards the realisation of the common interest, strictly linked to the idea of the good of the community, while the second aimed to realise private interests—individuals guided by it were egotists unable to apprehend, or able to apprehend but unable to realise, the ideal of the common good.

How differently is this issue presented by Bradley. Here, both wills —the particular and the universal—have been differentiated, though

---

[32] One of the few scholars to see in Bradley the first idealist who tried to develop and modify Rousseau's concept of the general will was John Henry Muirhead (J.H. Muirhead, *Recent Criticism of the Idealist Theory of the General Will (II.)*, "Mind" 1924, Vol. 33, pp. 168–169).

not opposed. Each is assigned a different subjective but not objective scope. The universal will, characterising the moral, communal whole, expresses its claims on individuals. The particular will, on the other hand, independently of the nature of the goods it aims to realise, is the will of individuals. The question of whether it belongs to egoists, altruists or patriots is not prejudged here.

What import does this seemingly trivial discrepancy have? The consequences are significant. For while the Rousseauian general will could take the form of a moral disposition, a concrete way in which citizens perceive their roles within the life of society, in Bradley the particularism of the will is inevitable. In the *Social Contract*, the emphasis was decidedly on the content of the will. To be guided by the precepts of the *volonté générale* was to desire the realisation of the common good. In the *Ethical Studies*, the situation is different. Here it is not so much the content, but the subject of the will that plays a central role. The goal of individuals is to fulfil duties linked to their position within the community. Only "by willing ourselves as such, can we look on ourselves as organs in a good whole, and so ourselves good".[33] Here, virtue is no longer an internal disposition, but an external conformity to the community's precepts. Obeying them is a sufficient sign of subservience to the general will.[34]

Externality and autonomy are here understood in an entirely different manner than by Rousseau. The role of individuals is not to attempt to determine what is just. Individuals do not have to be independent from an external authority in their judgments in order to express the general will. The necessary condition for its expression is rather obedience to the socially constructed vision of the duties inseparably linked to one's station within society. And so, Bradley defined civic virtue as "either merely thought of as realising this universal [community—J.G.], or actually also doing so. 'This is my duty' means 'in this I identify, or am thought of as identifying, myself with right'".[35] The nature of this universe, similarly to that of the universal will, is deliberately left undefined. The community can expect the most varied acts on the part of its members, even those that in a long-term perspective are detrimental to it. Rousseau would find such a position unacceptable.

Bradley thus challenged the strict distinction between morality and legislation. It is impossible to invoke a moral duty that is different from a legal obligation. This is precisely why he criticised the liberal tend-

---

[33] F.H. Bradley, *Ethical Studies*, Oxford 1927, p. 182.
[34] *Ibid.*, p. 301.
[35] *Ibid.*, p. 208.

ency to differentiate rights from duties.³⁶ Right constitutes "an expression of that which is universal", a group of interdictions and precepts imposed on the individual by the community. "What is duty? It is simply the other side of right. It is the same relation, viewed from the other pole or moment. It is the relation of the particular to the universal, with the emphasis on the particular. It is *my* will in its affirmative relation to the objective will."³⁷ Bradley himself summarised his position on this issue in five theses:

> (1) It is false that you can have rights without duties. (2) It is false that you can have duties without rights. (3) It is false that right is merely negative. (4) It is false that duty depends on possible compulsion, and mere mistake that command always implies a threat; and (5) It is absolutely false that rights or duties can exist outside the moral world.³⁸

Duty therefore unequivocally commands: the particular will should incline to the universal, the individual should be an exponent of the morality of the community, an obedient citizen respecting custom and the letter of the law. This is why Bradley differentiated between the "real self" and the "false self". The first, as it is easy to guess, forms a part of the moral, communal whole by conforming to its precepts. The second gives in to its passions, it is ruled by "habits and desires opposed to the good will".³⁹ As a "false self" it is anarchic, "no unity, no system, no concrete universal".⁴⁰

3.2.2. ...congeries of the hopes and fears (Thomas Hill Green)

Let us proceed to another idealist formulation of the concept of the general will, this time not exempt from references to Rousseau. We will examine the thought of Green, who made it much easier for his readers to divine the nature of the general will. It is easy to indicate its main definition in the *Lectures on the Principles of Political Obligation*.

> It then needs to be pointed out that if the sovereign power is to be understood in this fuller, less abstract sense [...] it can no longer be said to reside in a determinate person or persons, but in that impalpable congeries of the hopes and fears of a people bound together by common interests and sympathy, which we call the general will.⁴¹

Defined in this manner, the general will appears to express a collection of individual emotional states determined by "common interests and

---

36 Ibid.
37 Ibid.
38 Ibid., p. 213.
39 Ibid., p. 182.
40 Ibid., p. 304; cf. ibid., p. 310.
41 T.H. Green, *Lectures on the Principles*, p. 70 (§ 86).

sympathy". It is an attribute of a group of people, which means that its expression should not be sought in the decisions of particular individuals. Defined by emotional states, it remains fundamentally inexpressible, since the process of articulating its postulates would equate to the intersubjectivisation of feelings.

The other definitions of the general will found in Green are no less instructive:

> [S]etting aside this fictitious representation of an original covenant as having given birth to that common 'ego' or general will without which no such covenant would have been possible;[42]

> [I]n those states of society, in which obedience is habitually rendered by the bulk of society to some determinate superior, single or corporate, who in turn is independent of any other superior, the obedience is so rendered because this determinate superior is regarded as expressing or embodying what may properly be called the general will;[43]

> [T]hough it may be misleading to speak of the general will as anywhere either actually or properly sovereign, because the term 'sovereign' is best kept to the ordinary usage in which it signifies a determinate person or persons charged with the supreme coercive function of the state, and the general will does not admit of being vested in a person or persons, yet it is true that the institutions of political society — those by which equal rights are guaranteed to members of such a society — are an expression of, and are maintained by, a general will.[44]

The general will forms the basis of any compact. As such, it predetermines the existence of all social pacts and political institutions. In the exercise of power, superiors rely on social consent, while the latter is based on the conviction that the precepts of the general will are realised through their actions. And therefore "habitual obedience" to authority depends on the effective satisfaction of the demands of the general will. The latter cannot be identified with the sovereign, and this because of the impossibility of attributing it to a particular person or group. However, it has to do with the concept of equality, since it supports institutions that establish and preserve legal egalitarianism.

> [W]e may call this person or persons sovereign if we please, but we must not ascribe to him or them the real power which governs the actions and forbearances of the people, even those actions and forbearances [...] which are prescribed by the sovereign. This power is much more complex and less determinate [...] but a sense of possessing common interests, a desire for common objects on the part of the people, is always the condition of its existence. Let this sense or desire — which

---

[42] *Ibid.*, pp. 91–92 (§ 116).
[43] *Ibid.*, p. 68 (§ 84).
[44] *Ibid.*, p. 74 (§ 93).

may properly be called general will — cease to operate, or let it come into general conflict with sovereign's commands, and the habitual obedience will cease also.[45]

The general will is linked to the notion of common interest. The unperturbed functioning of the superior is dependent upon the belief of the people that he expresses this interest, the "desire for common objects", which may be called the general will. It is upon this that the legitimacy of power rests. The superior whose precepts are in conflict with it, who ceases to express the common interest, also loses the "habitual obedience" of the people.

Based on the above fragments, let us attempt to compile a list of the potential positive designations of the general will. And so: 1) it has a sentimental character and as such is inexpressible; 2) it belongs to society as a whole, not to its individual members; 3) it forms the basis of all social and political pacts and 4) the basis for the legitimation of authority; 5) it supports institutions that guarantee the equality of citizens, and also 6) it has to do with the vision of the common interest as shared by them.

This enumeration of the characteristic traits of the general will constitutes an important, if preliminary, stage in the elucidation of the role played by this category in the whole of Green's thought. Since he himself saw it as a way of reconciling Rousseau's voluntarism with positivism, it seems appropriate to enumerate his objections to the main, in his view, representative of the latter tradition — John Austin.

3.2.2.1. Rejection of John Austin's positivism

When elaborating his own view of the general will, Green largely based it on a critique of Rousseau's thought on the one hand, and an opposition to positivism on the other. To both positions, clearly one-sided and on the surface impossible to reconcile, he attributed a limited cognitive value, though only after modifications which allowed them to be included within the same theoretical system. This was precisely the goal he set himself in the *Lectures on the Principles* — to avoid the limitations of the theories enounced by Rousseau and Austin (whose writings he considered to embody the positivist world view), while skilfully merging their conceptions. This is why it is necessary to present Green's opinion of Austin alongside his critique of Rousseau.

The critique of positivism constitutes the very core of Green's thought. How could it be otherwise with a speculative and systemic thinker, elaborating epistemological, metaphysical and ethical theories, even if his method was not exclusively *a priori*? This theoretical bagg-

---

[45] *Ibid.*, pp. 68–69 (§ 84).

age had to result in an opposition to the fundamental tenets of any form of positivism. Although this criticism pervades most of Green's political theses, some of them exhibit a near programmatic form of it. They appear mostly in *Lectures on the Principles*, particularly in the discussion of Austin's philosophy of law. Austin defined sovereignty in the following manner: "[i]f a *determinate* human superior, *not* in a habit of obedience to a like superior, receive habitual obedience from the *bulk* of a given society, that determinate superior is sovereign in that society, and the society (including the superior) is a society political and independent."[46] Green concentrated his critique on two claims implied by this statement: 1) sovereignty can be ascribed only to a specific person or persons, 2) "the essence of sovereignty [...] lies in the power, on the part of such determinate person or persons, to put compulsion without limit on subjects, to make them do exactly as it pleases."[47]

---

[46] J. Austin, *Province of Jurisprudence Determined*, London 1832, p. 200.

[47] T.H. Green, *Lectures on the Principles*, p. 67 (§ 83). John Dewey correctly drew attention to the fact that the definition of Austin's philosophy of law in these terms denotes a misunderstanding, or even ignorance, of it. For even though formulations similar to those used by Green do actually appear in John Austin's writings, it is not as if their force were not diluted by others. In reality, Austin's theory is much more convergent with Green's outlook than the latter supposed. The author of *The Province of Jurisprudence Determined* does not elude the problem of founding legislation in morality, clearly writing that "the governed [...] are also the superior of the monarch: who is checked in the abuse of his might by his fear of exciting their anger; and of rousing to active resistance, the might which slumbers in the multitude" (J. Austin, *[The] Province of Jurisprudence Determined*, p. 20). That which, according to Dewey, differentiates Austin's theory from Green's is the inept presentation, or rather the total omission, by the former of the issue of the relationship between morality and legality (J. Dewey, *Austin's Theory of Sovereignty*, in: J. Dewey, *The Early Works, 1882–1898*, Vol. 4: *1893–1894*, Illinois 1969, p. 82). In Dewey's opinion, it would have been more justified for Green to have chosen as the target of his attack the theories of the by far more positivist Henry Maine—whose principal work, *Lectures on the Early History of Institutions*, Green often referenced as an exemplary exposition of Austinianism (cf. T.H. Green, *Lectures on the Principles*, p. 68–70, § 84–87)—George Cornewall Lewis or even Thomas Hobbes himself, the precursor of this current of the philosophy of law (J. Dewey, *Austin's Theory of Sovereignty*, pp. 70–72; cf. M. Richter, *The Politics of Conscience*, p. 243). One further fact pleads for the acceptance of Dewey's thesis: in *The Province of Jurisprudence*, Austin differentiates between *de facto* and *de jure* government. Further still, he uses these terms in the same sense as Green (J. Austin, *The Province of Jurisprudence Determined*, pp. 372–374), writing for example that "every government properly so called is a government *de facto*. In strictness, a so called government *de jure* but not *de facto*, is not a government" (*ibid.*, p. 374).

Thinkers who, like Austin, seek the sources of sovereignty solely in the decrees of a person or group of persons are mistaken. The problem is not that the ruler, government or parliament cannot be considered the sovereign, but rather that the positivists understood this term in a completely unwarranted manner. The fact that there is a person to whom citizens render "habitual obedience", to use Austin's terminology, only proves that "we may call this person or persons sovereign if we please, but we must not ascribe to him or them the real power which governs the actions and forbearances of the people."[48] Designating them as the sovereign is justified only in the institutional sense, in the sense of Rousseau's *de jure* sovereignty. The functioning of this type of institution always depends on the general will. It is the general will that decides the fate of institutional sovereigns in the final instance: "it may fairly be held that the ostensible sovereign — the determinate person or persons to whom we can point and say that with him or them lies the ultimate power of exalting habitual obedience from the people — is only able to exercise this power in virtue of an assent on the part of the people, nor is this assent reducible to the fear of the sovereign felt by each individual."[49]

The above theses are not solely applicable to the democratic order, in which the *de jure* sovereign derives legitimacy directly from the *de facto* sovereign, the general will. Even authoritarian rulers, for as long as they are able to enforce obedience to their commands, consciously or not, rely for their rule on the consent of the will of the people. A lack of legitimation on the part of the subjects always results in a change of power. This does not need to take place immediately, yet the tension created by the alienation of the *de jure* sovereign from the *volonté générale*, by the chasm between the expectations of the citizens and the letter of the law, must in the end be resolved — as a final measure by civil disobedience or political revolution. "If a despotic government comes into anything like a habitual conflict with unwritten law which represents the general will, its dissolution is beginning."[50]

Yet Green's criticism of positivism should not be misunderstood. From the premises: 1) Austin saw the source of law in the decisions of a personal sovereign; 2) in his view, legislation gains legitimacy from obedience to a sovereign thus defined; 3) Green criticises this position,[51] and thus, if a personal sovereign is capable of enforcing obedience to his edicts, then the latter must be expressing the general will — the real

---

[48] T.H. Green, *Lectures on the Principles*, p. 68 (§ 84).
[49] *Ibid.*
[50] *Ibid.*, p. 73 (§ 90); cf. *ibid.*, pp. 102–103 (§ 132).
[51] *Ibid.*, p. 89 (§ 113).

sovereign, we can conclude that: 4) Austin's personal positivism has simply been replaced by Green's impersonal positivism, and so the decision of the individual with the precept of the general will. Nothing is further from the truth. Green's rejection of positivism is unconditional. However, it does not imply taking the opposing position — that of modern natural law theory.

But is it possible to take an intermediate position? Should we not agree with Leo Strauss that "[t]o reject natural right is tantamount to saying that all right is positive right, and this means that what is right is determined exclusively by the legislators"?[52] Green's works demonstrate that he is convinced that it is possible to work out a conception reconciling the fundamental premises of both these positions. The author of the *Social Contract* was not wrong when he claimed that the exercise of power requires the consent of the citizens. On the other hand, Austin was right in claiming that power can in a certain sense be identified with a sovereign government or ruling person, to whom "habitual obedience" is rendered. How is it possible to bring together these two perspectives? This shall be the subject of the next subsection.

3.2.2.2. Between Jean-Jacques Rousseau and John Austin

We have already noted that Austin bases his argumentation on two premises: firstly, that sovereignty can only be ascribed to "a determinate person or persons", secondly that "the essence of sovereignty [...] lies in the power, on the part of such determinate person or persons, to put compulsion without limit on subjects, to make them do exactly as it pleases."[53] Rousseau would have accepted neither, since in his view the general will cannot be reduced to the will of any single person. However, both Rousseau and Austin were partly correct. Though according to Green, existing interpretations of their theories are wholly unacceptable.

Rousseau correctly indicated that the citizens are the source of legitimacy. And Austin was not mistaken when stating that authorities are always embodied in individuals or groups of people. However, both made fundamental errors. On the one hand, the positivist premise that the sources of sovereignty can be sought only in the commands of a given person or institution is false. Every decision, in order to have true causal power, must be based on the "habitual obedience" of the people. Here, Green agreed with Austin. The error of the latter consisted in an insufficient inquiry into the sources of the said obedience. If Austin had not stopped at the analysis of *de jure* sovereignty, he would doubtless

---

[52] L. Strauss, *Natural Right and History*, Chicago, IL 1953, p. 2.
[53] T.H. Green, *Lectures on the Principles*, p. 67 (§ 83).

have noticed that if obedience was only forced and the respect of law was only based on fear, the sovereign would not stay in power long.[54]

Rousseau's position is also incorrect, since he took his desiderata too far. The contents of the *Social Contract* imply the impossibility of ascribing sovereignty to nations ruled undemocratically, or even to those functioning according to representative democracy. The admission of such disclaimers makes the concept of the general will a relic of the past, the tool of a utopian, Jacobin-revolutionary vision of political order, unsuitable for the modern theory of state and law. Meanwhile sovereignty need not be based on the conscious, rational opinions of citizens expressed through direct democracy, claimed Green. What is more, it need not be realised through voting at all. Green was more consequent than Rousseau in claiming that the general will is indestructible, "always constant, unalterable and pure".[55] It imposes no institutional conditions. It is always the basis of public order.

Rousseau's conception of the *volonté générale* requires at least two major modifications. Firstly, the rule of the general will does not require a democratic system. As the expression of societal beliefs as to the right shape of public order, it is always the source of the latter's legitimacy. Secondly, as the set of social "hopes and fears" and the resultant system of values and expectations on the part of citizens towards the representatives of authority, it need not take the form of verbalised desiderata, nor find its outlet in manifestos or political programmes. The acceptance of a political system manifests itself as conformity to the commands of authority, while disapproval, as civil disobedience.

3.2.2.3. Between positivism and jusnaturalism

Green's already mentioned critique of natural law theories highlighted the errors of modern thinkers who failed to make the distinction between "is" and "ought to be". They attributed rights to individuals on account of their being members of humankind, while

> there is a system of rights and obligations which *should be* maintained by law [...] and which may properly be called "*natural*", not in the sense in which the term "natural" would imply that such a system ever did exist or could exist independently of force exercised by society over individ-

---

[54] *Ibid.*, p. 93 (§ 118). This view was also shared by Bernard Bosanquet (B. Bosanquet, *Individual and Social Reform*, in: B. Bosanquet, *Essays and Addresses*, London 1899, p. 25).

[55] J.J. Rousseau, *Social Contract*, IV, I, p. 91.

uals, but "natural" because necessary to the end which it is the vocation of human society to realize.[56]

The proper theory of natural law "is not an inquiry into the process by which actual law came to be what it is; nor is it an inquiry how far actual law corresponds to and is derived from the exercise of certain original or natural rights".[57] Law cannot be justified genetically, only teleologically. The final criterion of its appraisal is, firstly, not the past but the future, and secondly, not a hypothetical humankind but the members of particular communities. For the idealists, this future was seen to require extensive moral and institutional reform.

This definition of natural law makes one inclined to ask about the possibility of evaluating various legislative systems according to the degree in which they conform to it. Can some of them be seen as emanating from human nature, while others as opposed to it? Can one call upon natural law to defend a particular type of legislation? It would seem so. However, in doing so, one should not appeal to inherent human properties, but rather to the purpose of human existence. Hence, only legislation facilitating the realisation of the human *telos*, moral perfection, can be considered as in agreement with *jus naturae*. Yet do not all laws fulfil this mission in a way proper to themselves, since all can be said to contribute to the moral development of the community? All play a part, either as "safeguards" of the community's moral achievements, or a deterrent, demanding the exercise of civic attitudes.[58] All of this is true, which is why Green sought the basis for the valuation of legislation not only in its goal, but also in how quickly the latter was advanced by it. Some statutes may accelerate the process, while others slow it down. This is the reason for Green's glorification of social-minded legislation. An interventionist policy that aims to implement the precepts of positive liberty is more effective for the moral development of citizens than liberal laissez-faireism. The latter halts the process of perfecting a large part of the population, unable to secure their livelihood, and therefore reduced to the level of animals, day by day fighting for survival. Only a developed social system allows one to retain and perfect one's humanity. And only this type of legislation can be deemed to be in accordance with *jus naturae*.

---

[56] T.H. Green, *Lectures on the Principles*, p. 17 (§ 9); cf. *ibid.*, pp. 22–23 (§ 20); P.P. Nicholson, *The Political Philosophy*, p. 93; A.D. Lindsay, *T.H. Green and the Idealists*, in: *The Social and Political Ideas of Some Representative Thinkers of the Victorian Age*, ed. F.J.C. Hearnshaw, New York 1967, pp. 160–162.

[57] T.H. Green, *Lectures on the Principles*, p. 22 (§ 19).

[58] *Ibid.*, p. 70 (§ 87).

3.2.3. ... a system of ideas (Bernard Bosanquet)

Of all the thinkers discussed here, Bosanquet's writings are those that offer the least resistance when attempting to better define the concept of the general will presented therein.

> We may identify the general will of any community with the whole working system of dominant ideas which determines the place and functions of its members, and of the community as a whole among other communities.[59]

> The general will itself is the whole assemblage of individual minds, considered as a working system, with parts corresponding to one another, and producing as a result a certain life for all these parts themselves.[60]

Bosanquet's general will has a structurally ordered character, and takes the form of a "system of dominant ideas", an "assemblage of individual minds". The systemic nature of these configurations is expressed in the coordination of their elements. The general will determines the place and function of individuals within the social structure as well as the relationship between the community and other groups. It is only through participation in the community and, more precisely, through the fulfilment of the duties attached to one's social position, that individuals can realise their "real wills".

> Thus the general will is only in part self-conscious, and in as far as an attempt is made to formulate it in judgements it seems to be fallible. For then it ceases to be fact, and becomes interpretation of fact.[61]

> [G]eneral will is a process continuously emerging from the relatively unconscious into reflective consciousness.[62]

Individuals are never fully conscious of its character, and so any attempt to describe it is doomed to failure. In spite of this, it continuously permeates the "reflexive consciousness", being an essential part of it.

> [M]ob, for instance, when they act as one man, under the influence of an identical sentiment of anger or cupidity. This is an irrational form of the general will, as a burst of feeling is of the individual will; but it is definitely general in so far as it is owing to the operation of the same sentiment in all the minds at once.[63]

---

[59] B. Bosanquet, *The Reality*, p. 325.
[60] Ibid.
[61] Ibid., p. 329.
[62] Ibid., p. 331.
[63] Ibid., p. 324.

> The process, through which the general will emerges "[i]s not essentially superficial nor sentimental. It is essentially logical".[64]

> The answer is drawn, I take it, from the conception of the general will, which involves the existence of an actual community, of such a nature as to share an identical mind and feeling. There is no other way of explaining how a free man can put up with compulsion and even welcome it.[65]

The general will can take both a rational and an irrational form. It does not belong exclusively to groups with strictly defined goals. It can be attributed to a mob, united by anger or cupidity, as long as these motives are present in the minds of all its members. However, it will then be irrational, and if a community is to be born of it, "superficial and sentimental" factors cannot lie at its base, but only those rational and logical.[66]

> But for a true comprehension of group-life it will always be necessary to refer its inward and spiritual side to something like the general will, and its outward and visible form to a complex of institutions, and thereby to set its outward and inward aspect in their true relation to each other and to the social unity.[67]

> [C]omplete reflective conception of the end of the State, comprehensive and free from contradiction, would mean a complete idea of the realisation of all human capacity, without waste or failure. Such a conception is impossible owing to the gradual character of the process by which the end of life, the nature of the good, is determined for man. The Real Will, as represented by the State, is only a partial embodiment of it.[68]

As the general will constitutes an "inward" principle that pervades social life, its "outward" counterpart is the set of institutions of sociopolitical life. These are, after all, two aspects of the same phenomenon, or more precisely, the same phenomenon once seen as the "inward" life of society, and then as its "outward" life. As the "real will", the general will is a "partial embodiment" of the ideal of human perfection. As the "ideal will", proper to an ideal state, one of its inalienable elements would be the vision of a perfectly developed personality. For the general will is comprised of an ideal of human nature proper to a given

---

[64] Ibid., p. 327; cf. B. Bosanquet, *The Philosophical Theory*, p. 172.
[65] B. Bosanquet, *The Function of the State in Promoting the Unity of Mankind*, in: B. Bosanquet, *Social and International Ideals. Being Studies in Patriotism*, New York 1967, p. 271.
[66] Cf. B. Bosanquet, *Liberty and Legislation*, in: B. Bosanquet, *Civilization of Christendom*, New York 1893, pp. 368–374.
[67] B. Bosanquet, *Introduction to the Second Edition*, in: B. Bosanquet, *The Philosophical Theory*, p. XXXI.
[68] B. Bosanquet, *The Philosophical Theory*, p. 141.

stage in the process "by which the end of life, the nature of the good, is determined for man".

> The social system under which we live [...] represents the general will and higher self as a whole to the community as a whole and can only stand by virtue of that representation being recognized.[69]

> [T]he administrative expression of the general will is not necessarily confined to *ad hoc* elective bodies, but may take any efficient and convenient shape without violation of the theory of democratic self-government.[70]

The social system reflects the general will, while this representation must gain acceptance. For the institutions of the community to function without obstacle, the consent of the persons subjected to them is necessary. It does not need to take the form of democratic voting, where citizens express their will through "*ad hoc* elective bodies". Institutions can also embody the general will when bypassing the *vox populi*.

3.2.3.1. Interpretations

Based on the fragments cited above, Bosanquet's view of the general will can be defined in the following way: 1) it has a systemic character; 2) it is composed of "dominant ideas"; 3) it is related to socially ascribed roles and stations, and the resultant rights and duties; 4) individuals are unconscious of it; 5) it emerges in a rational and logical manner; 6) its "outward" expression is the set of socio-political institutions; 7) its essential element is the ideal of the best life. This enumeration still leaves many doubts. Analogies with public opinion, variously understood, spring to mind. However, Bosanquet warned against false interpretations, preventively describing three potential errors in identifying the general will with:

1. Any decision by the members of a community — this is, according to Bosanquet, the error previously made by Rousseau in equating the general will with the will of all, the interest of the community with the interest of individuals, and thereby in fact reducing the first category to the second. Decisions can be regarded only as the "expression or consequence of the general will".[71] The general will itself is a system of ideas in perpetual motion,[72] impossible to identify with any particular moment: "no system of voting can secure its expression, because it does not exist in a form that can be embodied in a vote."[73]

---

[69] *Ibid.*, p. 186.
[70] B. Bosanquet, *Introduction to the Second Edition*, p. XXX.
[71] B. Bosanquet, *The Reality*, p. 325.
[72] Cf. B. Pfannenstill, *Bernard Bosanquet's Philosophy of the State*, pp. 235–236.
[73] B. Bosanquet, *The Reality*, p. 325.

2. Public opinion — the general will is above all based on factors of which individuals are not conscious; it "is not identical with public opinion, considered as a set of judgments which form the currently expressed reflection. [...] It may include these current notions [...] but it certainly includes much more, because the ideas that dominate the will do not always appear in reflection, or at least not with the importance which they have in life. The general will is more a system of wills than a system of reflections, and appears in action quite as much as in discussion".[74] There are at least two reasons against equating public opinion and general will: firstly, since "we are never thoroughly aware even of our own practical ideas",[75] it is impossible for us to comprehend the multiplicity of ideas operative within a community: "[w]e are not conscious, either of all the influences active in our will, or of its limitations";[76] secondly, since no one can mentally comprehend the totality of the social system, "no one, not the greatest statesman or historical philosopher, has in his mind, even in theory, much less as a practical object, the real development in which his community is moving."[77] Searching for the imprint of the general will on public opinion presupposes such a possibility.

3. "[D]e facto tendency of all that is done by members of the community" — "though — claims Bosanquet — it is much more like this than like a vote or a set of opinions";[78] the general will could be identified with such a tendency, if this notion referred solely to the ideas operating within a given society, and not also to other questions, not directly related to the ideal of the best life.[79]

---

[74] *Ibid.*, p. 326; cf. B. Bosanquet, *The Philosophical Theory*, pp. 266–267.
[75] B. Bosanquet, *The Reality*, p. 328.
[76] *Ibid.*
[77] *Ibid.*; cf. B. Bosanquet, *The Principle of Individuality and Value*, London 1912, p. 3.
[78] B. Bosanquet, *The Reality*, p. 326.
[79] Pfannenstill claimed that such a definition of the general will suggests an analogy with the concept of spirit (*Geist*) as developed by German sociologists — Werner Sombart, Max Scheler, Max Weber and Othmar Spann — or the "idea" of German neo-Hegelians — Julius Binder, Martin Buss and Karl Larenz (B. Pfannenstill, *Bernard Bosanquet's Philosophy of the State*, p. 236). Bosanquet himself openly admitted his debt to Gustave Le Bon, Émile Durkheim, Gabriel Tarde, among others (B. Bosanquet, *The Philosophical Theory*, pp. 39–44; cf. D. Boucher, A. Vincent, *British Idealism and Political Theory*, Edinburgh 2000, pp. 103–113), which would later prove one of the flashpoints in his relationship with Sidney and Beatrice Webb, who in their analyses tended to prefer the evolutionist and positivist perspectives, in particular drawing upon the work of Herbert Spencer and Auguste Comte (*ibid.*, p. 92–94).

While these negative definitions allow one to avoid errors of interpretation, they are only an initial step on the path towards understanding the nature of the general will. Its relation to dominant ideas, the state and morality still remains to be defined. The links between the general will and the first of these categories — which appears so frequently in this context, yet remains so opaque and ambiguous at first glance — will prove of particular importance.

What should we understand by the notion of dominant ideas? Many examples can be given, starting from the general and abstract, such as equality, liberty, subordination, dependence; and moving towards the particular, defining the precise places occupied by members of society: the ideas of fatherhood, motherhood, filiation, citizenship and so forth. The existence of society depends on the fulfilment of the functions defined by these ideas. Their set is always already ordered in some way. The smooth functioning of a community requires that it be so. For instance, it is necessary that the idea of sisterhood not be at odds with the idea of citizenship (see Sophocles' *Antigone*). Dominant ideas are those characterised by "logical capacity",[80] an exceptional capacity to harmonise the system (in case of liberal democracies, this harmonising role can be attributed to the idea of liberty).

Some scholars saw proof of Bosanquet's conservatism in the formulation of this conception. In Bosanquet's view, the stable functioning of society must be based on respect for its traditions, while the system of ideas as such should be free of philosophical abstraction divorced from social practice. Especially the dominant ideas, if they are to order the system, must be based on the historical experience of the community.

> Ideas do not spring from nowhere; they are the inside which reflects the material action and real conditions that form the outside. So that the common life shared by the members of a community involves a common element in their ideas, not merely in their notions of things about them, though this is very important, but more especially in the dominant or organizing ideas which rule their minds.[81]

The logical nature of the general will implies its progress towards a state of internal harmony, a relative ordering, and directedness towards a complete ordering. The extent of this ordering is reflected in the level of stability of the public order.[82]

Even the minds of individuals, by their assimilation of the contents which the general will is composed of, co-form a system. Although most citizens do not ponder the purpose for which their community

---

[80] B. Bosanquet, *The Reality*, p. 323.
[81] *Ibid.*, pp. 323–324.
[82] *Ibid.*, p. 327.

exists, the nature of the common good, the means of its realisation, or even the roles attributed to them within this process, they are still part of the "general scheme", whose goal is the realisation of the *bonum publicum*.[83] This system comes into being spontaneously. Since it is impossible to completely understand its complexity, it is also impossible to foresee and plan its development.[84]

In what manner is this system formed? The process of its emergence is twofold. On the one hand, it is subject to "practical organisation", on the other, to "reflective discussion". Practical organisation, the process of coordinating ideas, of which the individual is unconscious, plays a key role here. In it, specific ideas gain social acceptance, revolutionising the community's world view. Without a discussion, in which only few individuals normally take part, the social consciousness becomes dominated by certain ideas, which leads to changes in value hierarchies, as well as a redefinition of the ideal of the best life. "Every person is thus always being moulded into a logical unit much more than he is aware, and the causal opinions which he expresses do not really represent the content of his will or the process by which it is formed."[85]

Bosanquet attributed a much lesser significance to the second way in which the general will is formed. This proceeds thanks to "practical organisation", building on its effects, and consists in the "reflective discussion" of the meaning of ideas. Compared to the first way, it "ought really to be the same thing in a reflective form".[86] When individuals take note of contradictions between ideas operative within a community, they make a conscious effort to redefine them so as to make the system a relatively harmonious whole.

Each community has a system of ideas proper only to itself, presupposing specific goals and means for their realisation (under the guise of functions assigned to its members). Agreeing with the foreword to the English edition of Otton Friedrich von Gierke's *Political Theories of the Middle Age*[87] (penned by Frederick William Maitland), Bosanquet noted that "the real or general will is present in its degree in every co operating group of human beings. [...] Where two or more are gathered together with any degree of common experience and co-operation, there is *pro tanto* a general will."[88] Thus, families, social organisations, associations of workers or employers, political parties etc. all

---

[83] B. Bosanquet, *The Reality*, p. 320.
[84] *Ibid.*, pp. 328–329; cf. *ibid.*, pp. 329–330.
[85] *Ibid.*, pp. 329–330.
[86] *Ibid.*, p. 329.
[87] O.F. von Gierke, *Political Theories of the Middle Age*, transl. F.W. Maitland, Cambridge 1913.
[88] B. Bosanquet, *Introduction to the Second Edition*, p. XXIX.

have a will of their own. Every form of collective life is equipped with a system of ideas, with the dominant ones at the forefront. Each has its own system of values, effecting a fitting specification of functions among its members.

Since the coexistence of many general wills within one social body seems unavoidable, there arises the question of potential collisions. Bosanquet even argued that these are inevitable when the general will of the most extensive community, the state, is reformulated. The communities we are members of are like "boxes hidden one in another".[89] Conflicts between them are resolved by reference to the dominant ideas of the most extensive general will, that of the state. When there is a conflict between social perceptions of the duties incumbent on a parent and on a worker, for instance, as with the issue of the length of maternity leave or the guarantee of re-employment for women returning from such leave, the collision between the general will of the family (where the dominant idea should be the welfare of the offspring) and the general will of the workplace (where that idea could be profitability) will be resolved on the national level. In that case, depending on whether the dominant idea of the state is freedom of trade or balanced social progress, the dispute will be resolved to the advantage of one party or the other. Similar conflicts arise when the modification of one of the social ideals forces the readjustment of others.

The general will, understood as the "inward" life of the community, directly conditions its "outward" existence in the form of public institutions. The system of ideas necessarily contains the idea of the "best life", the realisation of which is the unchanging goal of individuals, who in turn expect the support of institutions within this field. When this idea is modified, the effect is always the expectation of a reform of the inter-human relations which serve to achieve it, for instance the institution of marriage, the regulation of commerce or of political participation. It is for this very reason Bosanquet attributed such weight to social recognition. In the end, institutions draw their legitimacy from the consent of the citizens. This consent may be "tacit",[90] since legitimation does not require the judgment of citizens.[91] Also undemocratic authorities, as long as they organise the public sphere in accordance with the idea of the "best life" and other dominant ideas, will continue to enjoy the acceptance of their citizens.[92]

---

[89] B. Bosanquet, *The Reality*, p. 330.
[90] B. Bosanquet, *The Philosophical Theory*, p. 174.
[91] B. Bosanquet, *Introduction to the Second Edition*, p. XXX.
[92] This is one of the main arguments against the charge of Bosanquet's political absolutism. William Sweet attributes particular weight to it, seeing it as proof of the liberalism of the author of *The Philosophical Theory* (W. Sweet,

3.3 Further history of the concept of the general will

To complete the picture of the place occupied by the category of the general will in British thought, it is necessary to illustrate its further history. It should be clear by now that the general will is at the core of idealist reflection on socio-political themes. Although not always explicitly referenced, it permeates the overwhelming majority of idealist political writing. We unfortunately lack the room here to show how it was alluded to by thinkers such as William Wallace, Henry Jones and David George Ritchie. We will be occupied with them further on, and only in a summary way, during our analysis of the idealist theory of law. Let us now focus on those thinkers who referred to the concept consciously and devoted a large part of their attention to it. As it will turn out, the main heroes of our considerations will not be the idealists themselves as much as the thinkers who followed the example of their works or engaged in a polemic with them, concentrating on the once widely-commented dispute between Hobhouse and Bosanquet — the controversy over the metaphysical theory of the state, as it is known in the relevant literature. Having described its essence, course and most important consequences, we will present the further history of the category of the general will, tracing its successive incarnations in the works of John Henry Muirhead and Hector James Wright Hetherington as well as the New Liberals — John Atkinson Hobson and Hobhouse.

3.3.1. Criticism. Controversy over the metaphysical theory of the state[*]

The idealist conception of the general will, together with a significant part of the idealist theory of state and rights, came under fierce criticism at the beginning of the twentieth century. The most notable dispute was between Bosanquet and Hobhouse, both because of its breadth and the number of voices heard in the discussion. On the surface Hobhouse, a declared social-liberal, the author of the still popular *Liberalism*,[93] and Bosanquet had a lot in common. A prolific writer, he dabbled in political journalism and also abandoned a university chair to take an active part in the promotion of social reforms, joining the staff of the liberal "Manchester Guardian" and later the social-liberal "Tribune". But what brought these two figures together most was

---

Idealism and Rights. The Social Ontology of Human Rights in the Political Thought of Bernard Bosanquet, Lanham–New York–London 1997).

[*] A part of this subsection has been published as *Bernard Bosanquet a Leonard Hobhouse – spór o metafizyczną teorię państwa*, „Politeja", no. 13 (1/2010), pp. 127–150.

[93] L.T. Hobhouse, *Liberalism*, New York 1911.

doubtless the master they shared — Green.[94] Both considered themselves faithful disciples and believed their thought to be merely an extension of his.

At the beginning of the twentieth century, these two thinkers and socio-political activists, Hobhouse and Bosanquet, became embroiled in a dispute fraught with consequences for the future of idealism and the concept of the general will. It began with the publication of Bosanquet's *The Philosophical Theory of the State* in 1899, a work which at the time was generally regarded as a statement of British Hegelian political theory.

At first, nothing foretold the criticism it would be subjected to. No one accused its author of absolutism. What is more, the first readings of *The Philosophical Theory of the State* suggested that it might legitimately be viewed as a manifesto of individualism, perhaps even excessively one-sided, since disregarding the significance of the role of the state in the lives of its citizens.[95] Of course, there were critical voices as well, but these came somewhat later.

It took the attention of a noted liberal authority to really cause an uproar and provide the impetus to rally the troops in the defence of democracy and liberalism against those who would condone dictatorship. It took someone to phrase his objections in a separate work, challenging Bosanquet's argument step by step. In other words, it took Hobhouse, who played this part perfectly. His *Metaphysical Theory of the State*, published in 1918, was a refutation of Bosanquet's and Hegel's political theories, striking the final blow at political idealism. Although Hobhouse's position was not that distant from those of Kant and Green, while his work contained a number of theses whose argumentation left much to be desired (for instance, the theory of moral and political evolutionism, in light of which twentieth-century democracies emerged through the gradual actualisation of a potential already imamnent in the ancient *poleis*[96]), his attack on Bosanquet had the effect of

---

[94] To illustrate the differences between Bosanquet and Hobhouse, Stefan Collini uses the terms Greenian "right" (Bosanquet) and "left" (Hobhouse), alluding to an analogous split among nineteenth-century Hegelians (S. Collini, *Hobhouse, Bosanquet and the State. Philosophical Idealism and Political Argument in England 1880–1918*, "Past and Present" 1976, No. 72, p. 107).

[95] J. Gibbon, *Review: The Philosophical Theory of the State*, "International Journal of Ethics" 1899–1900, Vol. 10, pp. 399–401; W.A. Dunning, *Review: The Philosophical Theory of the State*, "Political Science Quarterly" 1899, Vol. 14, pp. 530–533; J. Watson, *Review: The Philosophical Theory of the State*, "Queen's Quarterly" 1900, Vol. 7, pp. 320–322.

[96] L.T. Hobhouse, *Social Evolution and Political Theory*, New York 1911, pp. 126–148.

removing all metaphysics from politics, whether we speak of the humanitarian idealism of Kant's *Metaphysics of Morals* or the idealism of Hegel's *Philosophy of Right*, proclaiming the inevitability of wars. Striking at idealist philosophy *in toto*, Hobhouse also struck at the notion of positive liberty, anticipating Karl Raimund Popper's *The Open Society and its Enemies* by twenty-seven years, as well as a similar attack carried out forty years later by Isaiah Berlin in *Two Concepts of Liberty*.

As Hobhouse himself admitted, his inspiration for this foray against the idealist "apologists of dictatorship" was provided by a specific historical event:

> In the bombing of London I had just witnessed the visible and tangible outcome of a false and wicked doctrine, the foundations of which lay, as I believe, in the book before me. [...] Hegel himself carried the proof-sheets of his first work to the printer through streets crowded with fugitives from the field of Jena. With that work began the most penetrating and subtle of all the intellectual influences which have sapped the rational humanitarianism of the eighteenth and nineteenth centuries, and in the Hegelian theory of the god-state all that I had witnessed lay implicit.[97]

It is hardly surprising, then, that Hobhouse perceived Bosanquet's conception of the general will as a danger to freedom and democracy, especially the identification of the general with the "true will", opposed to the "actual wills" of individuals. That which for many could still have liberal implications in Hegel, for example the strict distinction between civil society and the state, was abandoned in *The Philosophical Theory of the State* and replaced by an identification of the state with society. Hobhouse could not have reacted differently to Bosanquet's book, because he regarded the political writings of Hegel as nothing short of a manifesto of conservatism, backwardness and an apology of the totalitarian state.

According to the author of *The Metaphysical Theory of the State*, there are two perceptions of the state: the democratic or humanitarian, where political institutions are merely a means for the attainment of non-political ends defined by the citizens, and the metaphysical, where the state itself is an end to be realised by means of its citizens. The first of these approaches allows rulers to be reproved for acting to the detriment of their subjects or humankind; in the second, the rulers determine standards of conduct, while their decisions are self-justified and are the indicators for how others should act.[98] Supporters of the demo-

---

[97] L.T. Hobhouse, *The Metaphysical Theory of the State: A Criticism*, London 1918, p. 6.
[98] *Ibid.*, p. 137.

cratic conception draw their conclusions from empirical evidence – the inescapable diversity of modern-day societies. This is why they reject metaphysical claims of the existence of a supra-individual whole, especially if this whole is ascribed a will, in particular a will superior to the wills of finite human beings. Nor do they see any reason to identify this whole with the state.[99] The "metaphysicians", on the other hand, teach that the "whole" has more reality than its "parts", and so should take precedence over them.[100] The "democrats" hold such theses to be magical thinking – completely untenable, even indefensible – refusing to grant them any cognitive value.[101]

A similar example of hypostatic error can be seen in the statement that the "real will" and the "actual will" can desire different things. But is there, ultimately, any other indication of what I want beyond my desire as such? And can will even be general? Can it, by definition, be anything other than particular? Can it reasonably be stated that from the fact that the system of ideas/general will is general, it follows that it is voluntary? Hobhouse answers all these questions in the negative.

These and similar idealist "absurdities" should not come as a surprise, Hobhouse claimed, since proponents of the "metaphysical theory of the state" rely nearly exclusively on theory, almost entirely ignoring practice. They do not take reality as it is but as it, in their view, should be. And it is precisely this view of an ideal society, against the voice of common sense, that they uphold as true, dismissing all factually existing communities as unreal or "actual", since entangled in conflicts and injustice. They write that reality develops in a planned and rational way, although every day we find evidence that human actions are spontaneous. Often, or perhaps even usually, irrational, uncoordinated and chaotic.[102] "[O]ur general charge against the method of idealism must be that it starts with and never corrects the fundamental confusion of the ideal and the actual."[103] It is thus primarily levelled against the Hegelian concept of the concrete universal,[104] intended to bring together the universal and the contingent.

However, the main, intentional target of Hobhouse's attack was not the "metaphysical theory of the state" in its broad sense, but rather the specific form it took in Bosanquet's work. Three of the latter's theoretical premises fuelled particular doubts in Hobhouse's mind: 1) that the true will of an individual consists in conforming to some kind of "real

---

[99] *Ibid.*, p. 30.
[100] *Ibid.*, p. 28.
[101] Cf. *ibid.*, p. 126.
[102] *Ibid.*, p. 81.
[103] *Ibid.*, pp. 22–23; cf. *ibid.*, p. 112.
[104] *Ibid.*, pp. 65–69.

will"; 2) that this "real will" is equivalent to the general will; 3) that the latter is embodied in the state. These, in Hobhouse's view, are the three key premises of *The Philosophical Theory of the State*, and at the same time its three most serious methodological errors.

The first ensues from two false theories, which it also tries to validate: the notion that human nature is richer than suggested by "actual" states of consciousness of individual people, and that there is an ideal, perfectly harmonious state of the human soul.[105] Hobhouse claimed that the first of these notions expresses an essential truth about the human condition, but does not in any way connect it with the will of particular individuals, still less does it imply rational reasoning or action. The second notion, on the contrary, takes the rationality of the will as its central concept, but is not supported by facts. It can therefore be considered a hypothesis at most, but should not be admitted as true under any circumstances. According to Hobhouse, when adhering to the rules of proper reasoning, these two conceptions cannot be joined. There is therefore no cognitive value to the thesis that individuals have a "real will", a fundamentally harmonious one, which they strive to realise, and which differs from their "actual will".

It is equally groundless to attempt to identify this alleged "real will" with the general will. "This argument confused identity of character with identity of continuous existence, the result of which was to set up a common self wherein the difference between one person and another is lost."[106] Due to selecting the incorrect terminology, and especially due to using the abstract concept of the general will, the "metaphysicians" inferred the existence of a being possessed of such a will.

Bosanquet's third crucial mistake lay in creating an arbitrary link between the general will and the state. It is true, says Hobhouse, that one can find arguments in support of such a link to society, as was in fact done by some philosophers inspired by Hegel's theory of right. And yet to attribute a general will to the state as such, and this is precisely what Bosanquet did, amounts to rejecting this formative relationship between custom and law, negating the possibility of any form of social pressure on the institutional and legal spheres.

The source of Hobhouse's opposition to such a "metaphysical" manner of philosophising about the state was not limited to methodological doubts. If the alarm needed to be sounded, it is above all because of the potential consequences of applying these "metaphysical" theories to socio-political practice. Several may be noted. The first is the depreciation of the individual and the subsequent dangers.

---

[105] *Ibid.*, p. 71.
[106] *Ibid.*

According to the "metaphysicians", individuals should not decide the desirable form of political order. What is more, they are not even competent to articulate their own desires. The socio-political system, this embodiment of the "real will", can evaluate the needs of individuals, and the optimal ways of satisfying them, better than the individual themselves.

Bosanquet wrote of the fulfilment of duties resulting from the social position of individuals as their "true freedom". Nothing could be more dangerous. Once this is admitted as a political tenet, no instance of civil disobedience, not even social consultation on any key political issue, will ever again be tolerated. If the idealist argumentation is deemed correct, democracy will permanently lose its theoretical justification. How to defend the liberal conception of freedom if, "[b]riefly, we are morally free when our actions conform to our real will, our real will is the general will, and the general will is most fully embodied in the state"?[107]

This and similar questions reveal the danger that Hobhouse believed to spring from the theories enounced in the pages of *The Philosophical Theory of the State*. Why should the future of the community be decided by people led astray by their "actual will", and so those who, according to Bosanquet, unconsciously act to both their and society's detriment? Why not make them happy, in spite of their own foolhardiness? They will eventually understand that it is for their own good, having attained a level of moral development at which they will be capable of grasping the blessings of positive liberty and the dangers of self-will. And even if they fail to understand this, should they not all the more so be denied the power to influence the fate of the community —since they are "incurably" irrational? After all, coercion as applied to irrational people is for their own good.

And at any rate, can one still speak of any sort of coercion if one accepts Bosanquet's central claims? To be coerced by society or the state means to be compelled by the general will, and so by the most harmonious form of the social system of ideas.[108] And what do all individuals strive for, if not precisely this inner harmony? It is no surprise that embracing Bosanquet's theory must inevitably lead to the acceptance of Rousseau's *dictum* that one can be forced to be free.

This entire anti-individualist argumentation is the simple effect of repeating at least two Hegelian errors. The first consists in identifying right with freedom. The same tendency to oppose "true freedom" to "false freedom", and to associate the former with moral perfectionism,

---

[107] *Ibid.*, p. 43.
[108] *Ibid.*, pp. 56–57.

which took the form of the improvement of individuals by conscious self-determination in the philosophy of Kant (in the form of obedience to the precepts of the categorical imperative) and later also that of Green, found an outlet, in Hobhouse's view, in the social and political paternalism found in the works of Hegel and Bosanquet.[109] Individuals do not require the freedom to search for means of self-realisation — these are "served on a platter" to them, as the customs and laws of the community. Why should they therefore stumble around, searching for the right course of action? The truths can be shown at any given moment. This anti-individualism is the result of adapting Rousseau's concept of the general will, although as Hobhouse underlined, not quite in keeping with the spirit of the original. For in the *Social Contract*, the concept referred to the renouncement of particular interests by individuals, in order to make the best political decisions for the community in abstraction to them. In *The Philosophical Theory of the State*, on the other hand, the notion of the general will denotes a certain whole, in which individual personalities are dissolved. The very term "individuality" is also redefined. It no longer refers to a deviation from the norm, but to what is merely an exemplification or embodiment of the common.[110]

The second Hegelian "mistake" inherited by Bosanquet is the confusion of law with right. The dialectical connection between these categories, still extant in Green's liberal theory, is absent in the works of Bosanquet, according to Hobhouse. Here law and right have been made equivalent. What are individuals allowed to do (that is, what do they have the right to do)? That which is permitted by law, and nothing more. One therefore cannot question legal regulations, arguing that they violate supra-legal rights (for example, those innate to the individual). This removes the grounds for any distinction between categories such as rightness, obligation, right, precept. The theories of Hegel and Bosanquet leave room only for precepts, whether social (coming from the sphere of the Hegelian *Sittlichkeit*[111]) or politico-legal (legislation). To act according to them is a virtue; to question their validity, an offence. My station and its duties embodies everything that is given and assigned to me as a citizen. It is also what citizenship is limited to.

This interpretation of the general will, as the source of moral precepts, leads to Bosanquet's already-mentioned equation of the state with society. Since both are governed by the same principles, the precepts emanating from the general will, then one cannot see social and

---

[109] *Ibid.*, p. 31.
[110] *Ibid.*, p. 32.
[111] *Ibid.*, p. 38.

political institutions as anything other than "external" manifestations of the same system of ideas constituting the social order. Hobhouse himself firmly rejected the claim of the identity of the state and society. According to supporters of the "democratic" theory of the state (among whom he counted himself), these two categories—state and society—even if they should not be directly opposed to each other, should certainly be distinguished. The state is only a tool in the hands of society. "The bony skeleton is necessary to the human body and in a sense holds it together, but it is hardly that which constitutes the life of the body, still less that which makes the life of the body desirable and possibly beautiful."[112]

Hobhouse leaned more towards Green's interpretation of the relationship between law and morality, or to put it another way, state and society. He was convinced that the primary task of state institutions was to embody, in legislation and political practice, principles that have gained social acceptance, inscribing themselves for good in the customs and moral beliefs of citizens.[113] In this approach, the state is merely a means to the achievement of ends defined by society and reflected in the commonly accepted system of values. Positing identity between means and ends, the state and society, Bosanquet committed an unpardonable, since clearly undemocratic, offence.

The other undesirable outcome of the "metaphysical" theory is the rejection of any universal standards of conduct. What is the state? A community held together by a common definition of reality, including similar fears and expectations in all of its members. What are law and the institutions of social and political life? Means serving to fulfil these expectations and provide protection against these fears. Where do these fears and expectations come from? From the historical experience of a given community, which takes the form of concrete ideas. The shape of social and political institutions is determined by tradition. And is there anything that differentiates nations one from another more than tradition? No, according to Bosanquet. This is why it is utterly abstract to talk of "human rights" or "natural rights" belonging to all members of the human race. The political version of this anthropological error of universalism rests on the postulate of guaranteeing legal protection to rights suggested by human nature. But it is impossible to establish universal legislation. In Hobhouse's view, this is the source of the great danger stemming from the application of the "metaphysical theory of the state" to political practice—the threat of militarism. Practically speaking, one can discern—in the criticism addressed by Hobhouse to

---

[112] *Ibid.*, p. 76.
[113] *Ibid.*, p. 86.

the author of *The Philosophical Theory of the State* — the restatement of arguments often used to combat Hegelianism. For on this point Bosanquet doubtless remained a faithful disciple of his German master, like him maintaining that war among nations is inevitable.

This does not mean that there are no differences between Hegel and Bosanquet. In the *Elements of the Philosophy of Right*, war is the principal means by which the general spirit develops, the victory of the nation representing a higher level of this development as the "*completion* of an act of comprehension is at the same time its alienation and transition. To put it in formal terms, the spirit which comprehends *anew* and which — and this amounts to the same thing — returns into itself from its alienation, is the spirit at a stage higher".[114] A fundamental role is therefore assigned to war. Without it, the general spirit could not perfect itself. In its historiosophical aspect, Bosanquet's political philosophy diverges significantly from Hegel's, hence the significance of conflict is fundamentally different in it. It no longer plays such a momentous role, and is merely the consequence of human weakness, specifically of the inability of communities to surpass the constraints imposed upon them by tradition. Military conflict no longer has a fundamental metaphysical meaning, being only an unfortunate side effect of human imperfection. Yet it cannot be avoided.

These were the main charges levelled by Hobhouse in his *Metaphysical Theory of the State*. Many other scholars, spurred on by its publication, made similar comments. The most important included Harold Joseph Laski, Alexander Dunlop Lindsay, Cyril Edwin Mitchinson Joad and Morris Ginsberg. Their arguments against Bosanquet's theories were frequently dissimilar, yet all of them were mere addenda to Hobhouse. It is probable that even without these additional voices, the political legacy of British idealism would have perished. This does not mean, however, that *The Metaphysical Theory of the State* provoked no opposition in intellectual circles. Although it was not the voice of Bosanquet himself, who never responded to Hobhouse's charges, the issue was taken up by other scholars, including idealists, such as Alfred Edward Taylor (1869-1945). In one of his articles,[115] while not uncritical of Bosanquet's theory, he mercilessly listed each of the mistakes of his adversary. Taylor claimed that Hobhouse had above all equated the real with the actual in a completely illegitimate way. It is true that from his nominalist point of view, any claims concerning the possibility of ascribing a higher degree of reality to certain abstract categories than to

---

[114] G.W.F. Hegel, *Elements of the Philosophy of Right*, p. 372 (§ 343).
[115] A.E. Taylor, *Critical Notice of Hobhouse's Metaphysical Theory of the State*, "Mind" 1920, Vol. 29, pp. 91–105.

human or objective existence must have seemed absurd. "But though any one is free to use the word 'real' in his own sense, if You choose to identify the Real with the actual, your identification makes nonsense of the writings not only of the philosophers who have spoken of an *ens realissimum* but of those of the poets who talk, for example, of 'Forms more real than living man'. We may say, no doubt, that Anselm or Shelley was talking mere nonsense, but at least they thought they meant something, and it might be worth while to try to find out what that something is."[116]

This is not the only error Taylor attributed to the author of *The Metaphysical Theory of the State*. Similar shortcomings can be found in Hobhouse's conception of individualism, defined by reference to an isolated individual.[117] In Hobhouse's opinion individuality, understood as independence from all influence, presupposes a person's ability to distance themselves from that which surrounds them. But this is nothing other than replicating the fundamental error of the "theories of the first look". In his criticism of Bosanquet, Hobhouse ought to have demonstrated that his understanding of freedom and individuality was erroneous, instead of axiomatically adopting an entirely different definition of these terms, to then attack the author of *The Philosophical Theory of the State* from precisely this position. This serious omission on the part of Hobhouse gave birth to successive mistakes in his argumentation. One cannot otherwise explain the transition he makes from the claim that the state has no purpose other than to ensure the welfare of individuals, to the thesis that individuals should be free to pursue goals they set for themselves. These statements are not connected by a relationship of implication.[118]

Although there were many more scholars arguing that Bosanquet's philosophy was fundamentally democratic (we should mention George Holland Sabine,[119] Charlie Dunbar Broad,[120] John Petrov Plamenatz,[121] Pfannenstill[122] as well as the last representative of British idealism fighting to defend its good name—Muirhead[123]), none of them attempted to defend his theory in a separate treatise. It is doubtless because of this

---

[116] *Ibid.*, p. 99.
[117] *Ibid.*, p. 100.
[118] *Ibid.*
[119] G.H. Sabine, *Bosanquet's Theory of the General Will*, "Philosophical Review" 1923, Vol. 32, pp. 639–649.
[120] C.D. Broad, *The Notion of General Will*, "Mind. New Series" 1919, Vol. 28, pp. 502–504.
[121] J.P. Plamenatz, *Consent, Freedom and Political Obligation*, Oxford 1968.
[122] B. Pfannenstill, *Bernard Bosanquet's Philosophy of the State*.
[123] J.H. Muirhead, *Recent Criticism of the Idealist Theory of the General Will*.

that subsequent generations of scholars became convinced that Hobhouse's work had gained the upper hand in the dispute over the metaphysical theory of the state. This belief in the anti-democratic and anti-liberal character of Bosanquet's political theories persisted for nearly eight decades. Also due to Hobhouse, it was assumed that a gulf separates Green, the democratic idealist, from Bosanquet, the absolutist idealist. The best proof this thesis was regarded as unproblematic is Herbert Marcuse's book *Reason and Revolution*,[124] long considered a correct, and critical, account of Bosanquet's Hegelianism. Marcuse writes that "[f]ar from being an apology for authoritarianism, Green's political philosophy can, in a certain sense, be designated as a super-liberalism."[125] Throughout his work, Green expresses the conviction that "the state should be submitted to rational standards, such as imply that the common good is best served through advancing the interest of free individuals."[126] However, none of these designations, in Marcuse's view, describe the thought of Bosanquet.

3.3.2. Continuation. John Henry Muirhead, Hector James Wright Hetherington, Leonard Trelawny Hobhouse, John Atkinson Hobson

Although many had stood up in its defence, the concept of the general will developed by Bradley, Green and Bosanquet did not have any noteworthy continuation within the idealist tradition. It is true that subsequent generations of idealists advanced socio-political conceptions that were close in content to those of their masters, recognising organicism and teleologism as essential components. And yet they rarely appealed to the concept of the general will. Or if they did, as for example Jones, writing at length of the minds of societies[127] and wills of nations[128] directed to the realisation of the common good,[129] or Ritchie, conceiving it as the foundation of all authority,[130] they did not devote much attention to it.

The last defenders of idealism to cultivate this concept were also the last faithful disciples of Bradley, Green and Bosanquet—Muirhead (1855–1940) and Hetherington (1888–1965). The first, although a sig-

---

[124] H. Marcuse, *Reason and Revolution. Hegel and the Rise of Social Theory*, London 1955.
[125] *Ibid.*, p. 392.
[126] *Ibid.*, p. 369.
[127] H. Jones, *The Working Faith of a Social Reformer and Other Essays*, London 1910, p. 98.
[128] *Ibid.*, p. 136.
[129] *Ibid.*, p. 247.
[130] D.G. Ritchie, *Darwin and Hegel. With Other Philosophical Studies*, London 1893, pp. 252–255, 259–260.

nificant part of his career was spent in Glasgow, where he first studied under Edward Caird and then held the post of a lecturer in ethics, not only had the opportunity to meet Green personally, but also to work with him for a short time while at Balliol College. His academic career then took him to Birmingham, Edinburgh and Berkeley. The author of a series of works on ethics (the foremost of which is *The Elements of Ethics*, once hailed as a breakthrough for idealist reflection on the issue of morality), he frequently joined forces with other scholars. He co-edited works with Jones[131] and Sarvepalli Radhakrishnan,[132] co-authoring one with Hetherington who, like Muirhead, also spent a great part of his career in Glasgow.

Hetherington was not as prolific a writer as Muirhead. His contribution to British learning lay more in the reform of academic institutions (his greatest services in this respect were to Royal Albert Memorial College which, thanks to his efforts, rose to the rank of the University of Exeter), rather than in the authorship of unforgettable works. His most important academic work was *The Social Purpose: A Contribution to a Philosophy of Civic Society*, co-penned with Muirhead. It is quite an unusual work, since it was written by two authors, one of whom (Hetherington) saw himself as a modifier of the other's ethical position. Nonetheless, this work presents a coherent picture, at least with respect to the general will. In it, we encounter the same situation as in the case of the three figureheads of British idealism, a link between a community's customs and its institutions and legislation: "customs and institutions [...] are not something foreign to the freedom of the will, but the organs through which it seeks to secure itself and make itself at home in the world of men and things",[133] "social institutions must be conceived of as standing for the more permanent ends of corporate life — ways in which the general will has 'set'."[134] The authors considered the latter to be nothing but "a universal element which acts as a unifying and controlling influence and constitutes [them the] habits",[135] bringing the actions of citizens into harmony and being conducive to their effective realisation of the *bonum publicum*. The attainment of a goal defined in this manner requires the constant improvement of social relations,

---

[131] *The Life and Philosophy of Edward Caird*, ed. J.H. Muirhead, H. Jones, Glasgow 1921.

[132] *Contemporary Indian Philosophy*, ed. J.H. Muirhead, S. Radhakrishnan, London 1936.

[133] H.J.W. Hetherington, J.H. Muirhead, *The Social Purpose. A Contribution to a Philosophy of Civic Society*, London 1918, p. 92.

[134] J.H. Muirhead, *The Elements of Ethics*, London 1912, p. 185.

[135] H.J.W. Hetherington, J.H. Muirhead, *The Social Purpose*, p. 84.

the gradual and planned enlightenment of community members as to the existence of a universal factor binding them into a social whole.

The general will as such can only attain its fullest embodiment when individuals come to identify their own good with the needs of the community as a whole.[136] Let us not, however — Muirhead and Hetherington warned — commit the error of reducing individual entities to the general entity — the state, the will of individuals to the general will; let us not stigmatise individualism in the name of social cohesion. We should remain conscious of the fact that in their political and social desiderata, citizens may express both non-egotistical interests and those transcending law and custom, thereby indicating the need for their reform.[137] Not only on this point did *The Social Purpose* resemble the works of the earlier idealists. Muirhead and Hetherington had a strikingly similar view of the general wills of communities, as determined exclusively on the local level and dependent on geopolitical conditions. They perceived the state as the "guardian and interpreter of the contributions of [individuals — J.G.] to this common purpose and endowed with the power necessary to secure their harmony and efficiency".[138]

Although Muirhead and Hetherington's book was the last idealist work to give serious consideration to the issue of the general will, it was not the last British work to concern itself with the subject. Surprisingly, it was the New Liberals — Hobhouse and Hobson — who turned out to be much more faithful disciples of Bradley, Green and Bosanquet than the idealists themselves. The first saw himself as a continuator of the thought of Green, the second spared no praise for Bosanquet.[139]

We have already discussed Hobhouse when examining his critique of *The Philosophical Theory of the State*. It is therefore fitting to devote at least a few sentences to Hobson. Born in Derby in 1858, a graduate of local schools and subsequently of Oxford University, he attached little weight to political and economic matters in his youth. In his later writings, he blamed this state of affairs on the laissez-faireist government of William Ewart Gladstone, who associated liberalism with educational reform, the extension of voting rights or the conduct of foreign affairs, but never with interference in the functioning of the market. It was not until he came to Oxford that Hobson had an epiphany; he himself cites the authority of Benjamin Jowett, Green and Mark Pattison (an

---

[136] *Ibid.*, p. 90.
[137] *Ibid.*, p. 91.
[138] *Ibid.*, p. 92; cf. *ibid.*, p. 283.
[139] J.A. Hobson, *The Social Problem. Life and Work*, London 1919, p. 274; J.A. Hobson, *The Crisis of Liberalism. New Issues of Democracy*, London 1909, pp. 76, 250.

Anglican minister and dean of Lincoln College, Oxford) as those who most shaped his socio-political views.[140] The sense of social injustice, heightened by liberal politics, was magnified during his stay in London, where he saw palpable evidence of the ravages caused by the free market economy.

Among the many convergences one can note between the lives of Hobson and Hobhouse, from our perspective, the most important is the fact that both referenced the concept of the general will, although not always calling it by this name. Hobson used the term interchangeably with "social will".[141] Hobhouse, on the other hand, a fierce opponent of Bosanquet, having distinguished the social from the general will, clearly preferred the former term, perceiving in the use of the latter the danger of having to admit the existence of a metaphysical state endowed with a will of its own, whose interest would stand above that of the individuals it was composed of.[142] In contrast to the general will —an attribute of an ontologically independent political entity—the social will is merely a collective term for the wills and minds of individuals bound together by acts of cooperation, and above all for the system of ideas constituting their effect.[143] "As there is a social thought, so there is a social will",[144] covering "all those modes of action that the existing constitution of society dictates, all the institutions that it maintains, all the customs that it prescribes".[145] This does not mean that there is a social mind, independent of the minds of members of society. The will is made social by the fact of its being based on current social relations. "[W]hen we speak of social thought, social will, or more generally of social mind, we [do not] imply a mystical psychic unity. [...] This term is simply an expression for the mass of ideas operative in a society, communicable from man to man, and serving to direct the thoughts and actions of individuals."[146] Such a mind manifests itself differently in different communities, imposing on each the existence of a plurality of institutions with their own proper ethea, and through these exerting its influence upon the individual. And since individuals participate in the life of many different institutions, the community

---

[140] J.A. Hobson, *Confessions of an Economic Heretic*, London 1938, p. 26.
[141] Which he described as the "spiritual unity of society", amongst other things (J.A. Hobson, *Work and Wealth. A Human Valuation*, New York 1926, p. VIII; cf. M. Freeden, *The New Liberalism. An Ideology of Social Reform*, Oxford 1978, p. 106; J.A. Hobson, *John Ruskin. Social Reformer*, Boston, MA 1898, p. 215).
[142] L.T. Hobhouse, *Social Evolution*, pp. 97, 196.
[143] M. Freeden, *The New Liberalism*, p. 106.
[144] L.T. Hobhouse, *Social Evolution*, p. 95–96.
[145] *Ibid.*, p. 96.
[146] *Ibid.*, pp. 96–97.

must also be composed of a plurality of minds or social wills,[147] and not single general will moulding all citizens into one.

> By the social mind, then, we mean not necessarily a unity pervading any given society as a whole, but a tissue of operative psychological forces [...], essentially of psychological character that arises from the operation of masses of men, and moulds and is in turn remoulded by the operation of masses of men; which has no existence except in the minds of men, and yet is never fully realised in the mind of any one man; which depends on the social relations between man and man, but takes full cognizance of the relation only in the higher stages of its development.[148]

The purpose of the social mind is to coordinate the actions of the members of a community, as well as of the community itself, taken as a whole in relation to other communities. The better developed the mind,[149] the greater its width and scope, thus, on the one hand, the further it reaches into the future and the past, attaining a profounder knowledge of the determinants of social change, and on the other, the greater its "clearness, articulateness, connectedness of perception and of thought",[150] the better this coordination. This mind, however — as Hobhouse repeatedly stressed — does not exist outside of individual minds. Its existence is conditional upon their consciousness of the bonds binding them together into a community.[151]

Hobhouse radicalised his position — which in spite of his persistent attempts still evoked the works of Bosanquet, which he so scorned — in *Development and Purpose*, finding the social mind and will to be more than merely the set of opinions and ideas of citizens.[152] Here, he defined "social mind" as "the Order formed by the operation of mind on mind, incorporated in a social tradition handed on by language and by social institutions of many kinds, and shaping the ideas and the practice of each new generation that grows up under its shadow".[153] The development of such an order is teleological. It evolves towards the ideal of social harmony, not so much in the minds of distinct individuals, as in communities developing over the course of generations.[154] Hobhouse

---

[147] *Ibid.*, p. 97.
[148] *Ibid.*, pp. 97–98.
[149] *Ibid.*, p. 98.
[150] *Ibid.*
[151] *Ibid.*, p. 99.
[152] See M. Freeden, *The New Liberalism*, p. 106.
[153] L.T. Hobhouse, *Development and Purpose. An Essay Towards a Philosophy of Evolution*, London 1913, p. 12; cf. *ibid.*, pp. 79, 84–86.
[154] *Ibid.*, p. 13.

understood this development as being fundamentally independent of the will of individuals.[155]

The same harmony, which Hobhouse perceived as an attainable goal in the perfecting of citizens and of the social mind, Hobson saw as embodied in every social structure.[156] On the other hand, where Hobhouse saw a community, Hobson merely discerned its germ. "[I]f our organic conception of society has any validity, the social will means more than this addition of separately stimulated individual wills."[157] The general/social will, in Hobson's view, is not a set of individual opinions on the purpose of social existence and the consensus taking the form of the ideas operative in society born thereof, but a spirit permeating the social and political body,[158] embodied — at least in a democratic state — in its "most definite and concrete instruments of social government, the political and administrative machinery of the state";[159] "in popularly-governed states [the general will] functions through public opinion and representative institutions."[160]

Hobson was much less sceptical than Hobhouse on the subject of the social mind and will. "[I]f the habits of thinking, feeling, and acting together among members of a nation thus bring their minds into a single mind which is dominated by thoughts and feelings directed to the ends of the whole of body politic, then we have the clear admission of a social organism on the psychical or moral side. This is the doctrine of the general will",[161] to which Hobson remained faithful. In accordance with it, the will of a community — not the musings and good intentions of reformers — is the ultimate foundation for all its transformations.[162] The general will is relatively autonomous from individual beliefs and designs.

These are not the sole similarities to be noted between the views of Hobson and those of the idealists (especially Bosanquet). His writings frequently give evidence of his sympathy for the concept of "my station and its duties". Praising civil virtue, he described it in terms of individ-

---

[155] *Ibid.*, p. 284.
[156] J.A. Hobson, *The Social Problem*, p. 72.
[157] J.A. Hobson, *Work and Wealth*, p. 302.
[158] J.A. Hobson, *The Social Problem*, pp. 144–145; J.A. Hobson, *Work and Wealth*, pp. 331–332, 337–340, 352; J.A. Hobson, *The Crisis of Liberalism*, pp. 77, 207, 217.
[159] J.A. Hobson, *John Ruskin. Social Reformer*, p. 220.
[160] J.A. Hobson, *Work and Wealth*, p. 351; cf. J.A. Hobson, *The Crisis of Liberalism*, p. 67.
[161] J.A. Hobson, *The Crisis of Liberalism*, p. 76.
[162] M. Freeden, *The New Liberalism*, p. 107; J.A. Hobson, *The Crisis of Liberalism*, p. 76.

ual sacrifice in the fulfilment of functions appertaining to a social infrastructure. "Social efficiency, for progress, really means the desire of individuals to merge or subordinate their separate ends of individuality. [...] Or adopting another formula which has its uses, it implies a conformity to the 'general will'."[163]

However, Hobson was somewhat more effusive than the idealists when sketching a picture of a reality governed by the precepts of the general will. Articulating his thoughts on the subject in one of his articles,[164] he portrayed an elitist and technocratic system of power, a community organised by experts, deriving information about the functioning of society from the citizens, in order to prepare solutions to remedy the inconveniences of social life.

As we can see, the concept of the general will had few twentieth-century idealist continuations. It did appear more than once on the pages of Ritchie's works or in Muirhead and Hetherington's *Social Purpose*. But it was never again to exhibit the intellectual freshness sensed so clearly in the works of Green and Bosanquet. Is this fact to be blamed on the then already apparent weakness of the concept, or the discouragement caused by Hobhouse's attack? Certainly not. Both Hobhouse himself and his doctrinal kin—the New Liberals—frequently employed Green's, and in the case of Hobson also Bosanquet's, notion of the general will. If we are to seek reasons for the low vitality of this idea, it is not in its weaknesses, but rather in the redundant character of the socio-political considerations of subsequent generations of idealists, none of whom set themselves the purpose of re-evaluating the thought of their masters. It is thus no surprise that in addressing the subject, they restated the theoretical pronouncements of Bradley, Green and Bosanquet, working within the same conceptual framework and usually adopting the same conclusions.

---

[163] J.A. Hobson, *The Social Problem*, p. 72.
[164] J.A. Hobson, *The Re-Statement of Democracy*, "Contemporary Review" 1902, No. 81, pp. 262–272.

Chapter Four

Idealism, the General Will and the Liberal-Communitarian Debate

Since we have already examined the charges brought by the idealists against the Rousseauian *volonté générale* and discussed their own modification of this category, considering it within the wider context of idealist political reflection, we can move on to the last of the issues under consideration. Let us therefore examine whether it is justified to view idealist thought, especially in its reformulation of Jean-Jacques Rousseau's key category, as capable of reconciling two feuding philosophico-political traditions: individualist and communitarian. To accomplish this, we must first identify exponents of a position conciliatory with respect to these traditions, extract the most important elements of idealist political philosophy, and finally verify whether it exhibits both individualist and communitarian traits.

4.1 Liberal communitarianism

Contemporary philosophico-political debate has become dominated by criticism of both the theoretical and practical implications of liberal theory. Communitarian, and to a lesser extent republican, charges have exposed a number of inconsistencies in the concepts of Rawls, Nozick and Ronald Dworkin. The front line of this conflict seems to extend between two camps of varying theoretical coherence. One one side, there are the communitarians and republicans (presenting a relatively coherent set of critical analyses of liberalism, based on postulates of the defence of communal traditions against the uniformising influence of liberal theory), although there is also ample room for socialists and post-Marxists (Ch. Mouffe), feminists (C. MacKinnon, M. Friedman, S.M. Okin) and postmodern liberals (J. Gray) in this camp. As adversaries, they have chosen the liberal supporters of the post-Enlightenment rationalism of Rawls, with the author of *A Theory of*

Justice in the lead, disciples of procedural liberalism such as Bruce Ackerman, and defendants of liberal law theory such as Ronald Dworkin. And although the charges brought by these opponents of procedural and deontological liberalism have often touched upon other matters, the most important, as cited in the relevant literature, have been those against the abstractness of Rawls' view of subjects as the discoverers of supposedly universal principles of justice. An excellent example of this type of critique is Sandel's *Liberalism and the Limits of Justice*. Its main claims have subsequently been repeated by other communitarians: Taylor, in the form of his "social thesis", MacIntyre in his criticism of the emotivist theory of personality, Walzer in his insistence on the cultural character of goods. Patrick Neil and David Paris have summed up this critique thus: "[l]iberal political theory, it is claimed, is excessively individualistic and insufficiently historicist. [...] [T]he liberal claim that society should be neutral regarding conceptions of the good is said to misunderstand the idea of community and the fact that liberal societies inevitably promote certain kinds of virtue and ignore others."[1] Republican accusations take a similar form, although they tend to focus on the practical implications of *A Theory of Justice*, in particular the dangers to the public sphere posed by its concept of subjectivity.

Some scholars, however, remark that the participants in this debate between the communitarian and liberal perception of citizenship tend to oversimplify liberal thought.[2] They claim that liberal and communitarian or republican concepts of the individual, liberty and law are not in fact separated by a chasm. Indeed, those who claim that the differences are irreconcilable are only demonstrating their own ignorance. This has been underlined by Thomas Spragens,[3] for example, according to whom treating atomistic individualism as a fundamental part of liberal theory, as the communitarians do, is a complete misunderstanding. It is true, Spragens says, that the conceptions of today's freethinkers, both libertarians and egalitarians, are founded on an individualistic methodology, recognising the primacy of rights over the good, exaggerating the worth of individuals and failing to appreciate the role communities play in the lives of their members.[4] But this has not

---

[1] P. Neil, D. Paris, *Liberalism and the Communitarian Critique: A Guide for the Perplexed*, "Canadian Journal of Political Science" 1990, Vol. 23, No. 3, p. 419.
[2] See J.T. Kloppenberg, *The Virtues of Liberalism*, Oxford 1998, p. 125.
[3] T.A. Spragens, Jr., *Communitarian Liberalism*, in: *New Communitarian Thinking: Persons, Institutions, and Communities*, ed. A. Etzioni, Charlottesville, VA 1995, pp. 37–51.
[4] *Ibid.*, p. 44.

always been so. From the seventeenth to the middle of the nineteenth century, liberalism had an entirely different outlook, as is clear from the writings of Locke, Antoine Nicolas Condorcet and Mill. The first considered the common good of citizens to be the fundamental purpose of the state, with education tasked with promoting virtues, appealing frequently in his reflections to the notion of natural law and never pronouncing himself in favour of absolute freedom. Condorcet and Mill, on the other hand, shared the belief that liberal society ought to contribute to the moral development of citizens and emphasised the need for social solidarity, as well as the importance of the community for the self-improvement of individuals.[5] It is an all too frequent mistake to compare these thinkers to Herbert Spencer, for whom any activity of the state was a threat to the freedom of its citizens. Locke, Condorcet and Mill did not examine the individual apart from the community or individual rights apart from obligations; they did not view relations between citizens and the state as fundamentally antagonistic, but as mutually beneficial. From this perspective, modern communitarianism does not seem to target — as some of its exponents might like to think — liberal thought *in toto*, but only its twentieth-century variety, hardly representative of the whole.[6] Were they still alive today, Locke, Condorcet and Mill would doubtless join in the critique.

A similar tone is heard in Taylor's essay, *Cross-Purposes: the Liberal-Communitarian Debate*, in which he defends the already mentioned claim that preferences cannot be directly derived from ontological positions. The choice between a pro-communal or pro-individualist standpoint is not inevitably dependent on the prior acceptance of atomism or methodological holism. This thesis is proven, Taylor argues, by the broad spectrum of positions found throughout the history of political philosophy, which have combined these two distinctions in all possible ways. For we know of: a) atomist individualists (Nozick), b) holistic collectivists (Karl Marx), c) holistic individualists (von Humboldt) and d) atomist collectivists (B.F. Skinner).[7] The contemporary liberal-communitarian debate completely ignores the last two positions, thereby enforcing the increasingly prevalent view that one can only choose between either a) or b). In a similar vein, Will Kymlicka in his book, *Liberalism, Community and Culture*,[8] points to the inappropriateness of drawing sharp distinctions between the liberal and communit-

---

[5] *Ibid.*, pp. 40–42.
[6] *Ibid.*, p. 47.
[7] Ch. Taylor, *Cross-Purposes: The Liberal-Communitarian Debate*, in: *Debates in Contemporary Political Philosophy. An Anthology*, ed. D. Matravers, J. Pike, London–New York 2003, p. 196.
[8] W. Kymlicka, *Liberalism, Community and Culture*, Oxford 1989.

arian traditions. He is mainly critical of Taylor, who holds that the "social thesis" can only support the communitarian politics of the common good, and not the liberal, deontological politics of normative neutrality.[9] According to Kymlicka, a social ontology does not have to stand in opposition to the neutrality of the state on questions pertaining to the good. The communitarian vision of a specific *common good*, determined by the tradition of a given community, is readily compatible with the liberal vision of community, "since its policies aim at promoting the interests of the members of the community".[10] Liberalism is therefore not at cross-purposes with ethical perfectionism, this being the main charge made by the republicans. The republican conception of the virtues (and also MacIntyre's), in which the worth of individuals resides in their effective contribution to the well-being of the community or in the realisation of their moral potential, can be combined with the liberal vision of community in several ways. Kymlicka distinguishes four such positions: a) deontological anti-perfectionism (Rawls), b) teleological anti-perfectionism (utilitarian liberals), c) deontological perfectionism (Marx) and d) teleological perfectionism.[11] The last of these most strongly disproves contemporary claims regarding the inevitable contradiction between liberalism, communitarianism and republicanism. And although Kymlicka does not list their representatives, in his earlier publications he frequently cites the names of Hobhouse, Green and John Dewey (referring to them — it is worth noting — as precursors of today's liberal communitarianism), in whose writings liberalism is merged with perfectionism and teleologism.

Taylor and Kymlicka are echoed by Stephen Macedo, Stephen Holmes and William Galston. The first, in his work *Liberal Virtues*, argues that liberal political theory can avoid the shortcomings it is accused of by its communitarian critics because it includes more than an instrumental notion of reason or a sceptical, relative view of life, and should therefore not be identified with atomism or the community as superficially understood.[12] The second is alarmed by the amnesia prevalent among today's liberals.[13] He is not surprised that communitarians have, in the search for their own identity, opposed their conceptions to the

---

[9] Ch. Taylor, *Atomism*, in: idem, *Philosophy and the Human Sciences*, Cambridge 1985, p. 188.

[10] W. Kymlicka, *Liberalism, Community and Culture*, p. 76.

[11] D. Weinstein, *The New Liberalism and The Rejection of Utilitarianism*, in: *The New Liberalism. Reconciling Liberty and Community*, eds. A. Simhony, D. Weinstein, Cambridge 2001, p. 181.

[12] S. Macedo, *Liberal Virtues*, Oxford 1990.

[13] S. Holmes, *The Permanent Structure of Antiliberal Thought*, in: *Liberalism and the Moral Life*, ed. N. Rosenblum, Cambridge, MA 1989.

deontological liberalism of Rawls, recognising him as the *pros hen* of contemporary liberal thought and depicting his philosophy as ridden with contradictions. Holmes displays less acceptance for the theses of the "early" Rawls, Ronald Dworkin and Nozick, who defend as exclusively liberal a position which cannot be equated with liberal thought. Not every liberalism must be based on the acceptance of the primacy of rights over the good, be hostile to teleological conceptions, the common good or positive liberty. Contemporary thinkers have a tendency to treat the liberal tradition ahistorically, ignoring the fact that it contains a wealth of possible interpretations of its key concepts such as liberty, individualism and community. And since both sides of the liberal-communitarian debate have replicated and reinforced precisely this distorted view of liberalism, it is hardly surprising that they have also failed to see the beliefs these positions potentially have in common.

The last of the scholars listed, Galston, in his work entitled *Liberal Purposes*, argues that there has never been such a thing as a purely procedural liberalism, actually seeking to establish the ideological neutrality communitarians denounce as destructive to communities, and conservatives hold to be merely apparent.[14] Liberalism is a doctrine based on a view of the good which places limits on the tolerance so often exaggerated by its opponents. It is therefore untrue that liberal thought excludes perfectionism. On the contrary, each of its forms presupposes a set of virtues which need to be practised by citizens. "Liberalism is committed to freedom, but it needs excellence. It is committed to freedom, but it needs virtue."[15] Among scholars to have made similar claims, Galston lists Judith Nisse Shklar, positing tolerance as one of the liberal virtues, Roger Smith and Nathan Tarcov, Jan Budziszewski, Harvey Mansfield, James Quinn Wilson and Spragens.[16]

The most radical opinions on the misrepresentation of the image of liberalism are voiced by Charles McCann who, in *Liberalism and the Social Order*, maintains that even thinkers generally regarded as "the most individualistic" of liberal individualists, i.e. Spencer, von Mises and Hayek, never embraced the views accredited to them by today's communitarians and conservatives, while their thought contains many of the essential features of the communitarian view of social reality.[17]

All of the above mentioned scholars point to the fact that liberal doctrine was not born in the nineteenth century, while the currently wide-

---

[14] W.A. Galston, *Liberal Purposes. Goods, Virtues, and Diversity in the Liberal State*, Cambridge 1991, p. 8.
[15] *Ibid.*, p. 11.
[16] *Ibid.*, pp. 215–216.
[17] Ch.R. McCann, Jr., *Individualism and the Social Order. The Social Element in Liberal Thought*, London–New York 2004, p. 215.

spread view that it has not undergone any significant changes in the course of its history is merely proof of ignorance or ill will on the part of those espousing it. The span of liberal theories is not limited to the narrow horizons of anti-teleologism and anti-perfectionism, characteristic of today's deontological liberalism. The author of *Sources of the Self* is not the only commentator to examine both earlier versions of the liberal-communitarian debate and the philosophical positions running counter to those of the two warring camps. Other scholars also list liberals from past eras, now either forgotten or misinterpreted, who combined the individualist and liberal perspective with the communitarian approach. Mill, for example, sometimes referred to as a communitarian liberal, is often cited in this context. He was classified as such by Alan Ryan,[18] who saw certain elements of Mill's world view, such as perfectionism and the consequentialist recognition of the primacy of the good over rightness, as placing him far from contemporary liberal thought (especially if we take the "early" Rawls to be its exemplary figurehead).[19] It is of course evident that Mill cannot be considered a proto-communitarian, since he believed that we are socially determined only to a small degree, treating the community as purely instrumental, a tool for improving citizens and making them happy. And so he did not attribute to it the key role that later communitarian thinkers did.

The characteristics qualifying Mill as one of the protoplasts of today's liberal communitarianism can also be found in other thinkers. After all, Mill had his continuators in the British liberal tradition, including — as Michael Freeden[20] and David Weinstein[21] tell us — representatives of what is termed New Liberalism. In the relevant literature this term is usually understood in two ways: narrowly and broadly. In the first case, it refers to the ideological reforms carried out within the British Liberal Party at the beginning of the twentieth century, as well as changes in the policy of the governments that originated from it. According to this definition, we should look for the beginnings of New Liberalism in the undertakings of the first government of William Ewart Gladstone (1868-1874), especially in its commitment to educational reform and the regulation of land ownership in Ireland (the Irish Land Act of 1870). This interventionist and social policy was continued

---

[18] A. Ryan, *Mill in a Liberal Landscape*, in: *The Cambridge Companion to Mill*, ed. J. Skorupski, Cambridge 1998, p. 530.
[19] *Ibid.*, pp. 528–529.
[20] M. Freeden, *The New Liberalism. An Ideology of Social Reform*, Oxford 1978, pp. 23–24.
[21] D. Weinstein, *The New Liberalism and the Rejection of Utilitarianism*, pp. 165–168.

by the next, second Conservative government of Benjamin Disraeli (1874–1880), which passed health and housing improvement laws, and was favourable to labour unions. But it was not until the governments of Herbert Henry Asquith (1908–1916) and Henry Campbell-Bannerman (1905–1908), considered model examples of New Liberal practice, that the greatest social reform of the period was carried out in British legislation. This included a number of acts, such as the *Provision of School Meals Act* (1906), the *Children and Young Persons Act* (1908), the 1909 budget (called the *People's Budget*), the *Trade Boards Act* (1909) and the *National Insurance Act* (1911).

Meanwhile the term New Liberalism, in its broad sense, denotes a certain tendency within British liberal thought — opposed to the utilitarian and atomist tradition on the one hand, and what is known as the Manchester school of liberalism, on the other. Thinkers and activists subscribing to the New Liberal paradigm shared the belief that the state must intervene in the economy, so that the poorest are not left to fend for themselves. Their writings are permeated by the language of the common good, criticism of the particularism of various social groups, the idea of cooperation for the welfare of the whole society. It was their fundamental belief that each community was like a spiritual bond holding individuals together and constituting a fundamental component of their identity. Based on these two premises, the New Liberals concluded that individuals can only find happiness in the harmony of peaceful coexistence and by working towards the prosperity of society. This prosperity was not understood in strictly material terms. The purpose of a community was not the financial comfort of its members, but the improvement of their moral condition. Journalists, economists, philosophers and liberal theorists such as Hobhouse, Hobson, Ritchie, Charles Prestwich Scott, Charles Masterman or William Clarke are considered to be representatives of New Liberalism taken in this sense. Although the movement had its origins in Great Britain, its adherents could also be found beyond Britain's borders. Dewey, Guido De Ruggiero, Albert Lange, Karl Vorländer and Max Weber are only the most prominent of these.[22] Frequently, as a result of extending the definition of New Liberalism, some thinkers of the mid and late nineteenth century are also regarded as New Liberals. These usually include Mill, Green or even Bosanquet, who however, due to his negative

---

[22] A. Vincent, *Liberalism and Citizenship*, in: *The Edinburgh Companion to Contemporary Liberalism*, ed. M. Evans, Edinburgh 2001, pp. 54–55, 57; A. Vincent, *The New Liberalism and Citizenship*, in: *The New Liberalism. Reconciling*, p. 206.

attitude towards state interventionism, is often put at a significant distance from the social-liberal tradition.

New Liberal thinkers are sometimes described as the forerunners of contemporary liberal communitarianism. But if we are to avoid the error of anachronism, we can only speak of liberal communitarianism *par excellence* in reference to contemporary thinkers. The position is chiefly ascribed to some thinkers representing both sides of the liberal-communitarian debate. On the liberal side, such a conciliatory, liberal-individualist-communitarian tone is discerned by some in the work of the "late" Rawls. The author of *Political Liberalism* could be viewed as communitarian in his belief in the irreducible complexity of social and political reality, with various communities preferring different conceptions of the good, as well as his doubts as to whether it is possible or worthwhile to formulate a universal ethical theory. A similar attitude towards community characterises the writings of such liberal thinkers as Allen Buchanan,[23] Gerald Dworkin,[24] Joel Feinberg[25] and Amy Gutmann.[26]

In the communitarian camp, liberal leanings are often ascribed to Michael Walzer, Taylor and Amitai Etzioni. Why these thinkers in particular? Above all, due to their acceptance of democratic liberalism as the proper platform for the communalisation of politics. They are not primarily interested in denouncing the philosophical and ideological gains of modernity, which would be tantamount to negating modern forms of self-government (as MacIntyre does), but rather in formulating a critique of those figures of liberal thought that could be blamed for the perversion of the fundamental ideas of the modern era through naturalism, egotistical individualism, instrumental rationalism and relativism. Like the "late" Rawls, they believe that the concept of the good is dependent on cultural context and accept liberalism as a platform for cooperation between individuals. They only want to go as far as the "communitarian amendment" of liberalism. According to Walzer "no communitarian critique, however penetrating, will ever be anything more than an inconstant feature of liberalism",[27] "[l]iberalism is a self-subverting doctrine; for that reason, it really does require periodic

---

[23] A.E. Buchanan, *Assessing The Communitarian*, "Ethics" 1989, Vol. 99, pp. 852–882.

[24] G. Dworkin, *The Theory and Practice of Autonomy*, Cambridge 2008, pp. 3–48.

[25] J. Feinberg, *Liberalism, Community and Tradition*, "Tikkun" 1987, Vol. 3, pp. 38–41.

[26] A. Gutmann, *Communitarian Critiques of Liberalism*, "Philosophy and Public Affairs" 1985, Vol. 14, pp. 308–322.

[27] M. Walzer, *The Communitarian Critique of Liberalism*, "Political Theory" 1990, Vol. 18, No. 1, p. 6.

communitarian correction."[28] Walzer's opposition to the liberal "language of rights" and ethico-political universalism which depreciates local solutions on these levels, his social particularism, are merely proof of his "soft anti-liberalism" and leave ample room in his writings for praise of the modern social-liberal state. Walzer is not put off by liberal society as such, with its alleged atrophy of the key values crucial to participation in communities, but rather by the universalist manner of its defence and legitimation, violating the factual plurality of lifestyles and conceptions of the good and of justice. He therefore turns out to be a liberal-communitarian perspectivist, or even relativist, but not an anti-liberal communitarian. Taylor, also, is not out to undermine the theoretical foundations of liberal society, but proposes their reform. Contemporary neo-Kantian, procedural approaches to liberalism should be replaced with a *quasi*-Hegelian anti-universalism, implying institutional decentralisation. We should not strive to create a cultural monolith in place of the mosaic of contemporary societies. Instead, we should decentralise them, leaving their constituent parts considerable freedom regarding their goals. We should mould the liberal state into an agora where different views of the good and of justice can be debated. Let us come together in a multicultural society without replicating the illusory visions of a liberal, uniform universalism.

Such projects of an anti-universalist correction of liberalism, born in the aftermath of the communitarian offensive, have gained a wide group of supporters. This was not only due to the communitarians themselves, or to their doctrinal kin, the republicans. Strikingly enough, their central theses overlapped with those of their intellectual adversaries, the postmodernists. What these two groups shared was their opposition to the post-Enlightenment, uniformising aspirations of modern liberal theory. The representatives of both saw in them a danger to the freedom of self-determination and development. It is impossible, however, to view them as a single anti-liberal front. Because what the communitarians demanded was freedom for communities and cultural traditions, while the postmodernists were in favour of voluntarism and individualism, opposing the allegedly universal (e.g. Rawlsian principles of justice) and objective (e.g. community-sanctioned rules of conduct) origin of moral laws and viewing them as oppressive. Although united by a certain type of anti-universalism, each group criticised universalism from a different perspective: the communitarians from the objective and the postmodernists from the subjective. In spite of the apparent impossibility of merging the two approaches, the relevant literature provides examples of thinkers who are sometimes designated

---

[28] *Ibid.*, p. 15.

both as postmodern and communitarian liberals. This is mostly the case with proponents of pluralism, with Gray and Joseph Raz in the lead. Both were disciples of Berlin, whose antagonism to monistic philosophies, attempting to formulate a single theory capturing all manifestations of reality (especially if these had political implications) led to his positive appraisal of cultural diversity, both political and ethical. Like his master, Gray maintains that liberalism should defend this plurality of world views rather than seek to impose the yoke of an ethico-political uniformity. The author of *Two Faces of Liberalism* proposes his own brand of *modus vivendi* liberalism (claiming to draw on the ideas of Hobbes[29]) — a liberalism not of unity but of ideological difference, in which institutions growing out of the liberal tradition serve as a platform for debating values without imposing specific solutions. What is communitarian about this is the belief in the profound complexity of social phenomena, making it impossible to subsume all values under a single ethico-political theory or to formulate a coherent theory providing a solution to all questions of a moral nature.

Is it possible to extract any characteristic features from the above examples of the liberal-communitarian position? This is certainly doubtful. Since we lack an unequivocal definition, both of communitarianism and liberalism, it is hard to expect the conciliatory position to have one. Yet a number of factors provide grounds for optimism, as far as the presentation of such a *differentia specifica* is concerned. Firstly, it is a fact that liberal communitarians, both in their critique and in the resulting modification of liberal theory, focus only on one of its forms. Their conceptions are united in the acceptance of liberal society as the basis for resolving ethical disputes. As David Miller argues, this entails the recognition of "the importance of autonomous choice: whichever way of life a person follows, it is important that he or she should have chosen to follow it after reflection on alternatives, rather than simply having been inducted into it, through a Jesuitical upbringing, for instance".[30] Secondly, there is the opposition to abstract universalism, the latter today most vividly epitomised by the writings of the "early" Rawls, as well as by Kant's ethical conceptions at the juncture of the eighteenth and nineteenth centuries. In its place appears the communitarian belief that "both the availability of a spectrum of ways of life and the capacity for autonomy depend upon a communal background."[31] Finally, representatives of the "third way" between the conflicted trad-

---

[29] J. Gray, *Two Faces of Liberalism*, New York 2000, pp. 5–20.
[30] D. Miller, *Communitarianism: Left, Right and Centre*, in: *Liberalism and Its Practice*, ed. D. Avnon, A. de-Shalit, London–New York 2005, p. 142.
[31] *Ibid.*

itions of communitarianism and liberal-individualism take notice of the inescapable cultural diversity of modern Western societies. They believe that different communities, with different ethical and political traditions, should be governed according to those and not by precepts derived from abstract philosophical theories. In this respect, liberal communitarians place an emphasis on specific common goods, which different communities envision in ways proper to themselves, thereby depreciating the politics of uniform legislation. "The key idea in the liberal communitarian vision of things", writes Miller, "is that a political society should be made up of a plurality of communities which ought as far as possible to have the character of voluntary associations."[32] To these three essential characteristics of liberal communitarianism we may optionally add one more: ethical perfectionism, which nonetheless runs counter to the anti-essentialism and subjectivism of certain varieties of liberal communitarianism, especially those associated with postmodernism. In the next section, we will try to determine whether these characteristics of liberal communitarianism can be ascribed to British idealism, and thus whether scholars are correct in viewing its proponents as the forerunners of the "late" Rawls, Taylor, Walzer and Gray.

4.2. Is idealism liberal-communitarian?

The recent renewal of interest in British idealist thought has not been limited to a discussion of its features or to reprinting the works of its major exponents. Some of the new approaches to idealism have emphasised its strikingly novel character, not in the context of problems prevailing at the end of the nineteenth and the beginning of the twentieth century, but also in relation to later philosophical and political debates. Next to a discussion of idealism's part in the doctrinal shift that took place within the liberal tradition at the beginning of the twentieth century, i.e. the transition from Manchester liberalism to New Liberalism, the most important theoretical issue we face appears to be the idealist position on the relationship between the individual and the community, as well as the manner in which this feeds into the liberal-communitarian debate. In this section, we shall present the current state of research on this problem, analysing the work of scholars who have, first and foremost, emphasised the liberal-communitarian character of idealist thought. We shall examine works by Gerald Gaus,[33] Rex

---

[32] Ibid.
[33] G. Gaus, *Bosanquet's Communitarian Defence of Economic Individualism*, in: *The New Liberalism. Reconciling*, pp. 137–158.

Martin,[34] Avital Simhony,[35] William Sweet[36] and Weinstein,[37] all of whom agree that by the beginning of the twentieth century, thinkers associated with the British idealist movement had put forward the same charges against liberalism as the communitarians did over half a century later. In doing so, they were not rejecting liberalism as such, but merely one of its forms, impossible to reconcile with the primacy of the community over the individual, of ethico-political contextualism over universalism and of concrete goods over abstract rightness. Unlike the communitarians, they did not abstain from formulating their own theory of law, consciously combining the "language of rights" with the "language of the common good". Rather than viewing rights and communities as in conflict (a view proper to the communitarian perspective and especially present in the writings of Sandel), idealists sought to reconcile both sides of the debate, thereby producing a "liberal, albeit non-individualist, theory of rights".[38]

It is to Green (Martin, Simhony and Weinstein) and Bosanquet (Gaus, Sweet) that we owe the idealist theory of rights. Most of the scholars who assign a key role to the author of *The Philosophical Theory of the State* in this respect cite his opposition to the universalist implications of liberal juridical conceptions, in particular the abstractionism of human rights or the various attempts to codify international relations. Sweet, the greatest contemporary populariser of Bosanquet, considers the originality of his theory of rights to lie in his conception of their sources and nature. All rights, Bosanquet claims, depend on social recognition, and remain inextricably bound with the common good of the people, as well as their *telos*, moral perfection.[39]

Bosanquet's liberal communitarianism is also diagnosed by Gaus, who emphasises the role played within the doctrinal development of New Liberalism by the fusion of organicist metaphysics and economic

---

[34] R. Martin, *T.H. Green on Individual Rights and the Common Good*, in: *The New Liberalism. Reconciling*, pp. 49–68.

[35] A. Simhony, *Rights that Bind: T.H. Green on Rights and Community*, in: *T.H. Green. Ethics, Metaphysics Metaphysics and Political Philosophy*, eds. M. Dimova-Cookson, W.J. Mander, Oxford 2006, pp. 236–261; A. Simhony, *T.H. Green's Complex Common Good: Between Liberalism and Communitarianism*, in: *The New Liberalism. Reconciling*, pp. 69–91.

[36] W. Sweet, *Individual Rights, Communitarianism and British Idealism*, in: *The Bill of Rights. Bicentennial Reflections*, eds. Y. Hudson, C. Peden, New York 1993, pp. 261–277.

[37] D. Weinstein, *The New Liberalism and the Rejection of Utilitarianism*, pp. 159–183; A. Simhony, D. Weinstein, *Introduction*, in: *The New Liberalism. Reconciling*.

[38] W. Sweet, *Individual Rights, Communitarianism and British Idealism*, p. 261.

[39] *Ibid.*, pp. 263–268.

individualism effected in *The Philosophical Theory of the State*.[40] Society and its well-being are recognised here as a *conditio sine qua non* of individual perfection. The freedom to control one's fate and possessions is, surprisingly, not opposed to the pursuit of the moral *telos*, but in fact advances it. Yet freedom of action should never be absolute. Bosanquet oscillated between liberalism and communitarianism, just as he did between liberal and socialist thought. On the one hand, withholding the possibility of deciding about themselves from individuals deprives them of the chance to learn to act responsibly, which is an indispensable part of moral development. On the other hand, allowing unlimited freedom would deepen the social gulf between rich and poor, making it impossible for the latter to improve themselves. The common good is thus at odds both with socialist interventionism and liberal laissez-faireism, and at the same time requires the promotion of individualism *and* sensitivity to the needs of other citizens as well as those of the community as a whole.

Simhony makes the same claims with respect to the thought of Green. She examines his writings within the broader context of contemporary philosophical, political and legal distinctions, portraying Green as the thinker who "shifted the idea of community (and the common good) to the conceptual heart of liberalism",[41] and thereby disproving advocates of the confrontational view of rights and communities. The latter maintain that the idea of rights presupposes an atomistic and egotistical view of individuals, that liberal doctrine presumes the existence of an insurmountable antagonism between individuals and communities, and that the liberal theory of rights only accounts for negative rights, while these only exacerbate the perception by individuals that their rights are curbed by their fellow citizens. According to the proponents of this view of liberalism, the difference between the liberal and communitarian perspective mirrors that between the "politics of rights" and the "politics of the common good".[42] The first must lead to the alienation of individuals from the community, thereby sanctioning and reinforcing social antagonisms, and also preventing the birth of any sentiment for the community. It is only the second type of politics that permanently grounds individuals in the life of the community, guaranteeing them a stable moral reference point and protecting against subjectivism and relativism. This gloomy diagnosis of the liberal perception of rights does not emanate solely from the writings of

---

[40] G. Gaus, *Bosanquet's Communitarian Defence of Economic Individualism*, p. 137.
[41] A. Simhony, *Rights that Bind*, p. 237.
[42] M.J. Sandel, *Introduction*, in: *Liberalism and its Critics*, ed. M. Sandel, New York 1984, p. 6.

anti-liberals. Liberals themselves have often maintained that the need for law emerges only once social ties have been corroded, the will to fight for the common good has weakened and the unity of the social organism has irrevocably been lost. Simhony attributes this view to Ronald Dworkin and Richard Flathman. At the same time, she notes that the camp of liberals arguing against it is nearly equally strong. Here she cites Jeremy Waldron, Alan Gewirth, and Raz.[43] Within this context she also points to Green, who reconciled rights and community long before the thinkers just mentioned, decisively rejecting the confrontational view (embodied in the nineteenth century by Spencer). In his works, the notion of right is coupled with a vision of citizenship engaged in the pursuit of the common good, individuals are permanently tied to the community and unable to fully abandon the values inherent in their cultural heritage, liberal right does not have a negative character, while liberal freedom is not to be equated with self-will.[44]

Elsewhere,[45] Simhony no longer sees the divide between liberalism and communitarianism as running between the politics of rights and the politics of the common good, but rather between two visions of the common good: "rightness–common good" and "goodness–common good", with the first based on the idea of right, and the second on the idea of the good life. The significance and relevance of Green's thought is, in Simhony's view, not only in the fact that he was the first to combine liberalism with the notion of the common good, but also in that his vision of the common good — although largely drawn from Kantianism — was not procedural but oriented towards the pursuit of a concrete good (the moral improvement of citizens). At the same time, Green did not reject liberalism, which would until then have been the standard consequence of embracing teleologism, but deliberately situated his reflections within that particular tradition. In this manner, long before the opposition liberalism–communitarianism or rightness–goodness was established, British idealism had already conciliated both perspectives within Green's thought.

Simhony points out essentially the same features of the idealist world view as those that Sweet found in the thought of Bosanquet. Departing from the "social thesis", Green is led to acknowledge social recognition as the basis of civil and political order. This is but a step from the "community of rights", a conception in which the uniqueness of social relations translates into the singularity of legislation, while the

---

[43] A. Simhony, *Rights that Bind*, pp. 241–243.
[44] *Ibid.*, pp. 244–249.
[45] A. Simhony, *T.H. Green's Complex Common Good*, p. 70.

legal system is founded on the general acceptance of legal regulations.[46] Simhony sees parallels here between the thought of Green and that of Taylor especially. Both formulated alternatives—to the contractualist tradition on the one hand, and to the absolutist tradition (viewing the community as a distinct ontological entity) on the other—thereby contriving a "third way" between the extremes of individualism and collectivism.[47] She finds similar parallels between Green and Raz, for whom community means unity of interest and hence reciprocity of rights, and not institutional support for individualism and competition.[48]

4.3 The idealist theory of rights

The above mentioned scholars all emphasise the significance of the theory of rights formulated within idealism. It is here that all that is essential within the context of the individualist-communitarian debate is contained. The "social thesis" proper to communitarian thought is joined here with the acknowledgment of recognition as the foundation of social order, an emphasis on the *bonum publicum* and its relation to the well-being of individuals; the positive functions of legislation are accentuated while the freedom of individual action is also underlined. The juridical theories of the idealists run counter to the belief in a fundamental antagonism between individuals and the state and to a similarly confrontational view of rights and communities.

With regard to their characteristic features, the legal conceptions of the British idealists display a considerable convergence with classical German philosophy, whose representatives were also suspended between positivism, natural law, particularism and universalism, individualism and the pursuit of the common good. The universalism of the German idealists, especially Kant and Hegel, derived from their rationalism. "[S]ince, considered objectively, there can be only one human reason, there cannot be many philosophies; in other words, there can be only one true system of philosophy from principles, in however many different and even conflicting ways men have philosophized about one and the same proposition."[49] In the case of Kant, this rationalism was especially manifest in his ethical and juridical theories. Hegel's was based on panlogism, the view that thought and being are

---

[46] A. Simhony, *Rights that Bind*, p. 249.
[47] Ibid., pp. 249–250; W. Sweet, *L'individu et les droits de la personne selon Maritain et Bosanquet*, "Études maritainiennes/Maritain Studies" 1990, Vol. 6, pp. 3–5.
[48] J. Raz, *The Morality of Freedom*, Oxford 1986, pp. 198–210.
[49] I. Kant, *The Metaphysics of Morals*, transl. M. Gregor, Cambridge 1991, p. 36.

one. This is the origin of his philosophy of history, within which the world's immanent *Weltgeist* systematically increases the freedom of finite subjects. The means to this end is the rationalisation of the public sphere, in which the arbitrary self-will of the initial rulers is replaced — through a similar spontaneity of action by an expanding group of citizens guided by their irrational will (*Willkür*) — by individuals beginning to realise the rational will (*Wille*) and finding their place in an ethical community, the state. Successive stages of this process lead to the attainment of higher stages of the reality of social relations. "What is rational is actual; and what is actual is rational"[50] — this maxim, whose possible interpretation illustrates the crux of the later dispute between the Hegelian "right" and "left", also captures the essence of Hegel's philosophy of history, in which the successive externalisations of the *Weltgeist*, attaining ever greater stages of rationality, also attain greater stages of reality.

Along with universalism and rationalism, German philosophy is pervaded by a sense of the relativity of legislation in the face of changing historical circumstances. This is especially pronounced in the historicist thought of Hegel, who does not admit the possibility of judging one's contemporaries from the standpoint of supposedly absolute knowledge, as Kant wanted to do with his universal measure of ethically correct conduct (categorical imperative formulas). The contextualism of Hegelianism combines well with both rationalism and universalism, producing a teleological view of reality aiming to fully realise its potential. The same path was taken by the British idealists, in whose writings rationalism and universalism come together with cultural and political contextualism, creating a theory of objective rights founded on custom and linked to the pursuit of the welfare of the social whole and of its individual members. Let us now examine the main features of the British idealist theory of rights: the theses concerning the recognition-based character of rights, their involvement in the pursuit of the common good and their positive nature.

4.3.1 The recognition-based character of rights

According to Green, every right involves two closely related elements: the claim by a person or group to "free exercise of some faculty" as well as the recognition of the validity of that claim by the community.[51] For

---

[50] G.W.F. Hegel, *The Elements of the Philosophy of Right*, transl. H.B. Nisbet, ed. A.W. Wood, Cambridge 2001, p. 20.

[51] T.H. Green, *Lectures on the Principles of Political Obligation*, in: T.H. Green, *Lectures on the Principles of Political Obligation and Other Writings*, eds. P. Harris, J. Morrow, Cambridge 1986, p. 108 (§ 139).

Bosanquet, a right "in the broadest sense" is a moral claim recognised by the community.

> Laws may be compared to the wood of a tree, or a skeleton of an animal, each of which is indeed a rigid framework, but has been entirely moulded by the growth of the flexible parts which seem to hang upon it. But the illustration is not strong enough. Wood or bone may die, and yet retain its strength; but a dead law has no strength at all, and a law can be a dead letter without being repealed. Law has its strength as well as its birth in the public will.[52]

This is why, in order to define the role of rights in the idealist tradition, it is necessary to examine both these ingredients—claim and recognition—separately, to then later define the relationships between them.

What is the claim to a right and where does it come from? The authors discussed here all agree that the immediate source of a claim is the desire for self-realisation, although each understands this differently. According to Green, individuals set up visions of a moral ideal, which they then strive to realise. There are many such visions—born in the minds of hedonists seeking fulfilment in succumbing to bodily whims, perfectionists attempting to master an ability particular to some domain of life, people aspiring to the role of fortresses guarding the orthodoxy of moral systems. Each of them, in spite of their differences, will need support from society to realise his chosen ideal, whether in the form of being able to obtain, consume or be guaranteed the ownership of goods, or simply by being "left alone" without interference as to the chosen way of life. Bosanquet considered the end of human effort to be the achievement of a harmonious and, as far as possible, developed personality. In Bradley's view, individuals can only attain fulfilment by participating in a whole which transcends their limitations, in other words, a community.[53] Both admitted that societal support was needed to achieve this state. They were thus critical of any thesis claiming that self-realisation was possible outside community. Self-fulfilment requires cooperation with others. Cooperation—the recognition of moral and legal subjectivity, while the condition for recognition is the appropriate content of the claim.

---

[52] B. Bosanquet, *The Philosophical Theory of the State*, London 1910, p. 188; B. Bosanquet, *Individual and the Social Reform*, in: B. Bosanquet, *Essays and Addresses*, London 1891, pp. 24–25; cf. B. Bosanquet, *The Notion of the General Will*, "Mind" 1920, Vol. 19, p. 81.

[53] F.H. Bradley, *Ethical Studies*, p. 174.

What makes a claim appropriate? The recognition by the community that it complies with the achievement of the common good.[54] "Rights then are claims recognised by the State [...] to the maintenance of conditions favourable to the best life."[55] This project is a derivative of the general will of a given community. It is little surprise, then, that according to both Green[56] and Bosanquet,[57] individuals are seldom conscious of it. Since they cannot have full knowledge of the congeries of the "hopes and fears" or the nature of the "system of ideas", they cannot be aware of the goals that these set. For a community to move in the direction desired by all of its members, it is not necessary that it be indicated and submitted for public debate. This is why it is so difficult to discover these goals, which does not mean that they cannot be known at all. Though still imperfect, their fullest expression is to be found in the community's morality, thus in the hierarchy of goods and values commonly accepted within a given community.[58]

If an individual lays claim to liberties that endanger the common good, the claim will not be recognised, while its author will be perceived as irrational and amoral.[59] We saw a similar argument before in the analysis of Green's view of the relationship between rights and morality. Since the evolution of rights must be preceded by an analogous development of morality, and morality should be understood as a set of prescriptions reflecting the desired nature of social relations within a given community, rights will always be based on a consensus as to admissible ways of realising oneself. Ways compatible with the general goals of society will be approved, while those that are even potentially subversive with respect to the dominant view of the τέλος (*telos*) will be rejected. The same holds true for governments: if they shape the public sphere in accordance with the claims ensuing from the general will, they will gain legitimacy, even when undemocratic.[60] Yet if they cling to the *status quo*, disregarding the changes taking place in the social consciousness, they will sooner or later be deposed. This is

---

[54] T.H. Green, *Lectures on the Principles*, pp. 113–114 (§ 144–145), 119–120 (§ 154–155), 135 (§ 172), 160–161 (§ 208–209); B. Bosanquet, *The Philosophical Theory*, p. 191.
[55] *Ibid.*, p. 188.
[56] T.H. Green, *Lectures on the Principles*, p. 96 (§ 121).
[57] B. Bosanquet, *The Philosophical Theory*, pp. 117, 155, 164, 202, 285.
[58] F.H. Bradley, *Ethical Studies*, p. 186; T.H. Green, *Lectures on the Principles*, p. 91 (§ 116).
[59] *Ibid.*, p. 159 (§ 208).
[60] *Ibid.*, p. 93 (§ 119).

how the belief in the representation of the general will and the common good constitutes the foundation of political order.[61]

"The state is for him [its member—J.G.] the complex of those social relations out of which rights arise."[62] The right thus reflects the nature of the social union, being a mirror that reflects its goals. In a similar spirit, Bosanquet affirmed that it is systemic in nature. It conceptualises desires and indicates the order of their realisation. The rights of individuals reflected in community legislation reveal and order the goals recognised as having value. In itself, the right is always local, belonging to a specific community, not to "mankind" or "human nature as such".[63] This view was shared by Bradley[64] and Green.[65] The purpose of a right is not to set up a political ideal, but rather to ensure the greatest possible perfection of a real community, whose form depends exclusively on the will of its members.[66] It is not by universal reasoning or international authorities that the contents of the legislative agendas of communities should be determined. If communities are to perform their basic task—perfect their members—their functioning must be based on general wills, "no rights are absolute, or detached from the whole, but all have their warrant in the aim of the whole."[67]

By analogy, rights and obligations are not allotted to community members irrespective of their function, but remain strictly connected to their social position. The same rights should not be enjoyed by everyone, because not everyone makes the same contribution to the common good. This is not merely the result of greater or lesser incompetence in performing one's functions. Some of them, though certainly useful, display a low value in terms of realising the common good.[68] No right is therefore inalienable, but belongs to an individual on account of his social functions and only as long as those functions are performed. A change in function entails a change in both rights and obligations.[69]

---

[61] *Ibid.*, p. 79 (§ 98).

[62] *Ibid.*, p. 110 (§ 141).

[63] B. Bosanquet, *Three Lectures on Social Ideals*, in: B. Bosanquet, *Social and International Ideals. Being Studies in Patriotism*, Freeport–New York 1967, pp. 196, 205.

[64] F.H. Bradley, *Ethical Studies*, p. 201.

[65] T.H. Green, *Lectures on the Principles*, p. 108 (§ 139); cf. *ibid.*, pp. 111–113 (§ 142–144).

[66] B. Bosanquet, *The Philosophical Theory*, pp. 198–199.

[67] *Ibid.*, p. 216.

[68] *Ibid.*, p. 191; cf. B. Bosanquet, *Kingdom of God on Earth*, in: B. Bosanquet, *Essays and Addresses*, p. 116.

[69] B. Bosanquet, *The Philosophical Theory*, p. 216; see W. Sweet, *Idealism and Rights. The Social Ontology of Human Rights in the Political Thought of Bernard Bosanquet*, Lanham, MD–New York–London 1997, p. 69. The indispens-

4.3.2 The common good

The nature of claims recognised by a community and reflected in its legal system is linked directly to its particular perception of the common good. Whether a claim is upheld depends on whether it contributes to the welfare of the whole.[70] Rights, Green wrote, can be ascribed to a person only as "a member of society, [...] in which some common good is recognised by the members of the society as their own ideal good, as that which *should be* for each of them".[71] Is the nature of the common good decided in advance, or do communities have unrestricted choice in this matter? How much freedom do societies have in defining a vision of their future? Based on what we have said so far, it seems clear that it is citizens who define the nature of the *bonum publicum*. This choice, however, is never a question of their autonomous decision, but rather the result of factors independent of them, in particular the traditions of the community, which form its general will, influencing the nature of the goods and values embraced. Yet more than by their contingent historical and geopolitical determinants, communities are determined by the nature of individuals themselves. After all, idealist ethics and political philosophy were based on a metaphysical view of human nature. These two factors: objective (the historical and geopolitical conditions) and absolute (the *telos* of human existence), define the general will and the well-being of the community.

Two characteristics can be ascribed to the common good as conceived by the idealists: its inalienable moral quality and its convergence with the realisation of the personal good of individuals.[72] The moral character of the common good springs from the fact that it is essentially a set of beliefs concerning desirable directions for self-realisation. As such, it is inextricably linked to the interests of community members. The desire for self-realisation, the motor of all human action, can only be fulfilled within a community. This binding of individual and communal interests led some scholars critical of idealism to accuse its proponents of putting forth tyrannical conceptions. The idealists seemed not

---

ability of recognition in the process of the establishment of rights also indicates a strict correlation between rights and duties (T.H. Green, *Lectures on the Principles*, p. 29, § 30, p. 85, § 107). The idealists turn out to be decidedly opposed to thinkers inclined to view rights as liberal and duties as exclusively oppressive (F.H. Bradley, *Ethical Studies*, p. 208; cf. T.H. Green, *Fragments on Moral and Political Philosophy*, in: T.H. Green, *Lectures on the Principles*, pp. 312–313, § 3).

[70] B. Bosanquet, *The Philosophical Theory*, pp. 82, 113.
[71] T.H. Green, *Lectures on the Principles*, pp. 25–26 (§ 25); cf. *ibid.*, pp. 103 (§ 132), 104 (§ 134), 106 (§ 136).
[72] W. Sweet, *L'individu et les droits*, pp. 5–6.

to have made provision for a situation in which the interests of the whole are at odds with those of its parts. This was sometimes construed as an attempt to sacrifice individual freedom on the altar of the collective. The individualism of Green, Bradley and Bosanquet's writings was largely ignored, along with their emphasis on the realisation of the human *telos*, and the interdependency between the institutional life of a community and the level of consciousness of its members. The individuals, seemingly subject to the dictates of the common good, in fact make the community a means of realising their plans, a tool always subservient to their will.

The category of the common good can be linked to the issue of social recognition in at least two ways. Firstly, the citizens' mutual recognition of their moral and legal subjectivity gives rise to a system of positive values and rights, which some[73] scholars see as an expression of the common good. As the author of the *Lectures on the Principles of Political Obligation* was frequently wont to suggest, communities tend towards the recognition of equal rights for all their members on all planes of existence.[74] In this context, the common good can be equated with a political system in which custom has the strongest influence on legislation (democracy) and with a legal system that guarantees the freedom to exchange goods, but also levels material inequalities when these stand in the way of the improvement of citizens (social liberalism). Maria Dimova-Cookson[75] has dubbed this procedural interpretation of the common good the "society of equals". There is much evidence against such a reading of the idealist view of the common good, however. After all, it implies proceduralism and anti-teleologism.[76] In its focus on principles of justice, rather than the communal *telos*, it contradicts the fundamental assumptions of idealist thought, ignoring its anti-Kantian and Aristotelian-Hegelian character. The liberal democratic system can be viewed as a condition for the realisation of the goal

---

[73] This perspective was especially emphasised by Simhony (A. Simhony, *T.H. Green: the Common Good Society*, "History of Political Thought" 1993, Vol. 14, pp. 122–145) and Maria Dimova-Cookson (M. Dimova-Cookson, *T.H. Green's Moral and Political Philosophy. A Phenomenological Perspective*, Basingstoke 2001, pp. 100–102).

[74] T.H. Green, *Prolegomena to Ethics*, in: T.H. Green, *Collected Works of T.H. Green*, ed. P.P. Nicholson, Bristol 1997, p. 222 (§ 209).

[75] M. Dimova-Cookson, *T.H. Green's Moral and Political Philosophy*, p. 102. It is here that Simhony discerned certain analogies with Rawls' theory of justice (A. Simhony, *Rights that Bind*, pp. 258–260; A. Simhony, *T.H. Green's Complex Common Good*, p. 78).

[76] M. Dimova-Cookson, *T.H. Green's Moral and Political Philosophy*, p. 102.

of communal existence, as Green[77] seems to have maintained, but it is never a goal in itself. This remark is equally true, if not more so, of the thought of Bradley and Bosanquet. The first associated the category of the common good with the realisation of "that which is universal in that which is particular", the second with the "best life" of individuals. According to both, the fulfilment of this mission is dependent on the performance of duties associated with "my station". Neither made any sweeping pronouncements as to the nature of these social roles or the nature of public order as a whole. Nor did they express any desiderata as to the specific structure of power relations. It therefore seems more appropriate to interpret the common good in a different manner.

The second reading of the common good emphasises the *telos* of human existence — moral perfection. Accordingly, the desirable social conditions are those that enable the moral development of individuals. No indication is given as to the nature of the ideals these should be based on, nor of their political form. These factors are dependent on the general will of the community, and so its traditions and historical experiences amongst other things. This substantialist interpretation is fundamentally different from the one we previously examined. It stipulates that it is not abstract procedures or political ideals that should determine the institutional development of communities.[78] "[T]he state is an institution for the promotion of a common good."[79] Not the right way of proceeding, but the *telos* embodied in a common vision of the good constitutes social life, at the same time enabling individual fulfilment.

4.3.3 Negative liberty–positive liberty. Negative rights–positive rights

In the writings of the idealists, the issue of the recognition and character of rights is tied in to the problem of liberty. They unanimously differentiated between the two types of liberty most frequently cited in philosophical and political discourse. The first of these is "juridical" liberty — as Green[80] called it — or "negative" liberty — as Bosanquet[81] and Bradley[82] termed it. This they understood in a spirit similar to that of the later philosophy of Berlin. Liberty is here equated with the freedom of self-determination, full autonomy and independence from others,

---

[77] T.H. Green, *Lectures on the Principles*, pp. 97 (§ 122), 120 (§ 155).
[78] See *ibid.*, p. 91 (§ 116); cf. *ibid.*, p. 95 (§ 120).
[79] *Ibid.*, p. 97 (§ 124).
[80] T.H. Green, *On Different Senses of "Freedom" as Applied to Will and the Moral Progress of Man*, in: T.H. Green, *Lectures on the Principles*, pp. 234–235 (§ 8), 240–241 (§ 17).
[81] B. Bosanquet, *The Philosophical Theory*, p. 124.
[82] F.H. Bradley, *Ethical Studies*, p. 57.

absolute self-will. Its enemies include the law, the state, fellow citizens mutually standing in the way of each other's attainment of chosen goals. Taking this perspective, we arrive at the position of the idiotic (from the Greek ἰδιώτης) individual, wholly indeterminate in his acts of volition.[83] This is no longer a man of flesh and blood, but a philosophical abstraction, as Bradley put it: "'free', because it is indifferent"[84] to all that surrounds it:

> if 'free' = 'free *from*', to be quite free is to be free from everything — free from other men, free from law, from morality, from thought, from sense, from — Is there anything we are *not* to be free from? To be free from everything is to be — nothing. Only nothing is quite free, and freedom is abstract nothingness. If in death we cease to be anything, then there first we are free, because there first we are — not.[85]

Advocates of this view are aware that absolute negative liberty is impossible in practice, if only because the freedom of some will always collide with the plans of others. To their mind, therefore, legislation is a necessary evil. Without it, most members of a community would quickly lose the possibility of self-determination, to the benefit of a stronger minority. Negative rights, thus rights which in the greatest degree contribute to the effective exercise of that independence, only ensure that all retain it to an equal extent, since all cannot retain it without limit. Their aim is not to realise the common good (if by that, one is to understand anything other than a conflictual compromise). Their purpose is not to impose a single vision of life and human nature, defining the means of distribution of goods, on the public sphere. Rather, they are founded on the belief that individuals are best equipped to ensure their own happiness, since they best know their needs and are the most determined to strive towards their fulfilment. It was this vision of individuals, community, freedom and rights that came to form the basis of the "theories of the first look" and utilitarianism.

The second type of freedom is "true" freedom — as Green[86] and Bradley[87] called it — "positive" or "political" freedom — as Bosanquet[88] and the author of *Ethical Studies*[89] defined it. According to the idealists, being guaranteed the freedom to do what one wishes with oneself and

---

83 Ibid., p. 12.
84 Ibid.
85 Ibid., p. 56.
86 T.H. Green, Lecture on "Liberal Legislation and Freedom of Contract", in: T.H. Green, Lectures on the Principles, p. 200.
87 F.H. Bradley, Ethical Studies, p. 56.
88 B. Bosanquet, The Philosophical Theory, p. 127.
89 F.H. Bradley, Ethical Studies, p. 57.

one's property does not mean that that which has true value will be realised. The assumption that everyone knows what is best for them turns out to be erroneous. For since the *telos* of human existence lies in moral perfection, only those who pursue it are truly free. Those who devote their lives to the pursuit of pleasure not only squander, sometimes irretrievably, the opportunity for self-realisation, but often deprive others of it through their actions. Green defined "true" freedom in a threefold manner, perceiving it as a "maximum of power for all members of human society alike to make the best of themselves",[90] "the liberation of the powers of all men equally for contributions to a common good"[91] and the "true end of all our effort as citizens [...], positive power or capacity of doing or enjoying something worth doing or enjoying".[92] Bosanquet wrote that "our liberty, or to use a good old expression, our liberties, may be identified with such a system [of rights—J.G.] considered as the condition and guarantee of our becoming the best that we have in us to be, that is, of becoming ourselves."[93] As one can see, each of these designations presupposes positive self-definition, and not self-will, as the foundation of freedom: "no man is so well able to do as he likes as the wandering savage. He has no master. There is no one to say him nay. Yet we do not count him really free, because the freedom of savagery is not strength, but weakness. The actual powers of the noblest savage do not admit of comparison with those of the humblest citizen of a law-abiding state. He is not the slave of man, but he is the slave of nature."[94]

True freedom should therefore be seen not as full liberty of action, but as the desire to realise strictly defined goods. It implies the need to bend one's will to the will of something greater than the finite human ego.[95] It may be the community general will speaking through "my station and its duties" (this "fuller freedom—Bosanquet wrote—which we [...] trace to its embodiment in the state"[96]) or it may be Bradley's views on the ideal of social and extra-social perfection. What is important is that the truly free person is the one pursuing their *telos*, consciously striving to attain moral perfection, and not—as the liberal

---

[90] T.H. Green, *Lecture on "Liberal Legislation and Freedom of Contract"*, p. 200.
[91] *Ibid.*
[92] *Ibid.*, p. 199.
[93] B. Bosanquet, *The Philosophical Theory*, p. 119.
[94] T.H. Green, *Lecture on "Liberal Legislation and Freedom of Contract"*, p. 199; cf. F.H. Bradley, *Ethical Studies*, p. 57.
[95] Cf. G.C. Bussey, M.D. Crane, *Bosanquet's Doctrine of Freedom*, "Philosophical Review" 1916, Vol. 25, pp. 723–724.
[96] B. Bosanquet, *The Philosophical Theory*, p. 127.

individualists would have it — the one capable of opposing everything to maintain the illusion of their independence and autonomy.

It is not so much the praise of negative freedom — something modern liberals have made their custom — as the opposition of negative right and freedom to positive right and freedom that is altogether groundless. Bosanquet was here nearly one hundred years ahead of Gerald MacCallum's thesis, expounded in his well-known article *Negative and Positive Freedom*,[97] positing the artificiality of Berlin's distinction between these two conceptions of freedom. For every definition of freedom presupposes a threefold schema. In speaking of freedom, we always touch upon the problem of the autonomy of a certain x from the actions of a certain y with regard to doing z. Meantime, in *The Philosophical Theory of the State*, Bosanquet holds that every concept of freedom presupposes a two-term relation: it is always "freedom *from* some things as well as freedom *to* others".[98] Thus a right that is outwardly only negative always already contains a positive aspect. "[T]he apparently negative has its roots and its meaning in the positive."[99] The criterion for accepting a certain conception of freedom, later made binding by law, is always a certain view of the good which one strives in this manner to realise. One must already presuppose the existence of worthwhile goals and goods, whose realisation and possession is understood to be good in itself. And if so, then right and freedom are always based on a view of universal needs implied by human nature, thus the *telos* of human existence.[100] Thinkers making an apology of "freedom from" have maintained that it safeguards the ability of everyone to make autonomous decisions about their own needs, but they did not take note of the theoretical meta-level on which this very notion of freedom had already been metaphysically grounded.

It is not the nature of freedom that is understood differently in the distinction between negative and positive freedom. For in both cases freedom consists in being obedient only to oneself. Freedom stands for a "condition relevant to our continued struggle to assert the control of something in us, which we recognise as imperative upon us or as our real self, but which we only obey in a very imperfect degree".[101] "The man is free who realizes his *true* self."[102] It is the nature of the category

---

[97] G.C. MacCallum, Jr., *Negative and Positive Freedom*, in: *Liberty*, ed. D. Miller, Oxford 1991, pp. 102–122.
[98] B. Bosanquet, *The Philosophical Theory*, p. 128.
[99] *Ibid.*, p. 127.
[100] *Ibid.*, p. 128.
[101] *Ibid.*, p. 118.
[102] F.H. Bradley, *Ethical Studies*, p. 57.

of "being determined only by ourself"[103] and the "true self" that is under discussion here. What are autonomy and self-determination? In what actions, performed under what moral disposition, are they realised? These are the types of questions that must first be answered by those participating in disputes on the nature of freedom. Clearly, one cannot escape metaphysical self-definition here. Belief in the existence of negative rights, thus those that establish a space of unhindered self-determination and, contrary to positive rights, impose no view of the good, is a liberal illusion.

The idealists viewed the "true self" — presupposed by every conception of freedom and rights — as morally perfect, a "whole self",[104] "the greatness and unity of life",[105] as Bradley and Bosanquet put it. Of course, this perfection may be understood in a number of ways. Some have mistakenly viewed it as the maximisation of pleasure. It is hardly a surprise, then, that they saw a limitation in those standing in the way of corporeal fulfilment, rather than seeing where these barriers to development were highest — within their very selves.[106] Negative freedom, i.e. uninhibited action in accordance with one's will, is an illusive freedom that makes no contribution to the realisation of the human calling.[107] It is nonetheless indispensable to every human being. "Freedom to" requires "freedom from". For the capacity for making choices rests on the ability to act freely. The freedom of self-realisation demands responsibility, awareness of the consequences of one's actions, while this cannot be learned unless one is free to dispose of oneself.

4.4 What became of the idealist theory of rights

The theory developed by Green and Bosanquet was continued in the works of their successors and followers. Their list most frequently includes Jones, John MacCunn (1846–1929), Edward Caird, Muirhead, Hetherington and Wallace. According to the first, a professor of ethics at the University of Glasgow, a community is moral in character, and so the limits of its power may only be defined according to a moral criterion.[108] Its task is to improve its members, it "supplies them with the means of a larger life, and extends and deepens the significance of their

---

[103] B. Bosanquet, *The Philosophical Theory*, p. 134.
[104] F.H. Bradley, *Ethical Studies*, pp. 68, 73–74; B. Bosanquet, *The Philosophical Theory*, p. 146.
[105] *Ibid.*, p. 135.
[106] *Ibid.*, pp. 119, 137.
[107] T.H. Green, *On Different Senses*, p. 228 (§ 1).
[108] H. Jones, *The Working Faith of a Social Reformer and Other Essays*, London 1910, p. 114.

individuality".¹⁰⁹ Jones was critical of both the radical collectivism of the socialists as well as of the individualism of classical liberals. Socialists would sooner annihilate the individual than perfect him, and liberals yearn for an explosion of self-will and the destruction of that which is common. Both fail to appreciate that individual identity presupposes the existence of community — "[a]s there is no cell or fibre of his physical organism which has not been borrowed and elaborated from his natural environment, so there is no element of his individuality which he does not owe to this social world within and upon which alone his rational nature can be sustained."¹¹⁰ Hence the efforts of the community and those of its members are guided by a single goal — the well-being of the social whole.¹¹¹ In *The Principles of Citizenship*, Jones defined citizenship as cooperation towards the common good, a cooperation requiring sacrifice, the readiness for which should be regarded as the greatest proof of patriotism.¹¹² He did not perceive freedom as opposition to institutions limiting our self-will, but a limited conformity to them the fulfilment of obligations associated with our station in the community. These stations, institutions and laws embody the vision of the common good particular to the members of a given community. They were created and continue to be based on their mutual recognition,¹¹³ reflecting their ethical spirit. Traditions shape communities, and provide a backbone without which they would disintegrate.¹¹⁴ This does not mean that we should never challenge the laws and ethos of our forefathers, but only that we should — when attempting to reform them — take notice of the communal past. The greatest sin of all reformers has always been to believe it possible to institute the rule of *a priori* laws — ignoring a community's existential context, seeking to create an ideal polity — without contradiction and injustice. The personalities of individuals cannot be separated from the environment they live in.¹¹⁵

In *The Ethics of Citizenship*,¹¹⁶ MacCunn emphasised the importance of universal political participation and the improvement of the material conditions of citizens as necessary to their moral improvement and the shaping of patriotic attitudes. Like him, Muirhead and Hetherington maintained that only a democratic state can fulfil this mission. "If the

---

¹⁰⁹ Ibid., p. 144.
¹¹⁰ Ibid., p. 278.
¹¹¹ H. Haldar, *Neo-Hegelianism*, London 1927, p. 360.
¹¹² H. Jones, *The Principles of Citizenship*, London 1919.
¹¹³ H. Haldar, *Neo-Hegelianism*, p. 358.
¹¹⁴ Ibid., p. 362.
¹¹⁵ H. Jones, *The Working Faith*, p. 48.
¹¹⁶ J. MacCunn, *The Ethics of Citizenship*, Glasgow 1894.

end of the State is [...] *self-government,* i.e. if it is the furthering of the good life, not only indirectly by the provision of external conditions, but directly, by the creation of an institution, participation in whose life offers to the individual the opportunity of attaining a finer quality of social will, then democracy may be not only the best but the inevitable form of political life."[117] The intention of these authors, however, was not to promote political universalism. Their writings are permeated by the same mixture of historicism and contextualism as that which appeared earlier in the works of Green, Bosanquet and Bradley. They did not see morality as something unchanging and absolute, but in constant development, where none of the stages can be judged from the perspective of another. Societies existing at the same time do not have to follow the same moral principles. Ethical progress, though always aiming in the same direction, takes different forms in different circumstances.[118] This is why the ethos of a community, embodied in its laws and institutions, is the only indicator of correct conduct. In the preface to the *Lectures on Birmingham Institutions,* Muirhead wrote that "institutions [...] represent the past efforts and the present cooperation of many individuals directed to a single and continuous purpose, and in this account may claim an individuality of their own or even a higher kind than of any single person."[119] Freedom is not associated with self-will but with the conscious observance of the precepts of the community. This does not equate to renunciation and sacrifice, but to joining others in an attempt to realise the common good.[120] It is this goal, and not allegedly universal rules of conduct, which constitutes the criterion actions should be judged by.[121] Subordination to the community, however, is not tantamount to a negation of individualism. The common good is always exclusively the good of individuals, a relatively perfect moral life and a harmoniously devised fullness of human potential. It "has a claim upon the individual because it corresponds to his own deepest need *to be an individual*".[122]

Edward Caird also understood freedom as the possibility of sacrifice in the name of the *bonum publicum*.[123] For it is only as members of a

---

[117] H.J.W. Hetherington, J.H. Muirhead, *The Social Purpose,* p. 249.
[118] J.H. Muirhead, *The Elements of Ethics,* London 1912, pp. 232–233.
[119] *Birmingham Institutions,* ed. J.H. Muirhead, Birmingham 1911, p. VII; cited after A. Vincent, R. Plant, *Philosophy, Politics and Citizenship. The Life and Thought of the British Idealists,* Oxford 1984, p. 28.
[120] J.H. Muirhead, *The Elements,* p. 163–164.
[121] *Ibid.,* p. 167.
[122] *Ibid.,* p. 180.
[123] E. Caird, *Lay Sermons and Addresses Delivered in the Hall of Balliol College, Oxford,* Glasgow 1907.

community that individuals can fulfil their most elementary need of moral self-perfection. Without community, there would be no morality. "We are *knowing* subjects only as we transcend our own individual existence, and regard it as an object among others in the one world. [...] In like manner, we are *practical* or *moral* subjects only as we are conscious of ourselves as members along with others of one society, and are able, therefore, to view ourselves like them, impartially, with reference to the ends of the society."[124] This does not necessarily imply total subordination to the community. By depriving individuals of the right to choose and to rebel against the institutional *status quo*, we make the same mistake as collectivist socialists, who would spiritually annihilate individuals out of concern for their well-being. "If the individual apart from society is an abstraction, society apart from individuals is no less an abstraction."[125]

Meanwhile, Wallace in his *Lectures and Essays on Natural Theology* saw communities as something nearly sacred. It is only by being part of them that we obtain a chance to unite with the Absolute. They allow us to take control of nature, which threatens our external being, and of our own animal nature in the form of drives,[126] thereby ensuring both our physical subsistence and spiritual development. The sole criterion for judging various *modi vivendi* and institutional orders should be how well they achieve these two goals. In his essay *On Human Rights*, Wallace closely followed Green's[127] argumentation, stating that only a contribution to the realisation of the common good is a basis for the assignment of a moral and legal personality to individuals. Humans have no inherent rights solely on the basis of their nature. These may only be gained within collective life, and only after having demonstrated our usefulness to the common good.[128] The community is the ultimate arbiter insofar as internal order and the rights of its members are concerned, it assigns them their functions and obligations,[129] "the state, in short, must realize—Wallace wrote—that is the mortal God, and that in this world it should be ubiquitous and omnipotent."[130]

---

[124] E. Caird, *Critical Philosophy of Kant*, Vol. 2, Glasgow 1889, p. 369.
[125] H. Haldar, *Neo-Hegelianism*, p. 104.
[126] W. Wallace, *Lectures and Essays on Natural Theology and Ethics*, ed. E. Caird, Oxford 1898, pp. 200–202.
[127] H. Haldar, *Neo-Hegelianism*, p. 180; cf. W. Wallace, *Lectures and Essays on Natural Theology and Ethics*, pp. 213–254.
[128] W. Wallace, *Lectures and Essays*, p. 258.
[129] *Ibid.*, pp. 303–305.
[130] *Ibid.*, p. 263.

4.5 Determinants of the liberal communitarianism of the idealists[*]

In the previous chapters, we outlined the arguments of scholars ascribing a liberal-communitarian nature to British idealism. We also presented the rudiments of the idealist theory of rights, from which the fundamental features of the idealist political philosophy can be inferred. Taken together, they form the basis of a philosophy bridging traditional theoretical divides (especially with regard to the two modern paradigms of liberalism and communitarianism). These features should be taken to include; 1) Hegelian-Aristotelian teleologism, 2) the metaphysical grounding of politics, 3) ethical and political contextualism, 4) oscillation between relativism and universalism, 5) a critique of the concept of negative freedom, an apology of freedom as positive self-determination, oriented towards a specific purpose, and 6) individualism. Let us take a separate look at each of these.

4.5.1 Teleologism

Using MacIntyre's terminology, the idealists held that certain concepts, including the concept of man, are functional in nature. Thus, just as the definition of a watch partly overlaps with that of a good watch, humanity should be defined by reference to the ideal of the good man. This last is vastly different from all the imperfect stages in the development of human personality. Bosanquet expressed this thought in the following way:

> [t]he most ordinary conception of growth involves maturity, and the term 'nature' in Greek and Latin, as in English, can indicate not only what we are born *as*, but what we are born *for*, our true, or real, or complete nature. Thus the great thinkers of every age have been led to something like Aristotle's conception.[131]

Green and Bradley espoused a similar view. The former, in the *Lectures on the Principles*, foresaw the failure of liberal attempts to discover the essence of humanity from the point of view of its hypothetical beginnings, the natural state, noting that the goal of human life does not lie at its dawn, but at its term. It is implicit in every moral desideratum. For morality is always built on the distinction between "what is" and "what ought to be".[132] This thesis is repeated by Bradley: "[m]orality implies an end in itself"[133] whose pursuit is dictated by an inner imper-

---

[*] A part of this section has been published as *Between Individual and Community: On the Uniqueness of the British Idealists' Vision of Politics*, "Collingwood and British Idealism Studies" 2011, Vol. 17, No. 1, pp. 63–89.
[131] B. Bosanquet, *The Philosophical Theory*, pp. 122–123.
[132] T.H. Green, *Prolegomena to Ethics*, p. 90 (§ 85).
[133] F.H. Bradley, *Ethical Studies*, p. 65.

ative. The idealists were not sparing in their praise for the conceptions of Aristotle and Hegel, whose writings after all had given the best account of the goal of human life and of the role of the community in its attainment. Green, considered the first nineteenth-century thinker to have revitalised ancient thought in the British Isles,[134] and Bosanquet, his faithful disciple in this point, credited Plato and Aristotle with having formulated the first "true theory of rights",[135] involving the purpose-oriented development of the state, like an organism,[136] which Hegel merely continued in the modern age.[137] The author of the *Lectures on the Principles* regarded Aristotle's τὸ τί ἦυ εἶναι, which he translated as "what a thing has in it to become",[138] as the dictum revealing his fundamental idea. It is not genesis, but ousia that defines the essence of humanity.[139] It was following Plato and Aristotle that British philosophers posited perfection of character, the full actualisation of one's potential,[140] as the final goal of human development. This is also unmistakably reflected in the modern, neo-Aristotelian teleologism of MacIntyre, and stands in opposition to the deontological concepts of neo-Kantians such as Rawls or procedural liberals like Ackerman.

4.5.2 The metaphysical foundation of politics

The absence of British idealism from contemporary studies devoted to liberal thought is often due to this very feature. Although the last decades have seen a rehabilitation of Hegel's metaphysics, seldom still viewed as defence of the Prussian monarchy and increasingly regarded as in part, if not wholly, liberal, the view that metaphysically-founded theories should be excluded from the list of liberal conceptions is still prevalent. Metaphysical theories of the state and politics, the last of which was formulated (at least according to Peter Laslett) at the edges of liberal thought by Bosanquet at the beginning of the twentieth century, found their continuation in the notion of general consent in the "early" Rawls and Habermas, and were ultimately defeated by communitarianism and ontologically agnostic postmodern liberalism. Green, and in his wake Bradley and Bosanquet, combined the results of epistemological and ontological research in the formulation of their ethical

---

[134] B. Pfannenstill, *Bernard Bosanquet's Philosophy of the State*, p. 107.
[135] T.H. Green, *Lectures on the Principles*, p. 36 (§ 39).
[136] B. Bosanquet, *The Philosophical Theory*, pp. 5–7, 30–31, 123, 274; cf. B. Pfannnestill, *Bernard Bosanquet's Philosophy*, pp. 42–45.
[137] T.H. Green, *On the Different Senses*, p. 231 (§ 4).
[138] F.H. Harris, *The Neo-Idealist Political Theory*, New York 1944, p. 23.
[139] W.H. Fairbrother, *The Philosophy of Thomas Hill Green*, London 1900, pp. 16–17.
[140] *Ibid.*, pp. 80–82, 119–120.

and political theories. According to these thinkers, the ultimate view one construes of the state and of the duties of citizenship depends on the nature of the Absolute. It is precisely this philosophical construct — which some of the idealists (amongst others Green, Josiah Royce and Edward Caird) associated with the Christian God[141] — that bears on the direction and rate of development of our reality. It is unnecessary to add that this quasi-theological approach to politics is entirely alien to modern liberals, as it is to most communitarians, of whom only the "late" MacIntyre, with his clear preference for the Thomist tradition within Aristotelianism, accepts the universal import of Christian values against a relativist reading of Aristotle's ethical and political thought. Oddly enough, the second great continuator of the project to provide politics with a metaphysical foundation was the "early" Rawls. There are several points on which his thought coincides with that of the idealists. Above all, like the neo-Hegelians, Rawls combines essentialism with liberalism, seeing it as ultimately founded in the theses on the essence of humanity, as manifest in the psychological laws governing individuals in the original situation.[142] Hence, like Green, Rawls considered legislation that is in harmony with *jus naturae* to implement precepts derived from human nature. The practical implications of his philosophy, namely the acceptance of social-liberal democracy, also bring *A Theory of Justice* close to the works of Green (who, of all the idealists described here, leaned closest towards the spirit of liberal interventionism).

At the same time, the idealists and Rawls differ as to the nature of their metaphysics. For the author of *A Theory of Justice*, it is strictly Kantian and based on ethical apriorism and universalism, in addition to being premised on the existence of autonomous selves, attaining freedom in independence from heteronomous factors and in obedience to rational moral laws. Meanwhile, following Hegel, British thinkers rejected this paradigm in favour of admitting a strict correlation between individuals and heteronomous factors, above all the heritage of their communities and their current existential context.

4.5.3 Ethico-political contextualism

This is the characteristic which brings the idealists closest to communitarianism — which usually holds ethico-political norms as relative to the traditions of specific communities. In this aspect, it is no longer really Green, but rather Bradley and Bosanquet, with their concept of "my

---

[141] T.S. Sprigge, *The God of Metaphysics*, Oxford 2006, pp. 223–225.
[142] J. Rawls, *Theory of Justice*, Cambridge, MA–London 1971, pp. 136–138, 142–145, 153–156, 242–433.

station and its duties", that bear the closest resemblance to the neo-Aristotelianism of MacIntyre's *After Virtue*. For according to both the British thinkers and MacIntyre, virtue consists in the conscientious fulfilment of duties imposed by the community. It is also here that the idealists' rejection of Kant's *a priori*, formalist philosophy on the one hand, and of the contractualists' abstractionism and methodological idealism on the other, anticipates Sandel's concept of the unencumbered self, Taylor's "social thesis" and diagnosis of the dialogical character of human existence, as well as Walzer's vision of "spheres of justice". Individuals living outside the social order and capable, at least in theory (as Rawls' *Theory of Justice* presupposed), of distancing themselves from the entirety of a community's cultural heritage, passed down to them in the process of socialisation, of abstracting from their past experiences and social position, are a philosophical fiction, in practice as useless as it is dangerous. And if that is the case, then universal political and legal systems, whose purpose is to implement prescriptions derived from these ethical constructs, are afflicted with the same flaws. They should be rejected in favour of an ethico-political contextualism, the belief that the moral standards in place within a specific community should constitute the primary source of examples of conduct for its members. To lead a good life means to contribute to the well-being of the community; to be a good person means to be a good citizen, neighbour, husband, parent. There is no humanity outside of social roles—thus also no standards of ethical judgment outside the communal system of values.

Directly connected to this issue are the problem of recognition as the foundation of the social world as well as the key role played by the general will in creating a community's normative system. The idealists, anticipating Taylor's position, viewed the social world as having a dialogical character and therefore resulting from agreement between individuals, while its transformation is circumscribed by the community's linguistic resources, its "horizons of meaning".[143] They held that the general will—lying within the realm of irrational "hopes and fears" or the "system of ideas" which, though logical, remains unconscious— delimits possible paths for self-determination. The analogies are especially marked between the thought of Taylor and that of Bosanquet. For what is the "system of ideas" if not the "horizon of meaning", defining social roles, and above all determining the meaning of fundamental concepts. Citizenship, fatherhood, brotherhood, liberty, equality —the meaning of these words depends entirely on the complexity and order of the general will's elementary ideas. The self-understanding of

---

[143] Ch. Taylor, *Ethics of Authenticity*, Cambridge, MA–London 2003, pp. 37–41.

citizens also depends on it, since they define themselves above all in reference to their social roles. A marked difference is visible here with regard to *A Theory of Justice*, yet a similarity can still be discerned with the "late" Rawlsian conception of political liberalism. Instead of the earlier universalism of the two principles of justice, in his later works,[144] especially in *Political Liberalism*,[145] Rawls opted for the recognition of the irreducible complexity of modern democratic states, and consequently also for the creation of a public sphere within which particular ethical and ideological systems could coexist based on an "overlapping consensus" as to fundamental rules. He therefore no longer proposed universal ethical solutions, but departed from the undeniable diversity of societies. Hence the ethics and politics proposed here are those of coexistence, a consensus fundamentally limited to the conditions of coexistence, not universal, the only consensus acceptable to rational individuals. The similarity to idealist thought lies here in the acceptance of the unavoidable plurality of ethea, as well as the abandonment of attempts to transform the public sphere according to universal principles of justice.

4.5.4 Between relativism and universalism

In spite of making such decisive statements against the formalist universalism of Kantianism as well as contractualist conceptions supposedly demonstrated by thought experiments, the idealists did not succumb to relativism. They rejected both the liberal language of universal human rights and the Protagorean doctrine of *homo mensura*. And so, although they laid themselves open to the same charges as were later proffered against the communitarians, namely making the nature of morality dependent on the contingency of communal existence, they were able to withstand them thanks to the previously mentioned metaphysical foundation of their politics. This situation is perhaps best illustrated by Bradley's opposition to the relativist implications of "my station", giving rise to the need to recognise a supra-societal indicator of conduct. As a result, the author of *Ethical Studies* argued that ideals of social and extra-social perfection exist, which enabled him not only to bypass the charge of relativism but also that of the static character of idealist thought. It is only by invoking these ideals that one can explain social changes and the critique of established behavioural norms. The reader of Bosanquet and of Green finds himself in a similar situation. Both betrayed their universal leanings, notably by recognising that citi-

---

[144] J. Rawls, *Justice as Fairness: Political not Metaphysical*, "Philosophy and Public Affairs" 1985, Vol. 14, No. 3, pp. 223–251.
[145] J. Rawls, *Political Liberalism*, New York 1993.

zens may legitimately challenge the *status quo*. Does not every critique presuppose the existence of ideals, in whose name it is made, and alien to hitherto accepted socio-political practice? These do not have to be timeless, since the idealists denied the existence of such. Their content and significance change along with the cultural and historical context. In the writings of Bosanquet, these ideals, contending for the status of "dominant ideas" in the general will, were subject to constant reformulation. Liberty as such, Green demonstrated, became assigned to a wider social circle as individual morality evolved, thereby increasing its subjective scope, but at the same time witnessed a change of content, as the category of free actions came to include ever newer ones. This is particularly manifest in the evolution from the idea of negative liberty to that of positive liberty. Individuals, not content with having guaranteed their brethren equal freedom to act, gradually strive to ensure "true freedom" for themselves, namely ethical growth. In a similar fashion, equality evolves from an ideal ensuring equal treatment before the law into the idea of equal opportunity, involving the redistribution of resources to provide everyone with an equal chance to pursue "the best life".

The variability of life, caused by our dependence on heteronomous factors, does not undermine the claim that the goal of life is unique — moral perfection. Hence, the idealists inevitably balanced between recognising the moral authority of the community, changing and imperfect, and trust in one's own conscience, which allegedly represents the commandments of supra-social morality (although this always poses the risk of subjectivism). It is this factor, the hesitation between universalism and ethical relativism, being neither strictly liberal nor communitarian, that is present in both of these traditions. In the former, it is notably exemplified in the tension between resistance to the metaphysical foundation of politics and the simultaneous defence of the concept of universal human rights (for example the question of "generic values" and human rights in Gray,[146] Richard Rorty's stand against inflicting suffering and humiliation[147]). Among the communitarians, a similar tension appears in the thought of MacIntyre (the clash between ancient contextualism and Christian universalism), Taylor (the recognition of the cultural character of morality is here at odds with the vision of a universal moral minimum[148]), or — and which is less obvious amidst the relativist readings of this thinker — Walzer (the contrast

---

[146] J. Gray, *Two Faces of Liberalism*, pp. 12, 31–32.
[147] R. Rorty, *Contingency, Irony, and Solidarity*, Cambridge 1989, pp. 91–93.
[148] Ch. Taylor, *Sources of the Self. The Making of the Modern Identity*, Cambridge 1989, pp. 4–5.

between the claim that value systems have a social origin and the claim of the existence of universal human rights[149]).

4.5.5 Criticism of the concept of negative freedom

The connection between idealist and communitarian thought is most clearly visible in the problem of freedom. For although the liberal tradition has also at various points maintained the idea of freedom as positive self-determination, it has usually given priority to freedom understood as independence from others. Even Rawls' conception, social-liberal and interventionist in its practical dimension, laid an emphasis, in the first principle of justice — "[e]ach person is to have an equal right to the most extensive total system of equal basic liberties compatible with a similar system of liberty for all" — on the freedom of self-determination, and as per the author's intent, without imposing a specific perception of the good life on individuals, but rather admitting a plurality of life plans. Similarly Habermas, yet another liberal thinker charged with *quasi*-metaphysical universalism, in his *Facts and Norms* emphasised the plurality of ethical and ideological perspectives.[150] The inevitable contamination of all practical discourse with particularisms persuaded Habermas to abandon hope of a rational, *a priori* foundation for ethics and politics. The universal pragmatism of language and the establishment of an "ideal speech situation", where the ability of the discourse participants to distance themselves from ideologies and experiences that "constantly disrupt" communication is implied, advocated by Habermas as early as the *Theory of Communicative Action*,[151] are here abandoned in favour of the claim that it is impossible to overcome the real limitations of individuals and therefore to attain full consensus on moral and political issues.

British idealism runs counter to the liberal theory of freedom. Its exponents clearly favoured "positive", "true", "political" freedom, its ideal exemplified not in self-will but in a specific type of ethical self-determination. To be free is not to dispose of oneself and of one's property as one pleases. The term can only be applied to an individual doing that which is worth doing, without squandering the opportunity for further self-realisation by acts of pure self-will. Besides, "freedom from" all dependence is a pure fiction, since it implies the Cartesian conception of the subject, capable of distancing himself from past

---

[149] M. Walzer, *On Toleration*, New Haven, CT–London 1997, pp. 5–6.
[150] J. Habermas, *Between Facts and Norms. Contributions to a Discourse Theory of Law and Democracy*, transl. W. Rehg, Cambridge, MA 1996.
[151] J. Habermas, *Theory of Communicative Action*, transl. Th. MacCarthy, Vol. 1–2, Boston, MA 1984.

experiences, of doubting all things, while maintaining his identity. One cannot, the idealists argue, detach oneself from past experiences and attain a post-conventional level of moral development (as presumed, amongst others, by Habermas) characterised by cool and impartial judgment of the morality one has been brought up to respect. One cannot escape social determination and free oneself fully from the influence of others. The transcendental Kantian subject, with its discovery of *a priori* ethical principles, was also accordingly dubbed a fiction with no equivalent in the real world by the British idealists.

One can find convergence here between the idealists and the communitarians, especially Taylor. In the essay *What's Wrong with Negative Liberty?*,[152] Taylor distinguished two possible approaches to freedom, understood, respectively, as an *exercise-concept* and an *opportunity-concept*.[153] The first of these reflects Berlin's "freedom to", defined as the use of opportunities to develop one's personality. The second overlaps semantically with "freedom from", as exemplified in absolute self-will. However, Taylor notes, these two notions cannot be strictly disassociated from each other, since one may imply the other. The freedom of "opportunity" does not have to equal independence from other people. It can refer to independence from one's limitations, implying the requirement of more intensive work on oneself, deriving its ideal from that of a flawless personality. Similarly, if "freedom to" is not to be equated with submitting oneself to the government of those who are more enlightened (as regards human nature or suitable directions of self-realisation, for example), and it does not have to be understood in this way, then it should be founded on the notion of "opportunity" as the basis of an independent search for one's *telos*. Nonetheless, out of these two notions of freedom, only one withstands the charge of performative contradiction. The first one, negative (proper to the thought of Hobbes and Bentham, amongst others) cannot stand as an independent theoretical construct:[154] "we cannot defend a view of freedom which does not involve at least some qualitative discrimination as to motive."[155] And since advocates of the notion of freedom as "opportunity" consider every act that influences an individual's decision a form of restraint, they will interpret all discrimination as to motive as interfering in self-willed agency. They are, however, mistaken in their reasoning. Not all opportunities, says Taylor, have the same worth.[156] There

---

[152] Ch. Taylor, *What's Wrong with Negative Liberty?*, in: Ch. Taylor, *Philosophy and the Human Sciences. Philosophical Papers 2*, Cambridge 1990, pp. 211–229.
[153] *Ibid.*, p. 213.
[154] *Ibid.*, pp. 214–215.
[155] *Ibid.*, p. 217.
[156] *Ibid.*, p. 219.

are desires that we can renounce without losing our identity, and which are therefore accidental to our being ourselves, whilst there are also those we must fulfil to remain who we are. When these two types of desires come into conflict, necessitating a choice, it is a mistake to maintain that each of the options is of equal weight. If I sacrifice my marriage in order to spend time at the local pub, I sacrifice a desire essential to my personality — my relationship to someone very close — in favour of something completely inessential to my being as a whole. Maintaining that each of these has the same value, thus that in realising either I am equally free, is pure nonsense.[157] If I elect an unimportant disposition, putting my very identity at risk, it means I have erred in my practical reasoning. Hence if freedom is to be defined as independence, it should not only exclude dependence on others, but also on our own defects steering us towards unreasonable choices. The concept of freedom should thus be redefined and seen to consist in "the absence of internal or external obstacle to what I truly or authentically want",[158] because "the internally fettered man is not free".[159]

There are many points on which Taylor's reasoning parallels that of the idealists. Firstly, British thinkers also saw the interconnection between the negative and positive conception of freedom. Green held that positive freedom implies the negative, since self-realisation requires unrestrained choice, just as negative freedom makes little sense without positive. There is as little merit in self-will as such as there is in coercing someone for the sake of a good they are as yet unable to grasp. This is why those defining liberty as self-will must also account for a goal to be served by it. What remained merely implicit in the works of Green was clearly formulated by Bosanquet: "the apparently negative has its roots and its meaning in the positive."[160] Every conception of freedom is based on a view of human nature which it purports to realise in a way proper unto itself. Hence the true dispute about the nature of freedom is not concerned with the scope of admissible actions as such, but rather with the definition of truly authentic agency.

4.5.6 Individualism

In spite of the many charges against the idealists that have accumulated in the literature, proclaiming them to be collectivist in their outlook and ready to sacrifice individual freedom to an abstract or — worse yet — the

---

[157] *Ibid.*, pp. 220–221.
[158] *Ibid.*, p. 222.
[159] *Ibid.*, p. 227.
[160] B. Bosanquet, *The Philosophical Theory of the State*, p. 127.

sole ontologically self-sufficient being — the community, recent years have seen a number of opinions in favour of recognising the individualism of their thought. Although the scholars voicing these opinions often did not appreciate the conservatism of Green's, Bradley's and Bosanquet's writings, they were doubtless right to remark on their individualist implications. It is, however, not the type of individualism which has until recently been associated with the liberal perspective.[161] That type, based on a clear distinction between the private and the public sphere, considered the expression of one's self to be possible only within the first of these. According to this interpretation, found in its most comprehensive form in the works of exponents of the "theories of the first look", all interference by public institutions in the decisions of citizens violates their freedom of expression, hence also their individualism. Nevertheless, as Bosanquet argued, this is an approach which results in the paradox of political obligation. "We shall need a new individualism, vitalized through the groups. The member of a state will not be the unit of a crowd whether of persons or groups, but the full individual, the many-sided activity, revealed and realized in the system of groups."[162]

The idealists did not view the difference between the private and the public in such categorical terms. There is no way to separate me as a private person from myself as a citizen. Is there a different conceptual scheme I apply in my private, as opposed to my public, life? Am I guided by different ideals, hopes and values in the one and in the other? Can I, as a citizen, forget about my needs as an individual, and about the community I live in as a private person? The answer is no — the idealists jointly agreed. "The idealistic theory [...] starts frankly from the *law-abiding* citizen or, in other words, from the public-spirited individual, who manages even his 'private' affairs, of family or business or profession, with the clear recognition that they are his readiest and most effective channels for rendering service to the 'common good.'"[163] This is why neither freedom nor individualism can be examined separately from the social whole. Originality, invention, extra-

---

[161] To emphasise this difference, Simhony and David Weinstein use Alexandre de Saint-Cheron's and Pierre Leroux's distinction between individualism and individuality (See Y. Arieli, *Individualism and Nationalism in American Ideology*, Cambridge, MA 1964, p. 232). They apply the first term to the egotistical view of personality characteristic of contemporary liberal thought, and the second to the notion of the Subject improving himself morally by acts of recognition and cooperation with others (A. Simhony, D. Weinstein, *Introduction*, pp. 16–17).

[162] B. Bosanquet, *Introduction to the Second Edition*, p. LVIII.

[163] A.R.F. Hoernlé, *Idealism as a Philosophy*, New York 1927, p. 277.

ordinariness will never be virtues if they fail to contribute to the well-being of a group. Although he might be proud of his ability, the most gifted and brilliant of thieves cannot be considered a man truly free nor his activity a manifestation of individualism. The last of these, the idealists hold, does not consist in an apology of self-will or the expression of a pointless or harmful originality. Since individuals are defined by their social roles, their individuality must both require and imply community with others. The duties that come with social functions do not limit freedom or restrict individualism. If this were to be the case, people would have to be able to detach themselves from their past and current influences and to subject them to a severe judgment. And although the idealists allowed a certain amount of criticism of the sort, they maintained that the limits of personality and thus also originality are delimited by the social. And since the origins of individualism are social in nature, so too must be its goals.

Conclusion

Let us try to sum up our considerations, formulate the conclusions we have arrived at and indicate directions for the further examination of the subject of this book. We have traced the evolution of the concept of the general will, from its strictly theological exposition, its appearance in controversies regarding God's plan for salvation and the laws governing the world, to the emergence of its first social and political inclinations in the writings of Blaise Pascal, Nicolas Malebranche and Montesquieu, in order to analyse its nearly wholly politicised meaning in the works of Denis Diderot and Jean-Jacques Rousseau. We then proceeded to examine the political philosophy of British idealism, outlining its main claims and socio-political conceptions. We have also presented the idealists' critique of Rousseau, and finally indicated the modifications it was subject to in their works. We did not restrict ourselves to the three main representatives of the British idealist movement, but gradually expanded our exemplification of the idealist *Weltanschauung* to other thinkers, both those affiliated with idealism, as well as those doctrinally tied to New Liberalism. Finally, we presented the place of the discussed tradition in the context of contemporary debates between the individualist and communal philosophico-political perspectives. We attempted to formulate a definition and to exemplify the liberal-communitarian position, which was then compared to idealist thought. We presented and briefly discussed the set of features which, in our opinion, confirms the idealists' individualist-communal affiliations, making it possible to place them among the first codifiers of liberal communitarianism.

Let us now present the conclusions that can arise from these considerations. Have the theses formulated in the Introduction been appropriately validated? One of them proclaimed the inevitability of a dual reading of Rousseau's concept of the general will. We sought to justify it by distinguishing, on the basis of passages from Rousseau's works, two equally valid and mutually irreducible ways of interpreting the *volonté générale*: the politico-legal and the ethical. It was shown that each implies an entirely different type of community. In the first case, a political one, where the ideal of the general will is realised through the votes of the citizens, achieving its most perfect incarnation in the legislation enacted by them. The members of such a community are people of flesh and blood, not devoid of concern for their own good, and even egotistical in putting it above the common interest. In the second case, the ethical interpretation, we are faced with a view of community whose members are held together by indissoluble emotional bonds, where all fully devote themselves to the pursuit of the common good, being in fact unable to differentiate between the communal *volonté générale* and their own egotistical *volonté particulière*. This is the vision of an apolitical society whose ideal members, conscious of their part in labouring towards the well-being of the whole, conscientiously fulfil their duties, desiring nothing beyond the good of the common Self. Although it is possible to reconcile these two views — that of the community of virtue and that of the community of duty — recognising the former as a regulative idea guiding the operation of the latter, or a successive (most certainly unattainable) stage of its development, the dual interpretation of the general will cannot be eliminated without simplifying the political philosophy of Rousseau beyond what is justified.

According to the second of this book's key theses, the political philosophy of British idealism combined elements of the individualist and the communitarian position in its programme. This was justified in two parts. Firstly, we extracted those elements of the idealist position which are, to different degrees, proper to the contemporary traditions of liberalism and communitarianism: teleologism, the attempt to provide a metaphysical grounding to politics, ethico-political contextualism, vacillation between relativism and universalism, criticism of the concept of negative liberty, individualism. In describing each of them, we consequently demonstrated similarities between idealist thought and the answers to the same problems developed within contemporary approaches. Similar conclusions were suggested by the comparison of the above mentioned elements with three characteristic features of liberal communitarianism, presented by David Miller, namely the acceptance of liberal democracy as the proper platform for resolving ethical controversies, opposition to abstract universalism and the acceptance of the cultural and ideological diversity of modern-day societies.

We also fulfilled the goals designated as secondary in the Introduction. Here, as we will recall, we managed to present the idealist view of the general will and sketch out the history of the shaping of this category during the period preceding the writings of Rousseau. We also reconstructed the socio-political philosophy of British idealism, not restricting ourselves, in accordance with our initial assumption, to the three foremost representatives of this tradition, but supplementing the presented overview with the views of later authors and supporters. The last of these aims was even realised with a certain surplus, namely a wide-ranging analysis of the idealists' juridical views.

This much we have managed to achieve, at the same time fulfilling the objectives set out in the Introduction. Here, it is also worth taking a look at those subjects that have not been touched upon or that were merely alluded to. Above all, we did not follow the use made of the concept of the general will by some continental and American philosophers. The first group essentially includes only the German idealists: Immanuel Kant, Johann Gottlieb Fichte and Georg Wilhelm Friedrich Hegel. Much is known about their fascination — sometimes only youthful (Fichte, Hegel), sometimes lifelong (Kant) — with the Rousseauian general will, yet in spite of this, there are few comprehensive studies on the topic. Usually underlining issues that provide ammunition against the *Social Contract*, commentators rarely pay attention to the positive links between the political philosophy of Rousseau and the conceptions of these German thinkers.

Another omitted potential field of inquiry is the dependence between Rousseau's thought and Rawls' political project, as expounded in his *Political Liberalism*, in particular with regard to the concept of public reason. The *volonté générale* has on frequent occasions been regarded as a source of inspiration for Rawls' "overlapping consensus", reached by individuals who have rationally limited their political and legal claims in order to constitute a stable public order embodied in liberal democratic institutions. Rousseau's idea that citizens, guided by concern for the common good, can — without communicating with one another — all reach similar conclusions as to the actions to be taken bears a striking resemblance to the idea of a single reason binding the participants in the legislative process.

Similarities to the Rousseauian general will can also be glimpsed in Jürgen Habermas' and Joshua Cohen's deliberative democracy projects. Also here, the main analogy is the desire to create a platform for deciding the nature of the public good, accessible to individuals who differ in terms of their ethical and political views, but who, forced to coexist, freely reduce their expectations and claims out of concern for the common good. Such a debate is the culmination of the democratic decision-making process, which in turn — leading to the enactment of an appropriate law, consistent with the general will of a given society — provides legitimacy to a political system and the public order born thereof.

Unfortunately, attempts to systematise questions pertaining to the notion of the general will in its relation to the ideas of public reason and deliberative democracy have not exceeded the narrow bounds of a number of articles, published mainly in the 1980s.

Our omission of the above mentioned subjects was due to many factors, chiefly the need to narrow the topic of reflection down to a size permitting its treatment in a single volume. Comparing the general will to the concept of public reason, or judging of its potential use for theories of deliberative democracy, would require a significant further extension of analyses. We therefore remain hopeful that other scholars will take up the subject matter touched upon here, from where we have left off.

Bibliography

Arieli Y., *Individualism and Nationalism in American Ideology*, Cambridge, MA 1964.
Arnauld A., *Œuvres philosophiques de Antoine Arnauld*, ed. J. Simon, Paris 1813.
Austin J., *Province of Jurisprudence Determined*, London 1832.
Avnon D., de-Shalit A., eds., *Liberalism and Its Practice*, London–New York 2005.
Barker E., *Political Thought in England 1848 to 1914*, London 1928.
Baud-Bovey S., ed., *Jean-Jacques Rousseau*, Neuchâtel 1962.
Bayle P., *An Historical and Critical Dictionary Selected and Abridged from the Great Work of Peter Bayle, Vol. III*, London 1826.
— *Various Notes on the Occasion of a Comet*, transl. Robert C. Bartlett, Albany 2000.
Bengtsson J.O., *The Worldview of Personalism*, Oxford 2006.
Bentham J., *Works of Jeremy Bentham*, Edinburgh 1838.
Bosanquet B., *Aspects of the Social Problem*, New York 1895.
— *Civilization of Christendom*, New York 1893.
— *Essays and Addresses*, London 1891.
— *Les idées politiques de Rousseau*, "Revue de métaphysique et de morale" 1912, Vol. 20, pp. 321–240.
— *Life and Finite Individuality*, London 1918.
— *Principle of Individuality and Value*, London 1912.
— *Science and Philosophy and Other Essays*, ed. J.H. Muirhead, R.C. Bosanquet, London 1927.
— *Social and International Ideals Being Studies in Patriotism*, London 1917.
— *The Notion of the General Will*, "Mind. New Series" 1920, Vol. 19, pp. 77–81.
— *The Philosophical Theory of the State*, London 1910.
Bossuet J.-B., *An Universal History from the Creation of the World to the Time of Charlemagne*, London 1810.
— *Politics drawn from the Very Words of Holy Scripture*, transl. P. Riley, Cambridge 1990.

Boucher D., *The Creation of the Past. British Idealism and Michael Oakeshott's Philosophy of History*, "History and Theory. Studies in the Philosophy of History" 1984, Vol. 23, pp. 193–214.
Boucher D., Vincent A., *British Idealism and Political Theory*, Edinburgh 2000.
Bradley F.H., *Essays on Truth and Reality*, Oxford 1914.
— *Ethical Studies*, Oxford 1927.
Broad C.D., *The Notion of General Will*, "Mind. New Series" 1919, Vol. 28, pp. 502–504.
Buchanan A.E., *Assessing The Communitarian Critique of Liberalism*, "Ethics" 1989, Vol. 99, pp. 853–882.
Burgerlin P., *La philosophie de l'existence de J.J. Rousseau*, Paris 1952.
Burke E., *Reflections on the French Revolution*, London–New York 1910.
Cacoullos A.C., *Thomas Hill Green. Philosopher of Rights*, New York 1974.
Caird E., *Critical Philosophy of Kant*, Glasgow 1889.
— *Lay Sermons and Addresses Delivered in the Hall of Balliol College, Oxford*, Glasgow 1907.
Cassirer E., *The Question of Jean-Jacques Rousseau*, transl. P. Gay, New York 1956.
— *Rousseau, Kant, Goethe*, New York 1965.
— *L'Unité dans l'œuvre de J.J. Rousseau*, "Bulletin de la société française de philosophie" 1932.
Cell H.R., MacAdam J.I., eds., *Rousseau's Response to Hobbes*, New York 1988.
Chapman J.W., *Rousseau – Totalitarian or Liberal*, New York 1956.
Cobban A., *Rousseau and The Modern State*, London 1964.
Cole G.D.H., *Social Theory*, London 1920.
— *Conflicting Social Obligations*, "Proceedings of Aristotelian Society" 1914–1915, Vol. 16, pp. 140–159.
Collini S., Hobhouse, *Bosanquet and the State. Philosophical Idealism and Political Argument in England 1880–1918*, "Past and Present" 1976, No. 72.
Derathé R., *Jean-Jacques Rousseau et la science politique de son temps*, Paris 1970.
— *Le rationalisme de Jean-Jacques Rousseau*, Genève 1979.
Derrida J., *Of Grammatology*, tranls. G.C. Spivak, Baltimore, MD 1997.
Dewey J., *The Early Works, 1882–1898*, Vol. 4: *1893–1894*, Illinois 1969.
Diderot D., *Denis Diderot's The Encyclopedia: Selections*, ed. S.J. Gendzier, New York 1967.
Dimova-Cookson M., Mander W.J., eds., *T.H. Green. Ethics, Metaphysics and Political Philosophy*, Oxford 2006.
— *T.H. Green's Moral and Political Philosophy. A Phenomenological Perspective*, Basingstoke 2005.

Dunning W.A., *Review: The Philosophical Theory of the State*, "Political Science Quarterly" 1899, Vol. 14, pp. 530–533.

Durkheim É., *Le "Contrat Social" de Rousseau*, "Revue de Metaphysique et de Morale" 1918, Vol. 25, pp. 1–23.

Dworkin G., *The Theory and Practice of Autonomy*, Cambridge 2008.

Etzioni A., ed., *New Communitarian Thinking: Persons, Institutions, and Communities*, Charlottesville, VA 1995.

Evans M., ed., *The Edinburgh Companion to Contemporary Liberalism*, Edinburgh 2001.

Faguet É., *Rousseau penseur,* Paris 1912.

Fairbrother W.H., *The Philosophy of Thomas Hill Green*, London 1900.

Feinberg J., *Liberalism, Community and Tradition*, "Tikkun" 1987, Vol. 3, pp. 38–41, 116–120.

Fénelon F. de, *Œuvres philosophiques de Fénelon*, Paris 1845.

Ferrero G., *Pouvoir. Les génies invisibles de la cité*, Paris 1943.

Fichte J.G., *The Vocation of Man*, transl. W. Smith, Chicago 1931.

Fisher H.A.L., *The Common Weal*, Oxford 1924.

Fontenelle B., *Œuvres de Fontenelle*, Paris 1792.

Forsyth M., Keens-Soper M., eds., *The Political Classics. Green to Dworkin*, Oxford 1996.

Frankena W.K., *The Naturalistic Fallacy*, "Mind. New Series" 1939, Vol. 48, pp. 464–477.

Freeden M., *The New Liberalism. An Ideology of Social Reform*, Oxford 1978.

Galston W.A., *Liberal Purposes. Goods, Virtues, and Diversity in the Liberal State*, Cambridge 1991.

Gibbon J., *Review: The Philosophical Theory of the State*, "International Journal of Ethics" 1899–1900, Vol. 10, pp. 399–401.

Gierke O.F. von, *Natural Law and Theory of Society*, transl. E. Barker, Vol. 1–2, Cambridge 1934.

—*Political Theories of the Middle Age*, transl. F.W. Maitland, Cambridge 1913.

Gilden H., ed., *Political Philosophy. Six Essays by Leo Strauss*, Indianapolis, IN 1975.

Ginsberg M., *Is There a General Will?*, "Proceedings of Aristotelian Society" 1920, Vol. 20, pp. 89–112.

Gray J., *Two Faces of Liberalism*, New York 2000.

Gray J., Pelczynski Z.A., eds., *Conceptions of Liberty in Political Philosophy*, London 1984.

Green T.H., *Lectures on the Principles of Political Obligation and Other Writings*, ed. P. Harris, J. Morrow, Cambridge 1986.

—*Prolegomena to Ethics*, ed. P.P. Nicholson, Bristol 1997.

—*Works of Thomas Hill Green*, 3 vols, ed. R.L. Nettleship, London 1885-8.
Greengarten I.M., *Thomas Hill Green and the Development of Liberal-Democratic Thought*, Toronto 1981.
Gutmann A., *Communitarian Critiques of Liberalism*, "Philosophy and Public Affairs" 1985, Vol. 14, No. 3, pp. 308-322.
Habermas J., *Between Facts and Norms. Contributions to a Discourse Theory of Law and Democracy*, transl. W. Rehg, Cambridge, MA 1996.
—*Theory of Communicative Action*, transl. Th. MacCarthy, vol. 1-2, Boston, MA 1984.
Haldar H., *Neo-Hegelianism*, London 1927.
Harris F.P., *The Neo-Idealist Political Theory*, New York 1944.
Harris P., *Moral Progress & Politics: The Theory of T.H. Green*, "Polity" 1989, Vol. 21, No. 3, pp. 538-562.
Haymann F., *J.-J. Rousseau Sozialphilosophie*, Leipzig 1899.
—*La loi naturelle dans la philosophie politique de J.J. Rousseau*, "Annales" 1943-1945, Vol. 30, pp. 65-109.
Hazard P., *The European Mind 1680-1715*, transl. J.L. May, Middlesex 1964.
Hearnshaw F.J.C., ed., *The Social and Political Ideas of Some Representative Thinkers of the Victorian Age*, New York 1967.
Hegel G.W.F., *Lectures on the Philosophy of History*, transl. J. Sibree, London 1861.
—*The Elements of the Philosophy of Right*, transl. H.B. Nisbet, ed. A.W. Wood, Cambridge 2001.
Hobbes T., *Leviathan or the Matter, Form and Power of a Commonwealth, Ecclesiastical and Civil*, London 1887.
Hobhouse L.T., *Development and Purpose*, London 1913.
—*Liberalism*, New York 1911.
—*Mind in Evolution*, London 1901.
—*Morals in Evolution*, New York 1906.
—*Questions of War & Peace*, London 1916.
—*Rational Good*, New York 1921.
—*Social Evolution and Political Theory*, New York 1911.
—*Theory of Knowledge*, London 1896.
Hobson J.A., *Confessions of an Economic Heretic*, London 1938.
—*John Ruskin. Social Reformer*, Boston, MA 1898.
—*The Crisis of Liberalism*, London 1909.
—*The Re-Statement of Democracy*, "Contemporary Review" 1902, No. 81, pp. 262-272.
—*The Social Problem*, London 1919.
—*Work and Wealth*, New York 1926.
Hoernlé R.F.A., *Idealism as a Philosophical Doctrine*, London 1924.

d'Hondt J., ed., *Hegel et le siècle des Lumières*, Paris 1974.
Hudson Y., Peden C., eds., *The Bill of Rights. Bicentennial Reflections*, New York 1993.
Joad C.E.M., *Guide to the Philosophy of Morale and Politics*, London 1938.
Jones H., Muirhead J.H., eds., *The Life and Philosophy of Edward Caird*, Glasgow 1921.
Jones H., *The Principles of Citizenship*, London 1919.
— *The Working Faith of a Social Reformer and Other Essays*, London 1910.
Kant I., *Perpetual Peace*, New York 2007.
— *The Metaphysics of Morals*, transl. M. Gregor, Cambridge 1991.
— *Kant. Political Writings*, ed. H.S. Reiss, Cambridge 1991.
Kloppenberg J.T., *The Virtues of Liberalism*, Oxford 1998.
Krafft O., *La politique de Jean-Jacques Rousseau: Aspects Méconnus*, Paris 1958.
Krook-Gilead D., *Three Traditions of Moral Thought*, Cambridge 1959.
Kymlicka W., *Liberalism, Community and Culture*, Oxford 1989.
Lanson G., *L'Unité de la pensée de Jean-Jacques Rousseau*, "Annales de la société Jean-Jacques Rousseau" 1912, Vol. 8, pp. 1–12.
Laski H.J., *A Grammar of Politics*, London 1925.
— *The State in Theory and Practice*, New York 1935.
— *Bosanquet's Theory of General Will*, "Proceedings of the Aristotelian Society. Supplement" 1928, Vol. 8.
Laslett P., ed., *Philosophy, Politics and Society. A Collection*, Oxford 1956.
Leigh R.A., ed., *Rousseau after 200 years. Proceedings of the Cambridge Bicentennial Colloquium*, Cambridge 1982.
Levine A., *The General Will. Rousseau, Marx, Communism*, Cambridge 1993.
Lindsay A.D., *The Modern Democratic State*, London–New York 1943.
— *Bosanquet's Theory of the General Will*, "Proceedings of Aristotelian Society" 1928, Vol. 8.
MacAdam J., *What Rousseau Meant by the General Will*, "Dialogue" 1966–1967, No. 5, pp. 498–515.
MacCallum G.C., Jr., *Negative and Positive Freedom*, in: *Liberty*, ed. D. Miller, Oxford 1991, pp. 131–162.
MacCunn J., *The Ethics of Citizenship*, Glasgow 1894.
Macedo S., *Liberal Virtues*, Oxford 1990.
Machan T.R., *Classical Individualism*, New York–London 1998.
MacIver R.M., *Community. A Sociological Study*, London 1917.
— *The Modern State*, Oxford 1926.
MacKenzie J.S., *Introduction to Social Philosophy*, Glasgow 1895.
Maistre J. de, *Œuvres complètes de J. de Maistre*, Lyon 1886.
Malebranche N., *Œuvres complètes de Malebranche*, Paris 1837.
— *Treatise on Nature and Grace*, transl. P. Riley, Oxford 1992.

Man P. de, *Allegories of Reading: Figural Language in Rousseau, Nietzsche, Rilke and Proust*, New Haven, CT–London 1979.
Mander W.J., ed., *Anglo-American Idealism, 1865–1927*, London 2000.
Mander W.J., *British idealism. A History*, Oxford 2011.
Mandeville B., *The Fable of the Bees*, London 1729–1730.
Manser A., Stock G., eds., *The Philosophy of F.H. Bradley*, Oxford 1984.
Marcuse H., *Reason and Revolution. Hegel and the Rise of Social Theory*, London 1955.
Matravers D., Pike J., eds., *Debates in Contemporary Political Philosophy. An Anthology*, London–New York 2003.
McCann Ch.R., Jr., *Individualism and the Social Order*, London–New York 2004.
Mill J.S., *On Liberty and Other Writings*, ed. S. Collini, Cambridge 1989.
Miller D., ed., *Liberty*, Oxford 1991.
Montesquieu Ch., *Œuvres complètes*, ed. D. Oster, Paris 1964.
— *The Complete Works of M. de Montesquieu*, London 1777.
— *The Spirit of the Laws*, transl. Th. Nugent, New York 1899.
Morrow J., *Liberalism and British Idealist Political Philosophy: A Reassessment*, "History of Political Thought" 1984, Vol. 5, pp. 91–108.
Muirhead J.H., Hetherington H.J.W., *The Social Purpose*, London 1918.
Muirhead J.H., Radhakrishnan S., eds., *Contemporary Indian Philosophy*, London 1936.
Muirhead J.H., *Recent Criticism of the Idealist Theory of the General Will*, "Mind. New Series" 1924, Vol. 33, No. 130, pp. 166–177, No. 131, pp. 233–241, No. 132, pp. 166–175.
— *The Elements of Ethics*, London 1912.
Nadler S., ed., *Cambridge Companion to Malebranche*, New York 2000.
Neil P., Paris D., *Liberalism and the Communitarian Critique: A Guide for the Perplexed*, "Canadian Journal of Political Science" 1990, Vol. 23, No. 3, pp. 419–439.
Nicholson P.P., *A Moral View of Politics: T.H. Green and the British Idealists*, "Political Studies" 1987, Vol. 35, pp. 116–122.
— *Political Philosophy of the British Idealists. Selected Studies*, Cambridge 1990.
Pascal B., *Thoughts*, transl. W.F. Trotter, ed. Ch.W. Eliot, New York 1910.
Pfannenstill B., *Bernard Bosanquet's Philosophy of the State*, Lund 1936.
Plamenatz J.P., *Consent, Freedom and Political Obligation*, Oxford 1968.
Plant R., Vincent A., *Philosophy, Politics and Citizenship*, Oxford 1984.
Polin R., *La politique de la solitude. Essai sur la philosophie politique de Jean-Jacques Rousseau*, Paris 1971.
Pucelle J., *La Nature et l'Esprit dans la Philosophie de T.H. Green*, Paris 1960.

Pufendorf S., *De Iure Naturae et Gentium Libri Octo*, Londini Scanorum 1672.
Rawls J., *Theory of Justice*, Cambridge, MA–London 1971.
— *Justice as Fairness: Political not Metaphysical*, "Philosophy and Public Affairs" 1985, Vol. 14, No. 3, pp. 223–251.
— *Political Liberalism*, New York 1993.
Raz J., *The Morality of Freedom*, Oxford 1986.
Richter M., *The Politics of Conscience*, Cambridge 1964.
Riley P., *General Will Before Rousseau*, Princeton, NJ 1986.
— *Will and Political Legitimacy. A Critical Exposition of Social Contract Theory in Hobbes, Locke, Rousseau, Kant, and Hegel*, Cambridge, MA–London 1982.
— *A Possible Explanation of Rousseau's General Will*, "The American Political Science Review" 1970, Vol. 64, No. 1, pp. 64–88.
Ritchie D.G., *Darwin and Hegel*, London 1893.
Robinson J., *Bradley and Bosanquet*, "Idealistic Studies" 2000, Vol. 6, pp. 1–23.
Rorty R., *Contingency, Irony, and Solidarity*, Cambridge 1989.
Rosenblum N., ed., *Liberalism and the Moral Life*, Cambridge, MA 1989.
Rousseau J.J, *The Political Writings of Jean Jacques Rousseau*, ed. C.E. Vaughan, Vol. 1–2, Cambridge 1915.
— *The Social Contract and Other Political Writings*, ed. V. Gourevitch, Cambridge 1997.
— *Emile or On Education*, transl. A. Bloom, New York 1979.
— *Julie, ou la Nouvelle Héloïse. Lettres de Deux Amants*, Paris 1828.
— *Letter to D'Alembert and the Writings for the Theatre*, Lebanon, NH 2004.
— *Œuvres complètes de J.J. Rousseau avez des notes historiques*, Vol. 3, Paris 1835.
— *The Government of Poland*, transl. W. Kendall, Indianapolis, IN 1985.
— *The Social Contract and Discourses*, transl. G.D.H. Cole, London 1923.
Russell B., *History of Western Philosophy*, London 1947.
Sabine G.H., *A History of Political Theory*, Hinsdale, IL 1973.
— *Bosanquet's Theory of the General Will*, "Philosophical Review" 1923, Vol. 32, pp. 633–651.
Sandel M., ed., *Liberalism and its Critics*, New York 1984.
Santayana G., *Some Turns of Thought in Modern Philosophy*, New York 1933.
Simhony A., *T.H. Green: the Common Good Society*, "History of Political Thought" 1993, Vol. 14, pp. 225–247.
Simhony A., Weinstein D., eds., *The New Liberalism. Reconciling Liberty and Community*, Cambridge 2001.
Skinner Q., *Liberty Before Liberalism*, Cambridge 1998.

Skorupski J., ed., *The Cambridge Companion to Mill*, Cambridge 1998.
Spinoza B., *Complete Works*, transl. S. Shirley, ed. M.L. Morgan, Indianapolis, IN–Cambridge 2002.
Sprigge T.S., *The God of Metaphysics*, Oxford 2006.
Starobinski J., *Jean-Jacques Rousseau. Transparency and Obstruction*, Chicago, IL 1988.
Strauss L., *Natural Right and History*, Chicago, IL 1953.
Sweet W., ed., *The Moral, Social and Political Philosophy of the British Idealists*, Charlottesville, VA 2009.
— *Bernard Bosanquet and the Development of Rousseau's Idea of General Will*, "Man and Nature/L'homme et la nature" 1991, Vol. 10, pp. 179–197.
— *Idealism and Rights*, Lanham, MD–New York–London 1997.
— *L'individu et les droits de la personne selon Maritain et Bosanquet*, "Études maritainiennes/Maritain Studies" 1990, Vol. 6, pp. 141–166.
— *Was Bosanquet a Hegelian?*, "Bulletin of the Hegel Society of Great Britain" 1995, No. 31, pp. 39–60.
Taylor A.E., *Critical Notice of Hobhouse's Metaphysical Theory of the State*, "Mind" 1920, Vol. 29, pp. 91–105.
Taylor Ch., *Philosophy and the Human Sciences*, Cambridge 1985.
— *Philosophy and the Human Sciences. Philosophical Papers 2*, Cambridge 1990.
— *Sources of the Self. The Making of the Modern Identity*, Cambridge 1989.
— *Ethics of Authenticity*, Cambridge, MA–London 2003.
Thakurdas F., *Rousseau and the Concept of the General Will*, Calcutta 1976.
Thomas G., *The Moral Philosophy of T.H. Green*, Oxford 1987.
Tyler C., *Idealist Political Philosophy. Pluralism and Conflict in the Absolute Idealist Tradition*, London–New York 2006.
Vincent A., ed., *The Philosophy of T.H. Green*, Vermont 1986.
Voltaire, *Dictionnaire philosophique portatif*, Londres 1764.
Wallace W., *Lectures and Essays on Natural Theology and Ethics*, ed. E. Caird, Oxford 1898.
Walzer M., *On Toleration*, New Haven, CT–London 1997.
— *The Communitarian Critique of Liberalism*, "Political Theory", 1990, Vol. 18, No. 1, pp. 6–23.
Watson J., *The State in Peace and War*, Glasgow 1919.
— *Review: The Philosophical Theory of the State*, "Queen's Quarterly" 1900, Vol. 7, pp. 320–322.

Internet resources

http://www.papalencyclicals.net
http://www.thecounciloftrent.com
http://www.romancatholicism.org

Index

absolute idealism 82, 83
Ackerman, Bruce 141, 170
Alexander VII 10
Aristotle 53, 68, 73, 169, 170, 171
Arnauld, Antoine 9, 12, 19, on miracles 16, on general will 10, and Malebranche 10, 12
Arrow, Kenneth 2
Asquith, Herbert Henry 146
Augustine, St. 8, 9, 10, 11
Austin, John 58, 110, 111, 112, 113
Avnon, Dan 149

Bayle, Pierre 8, 12, 17, on occasionalism 19, 20, 21, Divine interventions 20
Bengtsson, Jan Olof 82
Bentham, Jeremy 63, 64, 65, 66, 67, 96, 98, 176
Berkeley, George 96, 134
Berlin, Isaiah 125, 149, 161, 164, 176
Besse, Guy 34
Beveridge, William Henry 3, 52
Binder, Julius 119
Bloom, Allan 32, 40
Bonald, Louis (Gabriel Ambroise) 94
Bosanquet, Bernard 2, 3, 4, 5, 52, 57, 59, 74, 83, 84, 105, 109, 114, 116, 117, 118, 119, 120, 121, 122, 133, 135, 138, 139, 146, 157, 159, 167, 169, 170, 171, 172, 173, 174, 178, on common good 160, 161, self-realisation 83, 84, 156, 159, 160, 175, 176, freedom 128, 129, 152, 161, 162, 163, 164, 165, 177, rights 130, 151, 158, social recognition 153, 154, 156, individualism 62, 63, 64, 65, 66, 67, 77, 78, 79, 80, 89, criticism of communal morality 90, 93, Rousseau 102, 103, 104, Hegelianism 37, 58, 73, 130, 131 Green 53, 56, Bradley 55, 56, 91, 92, 93, Hobhouse 123, 124, 125, 126, 127, 128, 129, 130, 131, 132, 136, 137
Bosanquet Robert Carr 79
Bossuet, Jacques Benigne 8, 12, 19, Providence 18, Cartesianism 18, and Malebranche 17, 18
Boucher, David 119
Bradley, Francis Herbert 2, 4, 5, 52, 54, 58, 73, 74, 77, 83, 84, 85, 88, 91, 92, 93, 105, 106, 107, 108, 133, 135, 139, 156, 157, 158, 159, 160, 165, 166, 167, 169, 170, 171, 173, 178, on Kantianism 59, 60, 61, self-realisation 83, 84, 87, 159, 160, 175, 176, sources of morality 85, 86, 87, social contract theory 72, freedom 161, 162, 163, *phronimos* 75, 76, and Bosanquet 53, 55, 56, Green 53, 54, 55
Broad, Charlie Dunbar 132
Brown, Borden Parker 82
Brown, Stuart 15
Buchanan, Allen E. 147
Buchanan, James M. 2
Budziszewski, Jan 144
Burgerlin, Pierre 28
Burke, Edmund 95
Burlamaqui, Jean Jacques 43
Buss, Martin 119
Bussey, Gertrude Carman 163
Butler, Joseph 98
Butterworth, Charles E. 40

Cacoullos, Ann R. 71
Caird, Edward 52, 54, 134, 165, 167, 168, 171

Index

Caird, John 72
Calvin, Jean 9, 21
Campbell-Bannerman, Henry 146
Carlyle, Thomas 52
Cassian, John St 9
Cassirer, Ernst 27, 28, 36
Cell, Howard R. 30
Chapman, John W. 38
Charity Organization Society 3, 55
Christian Social Union 52
citizenship, as a political project 34, 35, 38, 44, 102, 122, as an ethical project 50, 51, 119, 120, 166, *phronimos* as an ideal 75, 76, and duties 91, 92, 93, 106, 107, 108, 129, habitual obedience 112, 113, liberalism 141, 142, 144, 145, 153
Clarke, William 3, 146
Clauberg, Johannes 14
Clemens XI 10
Cobban, Alfred 41, 44, 45
Cohen, Joshua 182
Cole, George Douglas Howard 27, 31, 57
Coleridge, Samuel Taylor 52
collectivism 103, 154, 166
Collini, Stefan 65, 124
common good 34, 35, 47, 48, 49, 120, 121, and particular interests 23, 46, 51, 107, 133, 134, rights 153, 157, 158, 159, 160, 161, 162, personal good 153, 161, 167, social recognition 168, 178, as a form of political system 153, 158, 160, 161, and the best life 157, social recognition 160, liberalism 142, 144, 146, 150, 152, 153, communitarianism 150, 151, 152
communitarianism, and democracy, liberalism 140, 141, 142, 143, 144, 145, 146, 147, 148, 149, 150, British idealism 61, 150, 151, 152, 153, 154, 169, 170, 171, 172, 173, 174, 175, 176, 177, 178, 179
community, as a "moral person" 37, an aggregate 37, 61, 65, 66, 67, 77, 104, 105, community of Clarens 50, 51, two visions of community in Rousseau 48, 49, 50, 51, and moral development 90, 115, 128, 131, 142, 152, 157, 161, 169, 170
Comte, Auguste 119
Condorcet, Antoine Nicolas 142
Constant, Benjamin 94, 102
Crane, Marion Delia 163

De Ruggiero, Guido 146
Decree on Justification 9
Demolets, Nicolas 22
Derathé, Robert 28, 37, 40, 41, 42, 43, 44
Derrida, Jacques 29
Descartes, Rene 19
de-Shalit, Avner 149
Dewey, John 111, 143, 146
Diderot, Denis 8, 24, on general will 25, 26, 27, "violent reasoner" 25, and Rousseau 24, 25
Dimova-Cookson, Maria 151, 160
Disraeli, Benjamin 146
du Bay, Michel 9, 10
Dunning, William A. 124
Durkheim, Émile 30, 119
Dworkin, Gerald 147
Dworkin, Ronald 140, 141, 144, 153

Eliot, Thomas Stearns 52
Eriugena, Johannes Scotus 9
eternal consciousness 83
Etzioni, Amitai 141, 147
Evans, Mark 146
evolution 65, 66, 119, 124, of moral ideals 83, 88
Faguet, Émile 38
Fairbrother, William Henry 170
Faustus of Riez 9
Feinberg, Joel 147
Fénelon, François 8, 12, 17, 19
Ferrero, Guglielmo 30
Fichte, Johann Gottlieb 49, 52, 53, 70, 96, 182
Fisher, Herbert Albert Laurence 74
Flathman, Richard 153
Fontenelle, Bernard 12, 19, 22
Frankena, William K. 67
Freeden, Michael 64, 136, 137, 138, 145
freedom 10, 81, 82, 160, 167, 168, negative 102, 161, 162, positive 65, 161, 162, 163, juridical 161, true 103, 128, 129, 162, 163, and Divine grace 20,

21, and general will 33, 42, 51, 125, liberalism 62, 63, 64, 65, 66, 128, 142, 144, 152, 153, on two concepts of freedom 164, 165, idealist criticism of negative freedom 175, 176, 177
Friedman, Marilyn 140

Galston, William A. 143, 144
Gaus, Gerald F. 150, 151, 152
Gauthier, David 2
Gay, Peter 36
Gendzier, Stephen J. 25
general will, and Rousseau's concept of particular will 45, 46, 47, 48, custom 24, 47, 79, 106, 107, 108, 129, 134, 135, 136, 160, socio-political institutions 34, 35, 40, 50, 51, 76, 77, 78, 80, 82, 84, 86, 89, 90, 92, 93, 105, 106, 109, 110, 122, 130, 160, natural law 38, 39, 40, 41, 42, 43, 44, 45, metaphysical interpretation 36, 37, 38, ethical interpretation 34, 35, politico-legal interpretation 33, 34, common good 34, 35, 46, 47, 48, 49, 51, 106, 107, 153, 157, 158, 159, 160, 161, democracy 43, 50, 51, 100, 101, 112, 113, 114, 122, *pacta sunt servanda* principle 40, 41, 42, 43, social mind 136, 137, 138, public opinion 118, 119, and *amour de soi* 34, 44, voting 33, 36, 38, 48, 50, 100, 101, 104, 114, 118, 119, dominant ideas 116, 118, 120, 122, 174, habitual obedience 109, 110, 111, 112, 113
Geulincx, Arnold 12
Gewirth, Alan 153
Gibbon, John 124
Giddens, Anthony 57
Gierke, Otto Friedrich von 37, 121
Gilden, Hilail 45
Ginsberg, Morris 13, 57, 131
Gladstone, William Ewart 135, 145
Goethe, Johann Wolfgang von 74
Gore, Charles 52
Gottschalk 9
Gourevitch, Victor 25
Grace 8, 9, 10, 11, 12, 14, 16, 17, 18, 30
Gray, John 140, 149, 150, 174

Green, Thomas Hill 2, 3, 4, 5, 52, 54, 59, 74, 88, 89, 105, 108, 109, 110, 134, 135, 139, 143, 146, 165, 167, 168, 169, 170, 171, 178, on moral duties and legal obligations 80, 81, 82, Rousseau 97, 98, 99, 100, 101, 114, social contract theory 67, 68, 69, 70, 71, 72, common good 159, 160, 161, eternal consciousness 83, freedom 161, 162, 163, 174, 177, legal positivism 110, 111, 112, 113, 114, rights 115, 151, 152, 153, 154, 155, 156, 157, 158, self-realisation 62, 83, 84, 88, 89, 159, 160, 163, 175, 176, 177, and Bosanquet 54, 55, 56, 124, Bradley 53, 55, Hobhouse 124, 129, 130, 133, Hegel 58, 73, Aristotle 61, 62, 68
Grotius, Hugo 39, 71
Gutmann, Amy 147

Habermas, Jürgen 2, 170, 175, 176, 182
Haldane, Richard Burdon 3, 52, 73, 74
Haldar, Hiralal 53, 166, 168
Harris, Frederick Philip 170
Harris, Paul 62, 99, 155
Hayek, Friedrich August von 144
Haymann, Franz 30, 40
Hazard, Paul 17
Hearnshaw, Fossey John Cobb 115
Hegel, Georg Wilhelm Friedrich 7, 37, 52, 53, 56, 58, 89, 97, 102, 124, 125, 126, 127, 128, 129, 131, 171, 182, and panlogism 154, 155, criticism of Kantianism 73, historicism 58, 170, on Rousseau 95, 96
Helvetius, Claude Adrien 48
Hetherington, Hector James Wright 5, 74, 123, 133, 134, 135, 139, 165, 166, 167
Hincmar 9
Hobbes, Thomas 24, 36, 37, 39, 40, 43, 49, 57, 68, 70, 71, 72, 94, 100, 102, 105, 111, 149, 176
Hobhouse, Leonard Trelavny 3, 5 , 52, 56, 123, 124, 124, 126, 127, 128, 129, 130, 131, 132, 133, 135, 136, 137, 138, 139, 143, 146
Hoernlé, Reinchold Friedrich Alfred 74, 178
Höffding, Harald 34

Index

Holland, Henry Scott 52, 132
Holmes, Stephen 143, 144
Hondt, Jacques de 95
Hooker, Richard 71
Hudson, Yaer 151
Humboldt, Wilhelm von 142
Hume, David 13, 96, 98, 99, 100
Hus, Jan 9

idealism, and rationalism 73, 154, 155, universalism 73, 75, 80, 81, 148, 149, 151, 154, 155, 169, 171, contextualism 54, 58, 73, 80, 81, 82, 90, 151, 155, 167, 171, 172, 173, 174, 175, 181, teleology 54, 68, 73, 82, 83, 87, 88, 169, 170, 181, historicism 58, 73, 87, 88, 167
individualism 35, 94, 103, 104, 124, 132, 135, 152, 160, and holism 54, 142, idealist criticism 61, 62, 63, 64, 65, 66, 67, 74, 96, 98, 99, 154, idealist restatement 166, 167, 177, 178, 179, and liberalism 141, 144, 147

Jansen, Cornelius 9
Joad, Cyril Edwin Mitchinson 56, 131
Jones, Henry 52, 74, 123, 133, 134, 165, 166
Jowett, Benjamin 135
Jurieu, Pierre 12, 43

Kant, Immanuel 36, 49, 52, 53, 58, 59, 73, 80, 87, 89, 96, 97, 98, 102, 124, 125, 129, 149, 154, 155, 172, 182
Kelly, Christopher 40
Kjellén, Johan Rudolf 24
Krafft, Olivier 29
Krook-Gilead, Dorothy 85
Kymlicka, Will 142, 143

La Forge, Louis de 12
Lanson, Gustave 27
Larenz, Karl 119
Laski, Harold Joseph 57, 131
Laslett, Peter 57, 170
Le Bon, Gustave Tarde Gabriel 119
Leibniz, Gottfried Wilhelm 12, 27
Leigh, Richard A. 36
Leroux, Pierre 178
Levine, Andrew 2
Lewis, George Cornewall 111

liberalism, classical 37, 53, 54, communitarian 140, 141, 142, 143, 144, 145, 146, 147, 148, 149, 150, *modus vivendi* 149, political liberalism 147, 173, New Liberalism 3, 52, 84, 135, 136, 151, idealist criticism 102, and the "language of rights" 151, universalism 57, 58, 148
Lindsay, Alexander Dunlop 56, 74, 115, 131
Locke, John 12, 39, 49, 71, 72, 94, 96, 97, 98, 99, 100, 102, 105, 142
Luther, Martin 9, 21

MacAdam, James 30, 36
MacCallum, George C. 164
MacCunn, John 165, 166
Macedo, Stephen 143
MacIntyre, Alasdair 141, 143, 147, 169, 170, 171, 172, 174,
MacIver, Robert Morrison 57
MacKenzie, John Stuart 52, 74
MacKinnon, Catherine 140
Maine, Henry 111
Mairan, Dortous de 22
Maistre, Joseph de 94
Maitland, Frederick William 121
Malebranche, Nicolas 8, 10, 12, 17, 18, 19, 20, 21, 27, 181, and occasionalism 12, 13, on natural laws 14, miracles 15, 16, and Arnauld 16
Man, Paul de 29
Mander, William 56, 83, 151
Mandeville, Bernard 34
Mansfield, Harvey, Jr. 144
Marcuse, Herbert 56, 133
Martin, Rex 71, 151
Marx, Karl 142, 143
Masterman, Charles 3, 52, 146
Matravers, Derek 142
McTaggart, John McTaggart Ellis 74, 82
Méthais, Pierre 95
Mill, John Stuart 63, 64, 65, 66, 67, 102, 146, as a liberal communitarian 142, 145
Miller, David 149, 150, 164, 181
Mises, Ludwig von 144

Montesquieu 8, 19, 21, 23, 25, 102, 180, on occasionalism 22, 27, and geopolitics 24, balance of powers 49
moral ideal 84, 85, 86, 87, 91, 92
Moreau, Denis 16
Morgan, Michael L. 68
Morrow, John 62, 99, 155
Moses 18
Mouffe, Chantal 140
Muirhead, John Henry 5, 52, 54, 74, 79, 106, 123, 132, 133, 134, 135, 139, 165
my station and its duties 74, 75, 76, 91, 92, 93, 94, 173, criticism 129, 138, 139

Nadler, Steven 13
natural law 13, 14, 15, 22, and general will 2, 24, 25, 26, 27, 29,39, 40, 41, 42, 43, 44, 45, idealist restatement 67, 68, 69, 70, 71, 72, 114, 115
naturalistic fallacy 72, 84
nature, as a historical concept 38, 39, 40, as a normative concept 38, 39, 40, and the state of nature 35, 94, 95, 100, and society 40, 41, 42, 72, human nature 88, 102, 103, 117, 118, 127, 130, 159, 162, 164, 177
Neil, Patrick 141
Nettleship, Richard Lewis 98
Nicholson, Peter P. 61, 62, 85, 86, 88, 104, 115, 160
Nozick, Robert 58, 140, 142, 144

Oakeshott, Michael 3, 52, 86
occasionalism 12, 13, 14, 19, 27
Okin, Susan Moller 140
organicism 58, 78, 79, 80, 166, 170

paradox of self-government 62, 63, 66, 103, 104
Paris, David 141
Pascal, Blaise 8, 9, 11, 12, 22, 27, 180
Pattison, Mark 135
Paul, St. 8, 11
Peden, Creighton 151
Pelagianism 8, semipelagianism 9
Pelagius 8
perfectionism, ethical 128, 129, 143, 150, and liberalism 143, 144, 145
Pettit, Philip 3

Pfannenstill, Bertil 77, 91, 97, 105, 118, 119, 132, 170
Pike, Jon 142
Pius VI 10
Plamenatz, John Petrov 36, 132
Plant, Raymond 167
Plato 79, 170
Polignac, Melchior de 22
Polin, Raymond 29
Pope Alexander 97
Predestination 8, 9, 10, 21
Priestley, Joseph 98
Pringle-Pattison, Andrew Seth 73, 82
Pucelle, Jean 68
Pufendorf, Samuel 23, 37

Quesnel, Pasquier 9

Radhakrishnan, Sarvepalli 134
Ratzel, Friedrich 24
Rawls, John 2, 3, 58, 140, 141, 143, 144, 145, 147, 149, 150, 160, 170, 171, 172, 173, 175, 182
Raz, Joseph 3, 149, 153, 154
recognition, social 69, 86, 122, 153,172 political 69,166, and self-realisation 81, 82, 85, 88, and rights 5, 70, 151, 153, 154, 155, 156, 157, 158, 166, common good 160, 161
Reiss, Hans S. 89
Republicanism 2, 97, 140, 141, 143, 148
Richter, Melvin 68, 111,
rights 39, 41, 42, 43, 65, 66, 67, 68, 69, 70, 71, 72, 73, 74, 77, 78, 128, 129, 130, 131, negative 108, 152, 153, 162, 164, 165, positive 17, 26, 42, 45, 69, 106, 113, 160, 164, 165, and social recognition 155, 156, 157, 158, 159, common good 159, 160, 161, duties 107, 108, 118, liberal-communitarian debate 141, 142, 144, 145, 148, 151, 152, 153, 154
Riley, Patrick 2, 7, 8, 11, 12, 14, 15, 17, 18, 19, 22, 35, 36
Ritchie, David George 52, 73, 74, 123, 133, 139, 146
Rivarol, Antoine de 94
Robespierre, Maximilien 8
Robinson, Jonathan 91
Rorty, Richard 174

Rousseau, Jean Jacques 1, 2, 4, 5, 7, 8, 11, 12, 17, 19, 22, 23, 28, 29, 30, 31, 33, 34, 35, 36, 37, 38, 46, 51, 53, 58, 62, 67, 71, 94, 95, 97, 98, 106, 107, 108, 110, 118, 128, 129, 140, 180, 181, 182, on ideal community 48, 49, 50, state of nature 39, 40, 41, 44, 100, sovereignty, 100, 101, 105, 112, 113, 114, *pacta sunt servanda* principle 40, 41, 42, 43, associations 50, plus-minus principle 49, 50, and democratic government 51, 63, organicism 103, 104, individualism, 94, 95, 96, 99, 100, 102, contextualism 44, 45, and Diderot 24, 25, 26, 27
Royce, Josiah 171
Runciman, Walter Garrison 2
Russell, Bertrand 30
Ryan, Alan 145

Sabatier de Castres, Antoine 94
Sabine, George H. 43, 132
Saint-Cheron, Alexandre de 178
Santayana, George 85
Scheler, Max 119
Schelling, Friedrich Wilhelm Joseph von 73
Scott, Charles Prestwich 3, 146
Sen, Amartya Kumar 2
Seth, James 82
Settlement Movement 3
Shaftesbury, Lord (Anthony Ashley Cooper) 97
Shklar, Judith Nisse 144
Simhony, Avital 89, 143, 151, 152, 153, 154, 160, 178
Simon, Jules 10
Skinner, Burrhus Frederic 142
Skinner, Quentin 37
Skorupski, John 145
Smith, Roger 144
social contract 41, 42, 43, 44, 81, 94, 95, 154, idealist criticism 58, 65, 66, 67, 68, 69, 70, 71, 72, 96, 100, 172, 173
socialism 2, 28, 54
Sombart, Werner 119
Spann, Othmar 119
Spencer, Herbert 63, 65, 66, 67, 102, 119, 142, 144, 153

Spinoza, Baruch 27, 39, 41, 68, 69, 70, 71, 72, 80, 94, 100
Spragens, Thomas A., Jr. 141, 144
Sprigge, Timothy S. 171
Starobinski, Jean 28, 35
Stirling, James Hutchison 52
Strauss, Leo 34, 43, 45, 113
Sweet, William 56, 102, 122, 151, 153, 154, 158, 159

Tarcov, Nathan 144
Tawney, Richard Henry 3, 52
Taylor, Alfred Edward 131, 132
Taylor, Charles 3, 141, 142, 143, 147, 148, 150, 154, 172, 174, 176, 177
Thakurdas, Frank 2, 30, 37
theories of duty for duty's sake 59, 60, 61, 84
theories of the first look 61, 62, 63, 64, 65, 66, 67, 77, 78, 102, 132, 162, 178
Thomas, Geoffrey 56, 57, 91
Toynbee, Arnold 3, 52
Toynbee Hall 52
Tyler, Colin 62, 93

Utilitarianism 53, 54, 55, 65, 73, 74, 96, 99

Vaughan, Charles Edwin 25, 43
Vincent, Andrew 83, 119, 146, 167
Vorländer, Karl 146

Waldron, Jeremy 153
Wallace, William 73, 74, 123, 162, 168
Walzer, Michael 3, 141, 147, 148, 150, 172, 174, 175
Ward, James 74, 82
Watson, John 73, 74, 124
Webb, Beatrice 3, 52, 119
Webb, Clement C.J. 82
Webb, Sidney 3, 52, 119
Weber, Max 119, 146
Weinstein, David 143, 145, 151, 179
Wilson, James Quinn 144
Workers' Educational Association 52
Wycliffe, John 9